Assessing children's
mathematical knowledge

Assessing children's mathematical knowledge

Social class, sex and problem-solving

Barry Cooper and Máiréad Dunne

Open University Press
Buckingham · Philadelphia

Open University Press
Celtic Court
22 Ballmoor
Buckingham
MK18 1XW

e-mail: enquiries@openup.co.uk
world wide web: http://www.openup.co.uk

and
325 Chestnut Street
Philadelphia, PA 19106, USA

First Published 2000

A catalogue record of this book is available from the British Library

ISBN   0 335 20317 5 (hb)   0 335 20316 7 (pb)

Library of Congress Cataloging-in-Publication Data
Cooper, Barry, 1950–
    Assessing children's mathematical knowledge: social class, sex, and problem-solving/Barry Cooper and Máiréad Dunne.
        p.   cm.
    Includes bibliographical references and index.
    ISBN 0-335-20317-5 (HB). – ISBN 0-335-20316-7 (PB)
    1. Mathematics–Study and teaching (Elementary)–England–
Evaluation.   2. Mathematics–Study and teaching (Elementary)–
England–Social aspects.   3. Mathematical ability–Sex differences.
I. Dunne. Máiréad.   II. Title.
QA135.5.C5955   2000
372.7'0942–dc21   99-21687
                                                                          CIP

Typeset by Graphicraft Limited, Hong Kong
Printed and bound in Great Britain by
Marston Book Services Limited, Oxford

Contents

List of figures

List of tables

Acknowledgements

The work reported here has been carried out over a period of several years. Most, though not all, of the research has been funded by the UK's Economic and Social Research Council (ESRC) (Grants: R000235863 and R000222315). We are grateful to the ESRC and also to the Higher Education Funding Council for England for financial support for our work. Without such funding work on this scale would be impossible.

There are many individuals whose contributions to the work reported here need to be recognized. Most importantly of all, several people have worked with us, at various times, on the ESRC projects. Nicola Rodgers worked with us for seven months, both conducting interviews with children and entering data. Her enthusiastic contribution has not been forgotten. We would also like to acknowledge the contributions of Beryl Clough, Hayley Kirby and Julia Martin-Woodbridge in transcribing so patiently our interviews with children. We would also like to thank all of the teachers and the children from six schools who have participated in our research programme. In particular, the heads of the mathematics departments in the secondary schools, and the headteachers and mathematics co-ordinators in the primary schools, provided us with much support, for which we are very grateful – especially given the stressful situations in which such individuals now work in English schools.

Various people have commented on previous accounts of the work. We would like to thank, in particular, Basil Bernstein, Jo Boaler, Andrew Brown, Margaret Brown, Leone Burton, Stephanie Cant, Paul Dowling, Pat Drake, Michael Eraut, Roger Gomm, Viv Griffiths, Martyn Hammersley, Colin Lacey, David Longman, Maggie MacLure, Monty Neil, John Pryor, Robert Stake and Harry Torrance. Needless to say, none of these is responsible for the weaknesses that remain. Several teachers, and one headteacher, in our research schools who have contributed helpful commentary must remain anonymous. We have also received helpful critical comments from various anonymous referees acting for the ESRC and for academic journals.

Chapter 4 is a revised and extended version of a paper initially presented to the Annual Meeting of the American Educational Research Association in New York in 1996, and was published in a shorter form by *Qualitative Studies in Education* in 1998 (reproduced with the kind permission of Taylor & Francis). Chapter 6 is a revised version of a paper originally presented to the Annual Conference of the British Sociological Association in York in 1997, and was subsequently published in a slightly different form in *Sociological Review* early in 1998 (reproduced with the kind permission of the Editorial Board of *Sociological Review*). We would like to thank both journals for allowing us to use this material here. Parts of Chapter 5 were originally presented to the Annual Meeting of the American Educational Research Association in Chicago in 1997.

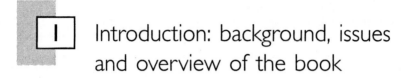

1 Introduction: background, issues and overview of the book

Changes in school mathematics and its assessment

In recent years, while the research reported in this book has been in progress, school mathematics has been a frequent topic of public discussion. Of course, periods in which school mathematics has been seen as in need of 'improvement' or 'reform' have occurred many times in the past. During such periods the practices of school mathematics are, relative to intervening times, no longer taken-for-granted. They are seen as failing children, or failing employers, or both (Cooper 1985a). The mathematics curriculum and its teachers are attacked by some critics for failing to adhere to the contents or 'standards' of the past (Ball 1994). At the same time, they may be under attack from others for failing to deliver the content and approach to mathematics required by the supposed 'needs' of a predicted future. Such needs are usually read off from some image of recent or emerging economic change (Cooper 1985a). Often, in parallel with these criticisms, there will be links made between school mathematics and broader educational issues, including children's classroom behaviour (e.g. Hayman 1975). It is not difficult to see why mathematics in particular should have been so often a matter of public debate. It has a long history as a high status school subject and, connected with this importance, has played a central role in the selection of children for higher education by means of public examinations. Children's supposed levels of intelligence have often been inferred from their attainments in school mathematics. Furthermore, the subject has been seen to be, and in many ways is, highly relevant to a variety of occupational roles, of lower and higher social status (e.g. Cockcroft 1982; but see Dowling 1998, for a critique of this view). It has also been the case, certainly until the relatively recent past, that the subject has been understood by most interested individuals and organizations as one in which correctness and incorrectness, and, via these, children's knowledge and understanding, are easy to identify. This belief has allowed the development of a testing industry in mathematics and the use of the products of this industry to make supposedly valid comparisons between individuals, schools and even nations (Stake 1992). In the case of England and Wales, in the past decade, there has been politically-driven reform of curriculum content, pedagogy and assessment resulting in a programme of national testing of mathematics, English language and science. The mass media now engage in an annual frenzy of school and district comparison, drawing on statistics of performance deriving from the administration of tests in these three subject areas at several points in a child's school career, and from examinations in a broader range of subjects at age sixteen. It is most often teachers, schools and children who bear the brunt of any resulting criticism, with little account being taken of any contextual factors. The tests themselves receive criticism only in professional and academic arenas.

In this book, we wish to redress the balance a little, by focusing on the various ways in which paper and pencil tests of mathematics may not reflect adequately what children actually know and understand of the subject. Researchers have shown, in recent years, that both adults and children are able to undertake arithmetical calculations outside of school, employing a variety of approaches not taught in school, even though they are apparently unable to produce similar results when faced with school problems and are required to use school-taught algorithms (Scribner 1984; Nunes *et al.* 1993). Our focus is a related one, but different in emphasis. Since the reaction against the abstract algebraic approaches favoured by the curriculum reformers of the 1960s, many influential voices working within mathematics education, whether within para-governmental institutions or within institutions producing future teachers, have favoured an approach to mathematics teaching and learning which has as a key focus the relating of work in mathematics to some version of the 'real world' (e.g. Cockcroft 1982; NCTM 1991). This approach is supported for a variety of reasons. For some, the main justification is motivational, based on a belief that children will find mathematics more interesting and relevant to their concerns if, for example, techniques of calculation are taught in the context of consumption or work – or, at least, via textual representations of such contexts. For others, the main motivation derives from the supposed needs of children as future consumers and workers. In England, much of the argument for a more 'relevant' and 'realistic' approach was disseminated to the world of education at large in the Cockcroft report (1982) on school mathematics. Subsequently, the Education Act of 1988 introduced a National Curriculum (NC) in England and Wales and, alongside this, a programme of national assessment of children's attainments at the ages of 7, 11, 14 and 16. This programme of assessment has comprised elements internal and external to the school, but, as a result of both political debate and practical experience of the original policy in practice, their relative importance has shifted (Cooper 1998b; Dunne 1998). As a result, by the middle of the 1990s, the main emphasis had moved from one focusing on assessment of children's work by teachers as part of their everyday classroom activities, to one focusing on assessment via the use of nationally designed paper and pencil tests marked by personnel external to the school in which the test was to be administered. The NC assessment tools were designed, under contract, mainly by university personnel previously experienced in mathematics education and who, as a result, seem to have carried with them, as one taken-for-granted assumption, the belief that 'relevance' and 'realism' were important aspects of educational practice in mathematics. As the 1990s progressed the designers of the assessment packages found themselves under increasing pressure to simplify the assessment tools and, in particular, to make more use of externally marked timed paper and pencil tests. This conjunction of factors led to tests being produced that consisted predominantly of items embedding mathematical operations in textually represented 'real life' situations.

Such 'realistic' test items can cause a variety of problems for children. They often require a greater amount of reading compared with 'non-realistic' items before the mathematical point can be addressed, which might be expected to disadvantage poorer readers. It has also been shown, in several research studies, that children frequently fail to apply 'realistic' considerations when it is defined as 'appropriate' that they do so by test designers (e.g. Verschaffel *et al.* 1994). (We discuss some of the characteristics of these studies in Chapter 3.) However, there is another potential problem generated for children by 'realistic' items, and one that has received much less attention in the research literature. Children, and especially those children who are less knowledgeable about the peculiar ways boundaries are drawn between school and everyday knowledge, will perhaps fail to demonstrate what they know and understand about mathematics as a result of drawing 'inappropriately', from the perspective of the test designers, on their 'everyday' knowledge of the world outside of the classroom (Cooper 1992, 1994b). This is one problem, alongside others, with which this book is concerned. In reporting the ways in which children cope with this 'boundary' problem, we pay attention to potential differences between boys and girls, and between children from different socio-economic backgrounds. We explain why below.

Research in mathematics education

Much research on children's understanding of mathematics has been carried out without reference to children's cultural backgrounds, often by psychologists or others using psychological frameworks of analysis. Notwithstanding the important tradition of work in cultural psychology (e.g. Cole *et al.* 1971; Cole 1996), revivified in recent years as a result of a renewed interest in the work of Vygostsky (e.g. Cobb 1994; Wertsch 1995), many researchers seem to have bracketed out extra-school cultural considerations in their approach to the study of children's problem-solving in school mathematics. As a consequence research findings are often presented in terms of some supposedly typical child, though, increasingly, results may be broken down by sex, either because of concerns with equality of opportunity or because of beliefs concerning sex differences in cognitive predispositions (e.g. Fennema *et al.* 1998). In the past, the lack of attention to culture may have resulted partly from a working assumption that children's cognitive development followed similar patterns everywhere. But, in the case of mathematics, it may also have been partly dependent on various tacit assumptions about mathematics itself, including assumptions concerning the universality of a discipline that many appear to believe to be above and beyond 'everyday' cultural differences. However, there are several reasons for believing that a consideration of cultural differences between children might allow us greater understanding of their success and failure in problem-solving in school mathematics.

First of all, it is important to note that mathematics, and school mathematics in particular, is not unchanging. Clearly, the content created and studied by university research mathematicians will change over time, and such changes will, via what Bernstein (1996) has termed recontextualizing processes, sometimes be reflected in changes in the content of school mathematics, though often only after a considerable time lag and after periods of conflict within the disciplinary group (Cooper 1983, 1985a). But, as we have already indicated, much of the change at school level only partly concerns the underlying mathematical operations themselves. Change in school mathematics is often about different matters. For example, around the period of World War II in England, a key focus of debate was the boundary between algebra, trigonometry and geometry with some individuals arguing for a more 'integrated' approach to the teaching of these three elements of the curriculum in the selective secondary schools. This desire to 'integrate' returned as part of the debate in the 1960s, where it became linked more explicitly with the wish of some reformers to introduce some modern abstract algebra into school courses. At the same time, some argued for a greater emphasis on 'realistic' applications of mathematics, wanting a weakening of the boundary between mathematics and 'everyday' and 'economic' concerns (Cooper 1985a). This demand appeared again in the early 1980s. There has also been an on-going debate over pedagogy between, at the extremes, those favouring the learning of algorithms and those favouring children's discovery and/or invention of mathematics for themselves (Ernest 1991).

This latter debate often seems to be driven as much by preferences concerning the supposed respective merits of established authority as opposed to popular democracy as by the nature of mathematical knowledge or the technical merits of various learning theories.

If we consider the elements of these debates – 'boundaries' within mathematics and between mathematics and 'everyday' matters, 'realism' with its associated question of whose 'everyday' concerns are to be represented in school mathematics, and the debate between supposedly authoritarian and democratic pedagogic approaches – we can see that the distinction between mathematics on the one hand and cultural matters on the other is not easy to draw. Indeed, 'culture' and associated ideas such as 'communities of practice' have begun in recent years to receive more attention within the field of mathematical learning and problem-solving. Some of this discussion has employed a rather restricted use of the 'culture' concept in which it is used to capture what are seen as defining elements in particular classroom approaches to mathematics or what it is that a teacher and his or her pupils share as a result of their work together (Davis 1989). Some of it, however, moves beyond this narrow concern to consider extra-school culture in relation to mathematical problem-solving, broadly conceived (e.g. Lave 1988). There has also been a growing literature on the relations between mathematics and its cultural context (e.g. MacKenzie 1981). There has been increasing discussion of ethnicity and mathematics (Shan and Bailey 1991) and, informed by feminist thinking, there have been claims that school mathematics typically has been 'gendered' in ways that favour boys over girls (e.g. Walkerdine *et al.* 1989). The latter claim, of course, only makes sense on the basis of assumptions about the ways in which boys and girls typically differ from each other, either in terms of cognitive predisposition or cultural identity. Turning to this side of the relation – the child – we can note that there has been a long tradition of analysing cultural differences between social groups with particular reference to their relevance for school achievement. Orientations to time, linguistic resources, orientations concerning 'abstraction', willingness to tolerate ambiguity, 'cultural capital' and many other factors have been discussed in the literature. Writers addressing these matters have often been attacked for characterizing the members of 'disadvantaged' groups in terms of a 'deficit', read off by comparing them with some other group presented as 'normal'. We would readily agree that sometimes this criticism is justified, but if carried too far it rules out a quite proper sociological concern with the consequences of the *relations* between a child's cultural resources, which are given on entry to the school, and what the school demands of the child as the conditions of his or her success. For a simple example, consider the child whose domestic language is 'B' but whose school demands the use of language 'A'. This child is not in any intrinsic sense linguistically deprived, but clearly is *relatively* deprived of a resource that the school demands for 'normal' progress to occur. It is true that the child's relative deprivation could be removed by a change in the school's linguistic medium of teaching and learning, though such a change might, of course, leave the child relatively deprived at a later stage of life. The key point here, however, is that, in the absence of such a change, the child is likely to do less well at school than speakers of language 'A', all other things being equal. Recent debates in California over the language of teaching, learning and assessment for pupils of 'limited English proficiency' illustrate the dilemmas that exist in this area.

There has been a neglect, especially within research on mathematics education, of the ways in which cultural differences between children from differing social classes might influence their success and failure in mathematics (Apple 1992, 1995a, 1995b). This is partly a result of a reaction against what were seen as 'deficit' theories and partly because of a relative falling away of concern with social class differences in educational achievement in comparison with the post-war period. Much more energy has been expended on the important areas of gender and ethnicity. But a little reflection on the existing literature on social class differences in attitudes to formal knowledge and problem-solving suggests that this area deserves further attention. For example, both Bernstein (e.g. 1996) in England and Bourdieu (e.g. 1986) in France have produced evidence which suggests, respectively, that both children and adults from the dominant and subordinate social classes of these societies differ considerably in their orientation to the boundary between 'everyday' and 'esoteric' knowledge. We return to their work in Chapter 4, but here we can just note the obvious potential relevance of such research to 'realistic' school mathematics. On the working assumption that their past research remains of relevance in more recent times, we can see that a shift to a curriculum and to assessment items that embed mathematical operations in 'everyday' contexts might not be neutral in its effects with respect to children from different social class backgrounds. We will show that it is possible that assessment via 'realistic' items might serve to exaggerate reported differences in mathematical understanding between the social classes. Furthermore, even if the details of these particular sociologists' claims were to be found wanting, either because of problems in their initial work or because of recent social and cultural change, the general point remains important. Changes in school subjects, and in assessment regimes in particular, should be examined not only from the point of view of their technical adequacy, that is their validity and reliability, but also in terms of the ways their demands intersect with the cultural resources of the various social groups confronted with them.

There a number of points we should add here, before describing the organization of this book. We know already, as a result of responses to our work at conferences, that there will be a few individuals within the world of mathematics education who will wish that we had not produced this account of the difficulties children experience with 'realistic' items. Such critics may be variously motivated. At worst, they may have a commitment to the merits of 'relevant' and 'realistic' school mathematics, which brooks no criticism. More acceptably, they may fear that those demanding a return to a regime emphasizing the rote-learning and testing of simple arithmetical algorithms may find support in the work reported here. We have some sympathy with this concern. However, practices in education must be considered in terms of a number of values simultaneously. Such values, for us, alongside those relating to pedagogy itself, include those relating to the fairness of assessment processes as well as to their technical adequacy. And, while we obviously have our own preferences concerning the nature of school mathematics, it remains crucially important, whatever current practice is, that any unintended effects it might have, with respect to either cognitive development or social selection, should be analysed with reference to evidence rather than personal preference. It may seem obvious to some, for example, that working-class children will benefit from 'relevant' or 'realistic' school mathematics, but perhaps we should check. Furthermore, even accepting that there may be good pedagogic or economic reasons for employing 'realistic' approaches in school mathematics, we still have much to learn about the ways in which their introduction, especially in the context of assessment, operates to mislead us about *which* children know exactly *what* mathematics. We hope this book proves a useful contribution to this understanding.

Organization of the book

Chapter 2 begins with a brief account of the origins and nature of the assessment regime for school mathematics in England at the time of our research. It then describes the research project on which this book is based. It ends with a discussion of two problematic variables, 'ability' and social class. Chapter 3 begins with a little history, looking at various claims concerning the relations between the 'abstractness' of mathematics and problems in the 'real world'. It then offers a critical account of some previous research on children's approaches to 'realistic' mathematics problems, before ending with an analysis of some of the peculiarities of National Curriculum test items and a brief discussion of one possible way of understanding children's responses to them. In Chapter 4, we employ the responses of two children to several 'realistic' test items in order (1) to illustrate the distinctive ways in which children might respond to such items, and (2) to introduce some key ideas from the work of Bernstein and Bourdieu on the manner in which individuals from different social class backgrounds might vary in their response to problem-solving situations. The chapter ends by providing a model of the ways in which culture might interact with assessment to produce 'differential validity'. In Chapter 5 we present two main statistical analyses of children's mathematical test performance at 10–11 years of age. Initially, after considering some technical problems concerning the reporting of achievement by NC 'levels', we present an overall analysis of performance by social class, sex, school and measured 'ability'. We then consider the ways in which children from various socio-cultural backgrounds perform on the two separate subclasses of items, which we have termed 'esoteric' and 'realistic'. In Chapter 6 we explore the responses of more than one hundred children to just two of the 'realistic' items previously discussed in Chapter 4, with two purposes. First, we wish to examine whether the possible social class differences in children's modes of responses pointed to in Chapter 4 exist across our sample as a whole. Second, we wish to consider whether some part of the social class differences in relative performance on 'esoteric' and 'realistic' items reported in Chapter 5 can be accounted for by the differentiated ways in which children interpret 'realistic' items. In Chapter 7 we explore the relationships between the overall achievement of 13–14-year-olds in the NC tests and a variety of factors. The chapter begins with an analysis of the distribution of children by our research schools to the hierarchically organized tiers of the NC tests. It considers the possible effects of the patterning of this distribution on measured achievement in the NC tests. The chapter then considers NC achievement in relation to sex, social class, school and measured 'ability'. In Chapter 8 we return to explore children's struggle with the meaning and demands of particular items. We begin with an analysis of the responses of both 10–11- and 13–14-year-olds to a data-handling item, which originally appeared in the Key Stage 2 tests. We then move to analyse the responses of higher attaining 13–14-year-olds to an item concerning probability. Our focus in this chapter is on the apparent tendency of some children to produce inadequately explicit responses to items requiring elaborated 'reasons' to be given for answers, and the consequences of this tendency for the validity of the assessment of these children's knowledge and understanding. In Chapter 9 we compare children's responses to two Key Stage 3 algebra items, which involve the constructing and simplifying of expressions. Our focus is on the ways in which the embedding of one of these tasks in an 'everyday' context leads to difficulties for some children in understanding the intended goal of the problem. We also consider the ways in which such difficulties are distributed by social class and sex. We turn now, in Chapter 2, to a description of our research programme.

2 | The research: origins, methods, issues

The research reported here had its origins in a concern that the initial test items produced for the National Curriculum (NC) in England might produce unintended difficulties for children, as a result of the ways mathematical operations were embedded in textually represented 'realistic' contexts (Cooper 1992, 1994b). A small pilot project was carried out in the summer of 1994, based on interviewing just 15 upper primary school children aged 10–11 years while they attempted, individually, to solve NC items. It was clear from this work that children were experiencing problems in negotiating the boundary between their 'everyday' and formal mathematical knowledge. In particular, it seemed that some test items, to be discussed in detail later, had the effect of leading children to draw 'inappropriately' on their 'everyday' knowledge in formulating their answers. As a result, these children failed to demonstrate mathematical understanding that their interview responses clearly showed that they had (Cooper 1995, 1998a, 1998b). This finding seemed to merit further investigation and, after the award of a grant from the Economic and Social Research Council, it became possible to examine children's responses to NC test items on a wider scale, both in test and interview contexts, and in both primary and secondary schools.

In this chapter we describe the initial design and subsequent practice of the research. We also discuss briefly the way in which we have categorized children by social class and our perspective on the measured 'ability' scores that we make some use of in our later analyses. First, however, we need to describe one or two aspects of the English National Curriculum in mathematics at the time of the research, and the development of the procedures for its assessment.

National Curriculum and assessment in mathematics

The UK Government made it clear in 1987 that there was to be a national programme of testing associated with the National Curriculum, which would be introduced in the 1988 Education Act. A Task Group on Assessment and Testing (TGAT) was set up to advise on its nature. As Ball (1990: 189) has shown, the nature of the membership of TGAT enabled an 'educationalist' voice to be 're-admitted . . . into the formal corridors of policy making'. TGAT's proposals (DES/WO 1988) are perhaps best seen as having been an attempt to argue for 'authentic assessment' in a context where key political forces were arguing for relatively simple paper and pencil tests of limited educational objectives as their preferred model of National Curriculum assessment. TGAT's proposed model emphasized continuous assessment by teachers (called Teacher Assessment – TA – in the UK), which would be moderated by externally set Standard Assessment Tasks (SATs) at the end of four Key Stages (KS) at the ages of 7, 11, 14 and 16. Curriculum subjects were to be set out via Attainment Targets (ATs) and associated Statements of Attainment (SoAs), with ten levels of attainment being specified. However, it is important to stress, given later developments, that TGAT did not intend that all the ATs would be tested via the SATs but rather that a limited number of 'profile components' (within which various ATs would be grouped) would be the focus of testing. Subsequent political debate over the proposals led to a shift towards the privileging of external assessment over continuous assessment by teachers. Notwithstanding this, the SATs were, in the initial stages, intended to be much more than paper and pencil tests. It was expected that they would involve a variety of practical and investigative activities.

The TGAT proposals did not only come under political attack however; teachers were also to express dissatisfaction about aspects of the assessment programme. As we noted above, TGAT had originally intended that the SATs would sample a range of ATs but not that there would be comprehensive coverage of all of them. The intended purpose of the SATs was to moderate, at the level of the class, a teacher's own continuous assessment of pupils. However, Government policy shifted this position to one where, by 1990/91, there was to be some written testing under controlled conditions of all pupils in each AT except where the nature of the AT made this 'inappropriate' (Brown 1992). In particular, Attainment Target 1: Using and Applying Mathematics has not been assessed via these tests (Schools Examinations and Assessment Council (SEAC) 1993a, 1993b). As a result of this political demand for more testing, and given the relatively complex test items to which TGAT's preference for 'authentic assessment' led, the initial trials of the NC tests led to considerable teacher disquiet over 'excessive' workloads (Torrance 1993). Eventually, this was to result in a teacher boycott of testing in 1993 with the consequence that although the tests were sometimes used by teachers with their pupils, in most cases their results were not reported to Government. The consequences of these shifts, coupled with the pressure on test developers to respond to such changes within very tight deadlines (Brown 1992, 1993), were that, by 1992, paper and pencil tests were being produced that involved contrived tasks which tended to compromise pedagogic 'good practice' as it had been set out in the influential Cockcroft Report on school mathematics of 1982 (see p. 22 this volume). In particular, some items in the Key Stage 3 (KS3) tests for 14-year-olds seemed likely to disadvantage pupils who took seriously the injunction to relate mathematics to the 'real world' (Cooper 1992). The pencil and paper tests for KS2 for 11-year-olds in 1993 seemed open to the same criticism and also seemed, via the marking scheme, to make the achievement of higher levels of NC attainment dependent on a child's capacity and/or willingness to avoid drawing on or referring to everyday knowledge when responding to the items (Cooper 1994b). Nevertheless, at least in terms of the sorts of examples discussed by some US researchers on assessment (e.g. Shepard 1995), these tests consist largely of performance assessment items. They often require the child to undertake the solution to a problem without any provision of a range of possible responses and they often require the child's understanding and/or process of working to be demonstrated in a written response. Furthermore, as a consequence of the move away from earlier concerns with 'modern' or structural algebra (Cooper 1985a, 1994a), the recent paper and pencil tests have had a preponderance of items that have 'realistic' settings. It is also important to note that, while there are multiple-choice items in these tests, they do not dominate the tests (see, e.g. Schools Examinations and Assessment Council 1993a, 1993b; Schools Curriculum and Assessment Authority 1994).

The main project

As we noted earlier, there were some good reasons to expect that the combination of relatively open-ended test items with 'real' contexts might produce a particular set of threats to valid assessment and that these threats might be expected to operate differently for children from different socio-economic backgrounds (Cooper 1992, 1994b; see also Morais et al. 1992, for relevant Portuguese evidence concerning science tasks).[1] Since the pilot work had suggested (see Chapter 4) that some children, when given a chance to reconsider their initial 'inappropriate' and – in terms of the NC marking scheme – incorrect response, could move to offer a correct response, the main project design was built around the comparison of children's responses in test and interview contexts. The collection of test performance data would allow us to explore the ways in which performance on NC items of various types differed by social class, sex, school and measured 'ability'. The interview data would enable us to explore whether, and in what ways, the test data validly represented the mathematical knowledge and understanding of children, both in general but also in relation to their membership of particular social groups. A brief description of the research follows. We expand details as necessary in later chapters.

We have employed both quantitative and qualitative methods. The basic strategy has been to use initially statistical analysis of children's performance on items in test situations to generate insights concerning broad classes of test items, e.g. items that embed mathematical operations in 'realistic' and 'esoteric' contexts respectively.[2] This has involved coding test items on a number of dimensions. These have included type of contextualization, 'wordiness', difficulty levels, attainment target, type of response required, and use of pictorial representation. Analyses of the relationships between social class, gender, measured 'ability', item type and performance have been carried out (Cooper *et al.* 1997). Some of these use the child as the case for analysis, others use the item itself. Alongside this approach we have used more qualitative analyses of children's responses to particular items in both the tests and the subsequent individual interviews to generate understanding of *why*, for example, 'realistic' and 'esoteric' items seem to be differentially difficult for children from particular socio-cultural backgrounds. This has involved the coding of children's responses on various dimensions, especially the child's use, whether 'appropriate' or not, of 'everyday' knowledge in responding to items. In parallel, informing and being informed by this work, a model of the way culture, cognition and performance on 'realistic' test items interact has been developed (Cooper 1996, 1998b). This model is described here in Chapter 4.

In each of three primary and three secondary schools we studied, Year 6 and Year 9 children (aged respectively 10–11 and 13–14 years) took three group tests in mathematics. Two of these were the statutory May 1996 key stage tests. The third, taken some four months earlier, comprised a test put together by us by drawing on previous NC items. It is important to note that, in order to maintain comparability across the years 1992–1996, we have worked within the 1991 NC framework for mathematics which comprised five Attainment Targets (National Curriculum Council 1991). One of these ATs, Using And Applying Mathematics, was not assessed via the tests. The remaining four comprised Number, Algebra, Shape And Space and Handling Data. For the same reason, and because we wished to throw light on the use of Statements of Attainment, we have also used the SoAs allocated to items where they are given by the test designers themselves and, in some analyses, have ourselves allocated SoAs to items from later tests where the official rubric had not given these. We have coded the SoAs for these latter items by comparison with previous officially labelled items.

Table 2.1 The primary and secondary school samples

	Number of children tested (February 1996)	Number of children interviewed	Number of teachers interviewed (one or more times)	Number of lessons observed
Primary schools				
School A	63	63	4	4
School B	44	44	3	4
School C	29	29	6	5
Total Primary	136	136	13	13
Secondary schools				
School D	254	50	6	10
School E	102	37	5	5
School F	117	36	4	5
Total Secondary	473	123	15	20

Our February 1996 tests were designed to cover a variety of item types and the four ATs listed in the previous paragraph. Our secondary test, like the statutory May 1996 test, was tiered by NC level. As a result there were four KS3 papers of overlapping 'levels of difficulty'. The February 1996 tests were marked according to the NC marking schemes by us, while the May 1996 tests were marked by official markers employed by Government. Between the administration of the test in February and the test in May we interviewed all of the Year 6 children and a 25 per cent sample of the Year 9 children while they worked individually through a selection of items from the February test. This allowed access to children's interpretations of the items and to their methods of solution. Furthermore, and this has been a crucial part of our approach, it was possible to allow children to reconsider their solution strategy and their answer itself in cases where they had initially chosen an 'inappropriate' 'everyday' reading of the meaning and requirement of the item. This has allowed us to explore the ways in which the use of a certain class of 'realistic' items can lead to the underestimation of children's actual existing knowledge and understanding (Cooper and Dunne 1998). In order to allow an examination of social class effects we have also collected information on parental occupations. The issue of parental occupations proved to be a sensitive one, especially in the secondary schools. Two of the three secondary schools required parental permission before children were allowed to supply this information. The third required that the question go directly to the home with the result that we gained this information for only 43 per cent of the sample in this school (School 'D' in Table 2.1). We also have children's scores on the three parts of the Nelson Cognitive Ability tests. The nature of the samples and the project's activities are set out in Table 2.1. The teacher interviews and the lesson observations were undertaken partly to gather teachers' accounts of the impact of testing and partly to gain some understanding of each school's approach to teaching mathematics.

We now turn to discuss measured 'ability' and social class.

Measured 'ability'

We have no doubt that part of the audience for this book will expect the use of data on 'ability' in our analyses. We are equally sure that another part of the audience will expect us to reject the use of such data on a mixture of theoretical and political grounds. Perhaps we can find a way of responding to both? What is it that verbal, quantitative and non-verbal Nelson Cognitive Ability Test (CAT) scores capture? Is it simply some underlying 'ability' and, if not, should we use these scores as central variables in our various analyses? There are several points to note.

First, the research programme from which this book derives was based on the working assumption that paper and pencil tests in mathematics might fail in many ways to capture what children actually know and understand and, furthermore, that part of this failure might be explicable in terms of differences of a broadly cultural nature between children from different social backgrounds. Clearly then, symmetry considerations alone would suggest that we would be – and are – wary of assuming that CAT tests can provide us with a gold standard for measuring 'ability'. In fact there is an enormous literature questioning the validity of various tests of 'ability' and/or 'intelligence' from a wide variety of perspectives. Among other problems, it seems likely that such tests reflect definitions of 'intelligence' favoured by particular social groups, usually the more powerful in society (Henderson 1976). It is also the case that the independent criterion used to validate the claims that these tests are tests of 'intelligence' or 'ability' is sometimes a measure of school achievement (Ryan 1972). Since school achievement is linked to such variables as social class, this approach to validation almost inevitably helps produce a test that, via a form of circular reasoning, favours children from those social groups who have been assessed by other means as performing better in the school system. There are also a variety of other problems with various well-known tests, although many of these concern the ways in which performance data have been collected, analysed and used rather than the tests *per se* (Gould 1984).

re also seem to be particular problems with the CAT tests them-
s. First of all, there is some doubt whether these tests are tests of
y' or tests of 'attainment' (a distinction that anyway can be difficult
end). Consider one edition of these tests. The quantitative battery,
ample, starts like this: 'In this booklet there are three tests that
will give you a chance to show *what you know* and *how well you think*'
(Thorndike and Hagen 1973: 3, our italics). A look at the items shows
that several of them are clearly knowledge-dependent, involving reference to minutes, hours, units of measurement for length, interest, etc.
Clearly a child's 'ability' here will be dependent on their knowledge of
these conventional measures and terms. Second, as with many tests that
require the child to choose one answer from a range, it is not obvious in
the case of several items that there is one incontestable correct answer
(Mehan 1973). Here, from the verbal battery, are three examples from
one page:

Most modern ships are _____ with radio telephones.

F blessed   G burdened   H equipped   J complete   K sailed

I find it hard to decide _____ to go or not.

A whether   B how   C but   D when   E if

He was sick and could not work to _____ his family.

A visit   B support   C hold   D cure   E save

Is it obvious that each of these has one best answer? We think not. Other
items require knowledge of the names of planets, religions, the names of
flowers and so on. On the face of it, the quantitative and verbal tests are
partly dependent on knowledge and, as such, are tests of attainment as
much as 'ability'. The non-verbal battery is different insofar as it is based
on reasoning about patterns and shapes, but even here children will
differ in their experience of such things and therefore in the degree to
which they are bewildered or otherwise by the items' demands.

Notwithstanding all these problems, various sociologists working in
the tradition of political arithmetic have used such 'ability' measures in
their work, both directly (e.g. Douglas 1964) and indirectly (e.g. Halsey *et
al.* 1980). Such usage enabled Halsey *et al.* (1980), for example, to demonstrate that working-class boys seem to have needed a higher IQ than
their service-class competitors in order to enter selective schooling in
England and Wales in the past (see Table 2.2 on p. 18 for definitions of
these social class categories). One way of interpreting these findings, for
those who suspect that 'ability' tests underestimate working-class 'ability' relative to service-class 'ability', is to regard Halsey's estimates of the
disadvantages suffered by working-class boys as minimal estimates of any

bias in the selective processes of schooling during the periods covered by his work. Such a position has some advantages, especially as it enables one form of critical analysis of school systems that present themselves as fair in their operation. A similar approach has been taken by those who have criticized the ways in which some local education authorities in the UK have awarded fewer selective school places to girls than their measured 'ability' would appear to justify (for an account of this debate, see Gipps and Murphy 1994). Such uses of the results of 'ability' tests are, of course, open to attack from those who wish to reject, in a more radical fashion, any attempt to recognize and account for individual differences in 'ability'. Children of 10–11 years of age are, however, likely to differ in respect of 'cognitive power'. We say this without wanting to prejudice any discussion of why. We also recognize that there needs to be continuing discussion of the forms of cognitive powers, which need to be distinguished (Gardner 1983) and of the social processes by which some of these powers, when realized as and in 'texts', become more highly regarded than others (Henderson 1976; Bourdieu 1986). Nevertheless, given the recognition that such differences between children exist, there is a need for some way of bringing their effects into analyses of performance on NC tests. In our case, the use of CAT scores will enable some statistical control to be exercised in the study of performance in mathematics tests. However, we remain sceptical about the adequacy of 'ability' tests as measures of such general 'abilities' as quantitative reasoning and, especially, about whether these tests are 'fair' across such groups as social classes and sexes. A more fruitful way of viewing these tests would seem to be to regard them as 'predictors of academic achievement' in given school systems, but only while remembering that these systems include, as a feature, existing relations between the socio-cultural background of pupils on the one hand and the cognitive demands of socially constructed curriculum and assessment systems on the other. As a consequence, insofar as 'ability' tests have been designed to correlate with the criterion of school achievement they are likely to be far from culture-free (Ryan 1972). If we employ CAT scores in our analyses with this proviso in mind, we may find ourselves being able to say something useful about, for example, the ways in which the NC mathematics tests do or do not, for variously defined groups, result in under or over-achievement when set against the prediction of achievement offered by the (not obviously culture-free) CAT scores. We will then, for this reason, make considerable use of CAT scores, but we will remind the reader occasionally of these issues and problems. We encourage readers to reflect carefully on the implications for any discussion that involves measured 'ability' of the two distinct views: either tests results are an indicator of some relatively pure and transferable 'ability' or they are indicators of likely achievement in the school system and as such have a built-in tendency to favour children from those social backgrounds who have previously performed better in schools, as a consequence of a variety of individual, social and cultural factors.

Social class

It is clearly not possible to analyse children's responses to test items by social class without employing some system of class categorization. There has long been, and still is, a vigorous debate about whether and how to undertake such categorization in social and educational research (e.g. Crompton 1993; Apple 1995a). We have employed the social class scheme developed by Goldthorpe and others (e.g. Erikson and Goldthorpe 1993) and, in particular, are coding children's social backgrounds in terms of the 'dominance' model as set out by these authors (Erikson and Goldthorpe 1993: 238). This general approach to the operationalization of social class is based on the assumption that clusters of occupations differentiated on a number of dimensions form meaningful social class groupings (Bourdieu 1987). It also takes account of employment status (whether employed, employee or self-employed, for example). The 'dominance' approach involves the further assumption that the family as a unit is what needs to be categorized, and that coding decisions should take account of the relative strengths of each parent's relation to the labour market. In the case of parents whose individual occupations would put them into different categories, full-time work overrides part-time work, and a higher status overrides a lower one. Such decisions, and the general approach itself, are clearly contestable. However, there is considerable evidence that such an approach captures what sociologists are concerned to describe by the concept of social class (Marshall *et al.* 1988) and, furthermore, exploratory statistical analysis suggested to us that the use of available competing categorizations (e.g. Ginn and Arber 1996: 488) would not produce any major differences in our findings.

We have data, inevitably of variable quality, on the current or most recent occupation of the parents/guardians of the children in our sample. Because of the difficulties of accurately describing both occupation and/ or employment status, we suspect that a proportion of our classifications will contain error. It is also the case that there is, at best, a simplification of social reality involved in attempting to characterize a child's familial context of socialization by a measure taken at one point in time. As Featherman *et al.* (1988) have shown, there is considerable occupational movement amongst parents of young children, and much of it is across the social class boundaries described by Goldthorpe. It is also likely that, to some extent, the 'effects' of social class which we discuss in this book are 'effects' of parents' educational careers, linked to their own origin

Table 2.2 Social class categories (Goldthorpe and Heath 1992; Erikson and Goldthorpe 1993)

Social classes	
Service class	
1	Service class, higher grade: higher grade professionals, administrators and officials; managers in large industrial establishments; large proprietors.
2	Service class, lower grade: lower grade professionals, administrators and officials; higher grade technicians; managers in small industrial establishments; supervisors of non-manual employees.
Intermediate class	
3	Routine non-manual employees
4	Personal service workers
5	Small proprietors with employees
6	Small proprietors without employees
7	Farmers and smallholders
8	Foremen and technicians
Working class	
9	Skilled manual workers
10	Semi- and unskilled manual workers
11	Agricultural workers

and destination class, i.e. of the distribution, in Bourdieu's (1994) terms, of educational capital (*capital scolaire*). Partly as a result of Featherman's findings and partly as a result of our sample size, we have chosen mainly to employ in the body of the book a three-category version of the chosen social class scheme, with the original 11 categories being collapsed into groupings previously described by Goldthorpe and his co-workers as the service class, the intermediate class and the working class. The details of these groupings are given in Table 2.2. We have collapsed categories one and two into a service class, categories three to eight into an intermediate class, and categories nine to eleven into a working class. We will occasionally, however, make use of the more differentiated 11-category scheme.

We have described the research and some of our working assumptions. We now wish, in Chapter 3, to discuss some previous research on mathematical problem-solving, especially in relation to 'realistic' contexts, before presenting, in the context of the pilot data, some key ideas from the work of Bernstein and Bourdieu in Chapter 4.

Notes

1 This claim concerning validity is dependent, of course, and in various ways, on what one takes to be school mathematics and, especially, how one views the boundary between mathematical operations and everyday knowledge (cf. Dowling 1991).
2 These have been defined as follows: 'realistic' items set mathematical operations in contexts involving everyday objects and people; 'esoteric' do not. A fuller account is given in Chapter 5.

3 | Children and 'realistic' test items: previous studies and National Curriculum test items

Introduction

Our research concerns the ways in which children interpret 'realistic' test items, and the consequences of their interpretations for their performance. There are two major ways in which children, when responding to such items, may fail to negotiate successfully the boundary between their 'everyday' knowledge and the 'esoteric' knowledge represented by mathematics as a formal discipline. On the one hand, they might fail to apply 'realistic' considerations when they 'ought' to. On the other hand, they might bring their 'everyday' knowledge to bear on a problem when it is 'inappropriate' to do so. We illustrate both of these possibilities in this chapter, but we begin with the former since it has received much more attention in the research literature to date. Our purpose is to illustrate certain problems and absences in the discussion within the field of mathematics education of children's 'failure' to use 'realistic' knowledge when solving 'realistic' mathematics problems in both ordinary classroom and research contexts. After discussing some of these problems by reference to the research literature on rather stereotyped word problems, the discussion is extended by reference to more complex 'realistic' NC items. Here the second problem, applying 'everyday' knowledge 'inappropriately' becomes the focus of our discussion. Before we begin this discussion, however, we present, as a context, a little history.

A little history

The proper relation between the 'everyday' and the 'abstract' in mathematical study is, of course, a frequent topic of debate. Consider these three quotes, spanning a period of more than 80 years:

Mathematics as a science commenced when first someone, probably a Greek, proved propositions about any things or about some things, without specification of definite particular things.

(Whitehead 1911/1948: 7)

It was only within the last twenty years or so that a definition of mathematics emerged on which most mathematicians now agree: mathematics is the science of patterns. What the mathematician does is study abstract 'patterns'. . .

(Devlin 1997: 3)

The satisfaction of achievement and the intrinsic beauty of mathematical relationships is sufficient justification for the course for more able pupils. For the rest of secondary school pupils we need a new and different approach, but not the same for all. The next twenty per cent of the ability range have some capacity for abstraction, and a course similar to some of the present [Certificate of Secondary Education] courses with an emphasis on the practical rather than the abstract mathematics would be suitable. Again, much more practice of basic arithmetic and some simple algebra would add to the pupils' confidence and their capacity to cope with work after school . . . For the rest of the secondary school pupils I think we must differentiate between the first three years, when the subject can be taught in the context of the classroom, and the other two years when I think there must be a much closer integration between the school and the outside world . . . To summarise, I think that much of the disorder in schools is because children are being asked to do work in all subjects, but particularly in mathematics, which is beyond their inherent capabilities, and this will continue until we recognise that different children need basically different courses . . . We must stop trying to teach abstract mathematics to all pupils, and concentrate on mathematics for some pupils and competence in arithmetic as a first priority for the majority.

(Hayman 1975: 147–8 and 153)

These three quotes raise some interesting questions. The first and second, separated by some 90 years, are both from books written by university researchers with the aim of increasing 'lay' understanding of mathematics. There is an explicit belief that mathematics is 'abstract' and perhaps an implicit belief that this abstractness can be made comprehensible for the 'general reader'. The third quote is taken from the Presidential Address to the Mathematical Association, given by Margaret Hayman in the mid-1970s.[1] At this time, she worked at Putney High School (a high status selective secondary school, and a member of the Girls Public Day Schools Trust). She was reacting to the changes in mathematics education that had occurred in England as a consequence of the conjunction of the 'modern mathematics' reform movement and the introduction of forms of comprehensive education. Like the other two writers, she also seems to believe that mathematics is an abstract discipline, but she apparently is quite convinced that only some children can contemplate this abstractness successfully. In fact, she claimed, discussing 'mixed-ability teaching', that 'in a class of thirty there may only be one really mathematical child' (Hayman 1975: 144). Perhaps she had no difficulty in recognizing which child this was as well as what his or her 'needs' were? Certainly it is clear in her talk that, for her, the children who were not 'really mathematical' were those who previously had gone 'from school to apprenticeships of some kind, where the work they had done at school was seen to be relevant and an adequate base from which to develop technical skills . . .' (Hayman 1975: 138).

Hayman's attack on what she saw as the introduction, for 'everybody' rather than a 'few', of the 'old grammar school course' can serve as an illustrative, if perhaps extreme, example of the various strident reactions in England in the early to mid-1970s to the effects on the curriculum of such projects as the School Mathematics Project (Cooper 1985a). One result of these specific attacks on 'modern mathematics', in the context of a generalized attack from the political right on comprehensive education (Ball 1990), was the setting up of a committee of enquiry on mathematics education (Cockcroft 1982), which argued strongly for mathematics courses to be well-differentiated by 'attainment' (Cooper 1985b; Ruthven 1986). Bringing together what had been said 'many times and over many years' it also argued, in the now famous paragraph 243, that mathematics teaching 'at all levels should include opportunities for:

- exposition by the teacher
- discussion between teachers and pupils and between pupils themselves
- appropriate practical work
- consolidation and practice of fundamental skills and routines
- problem-solving, including the application of mathematics to everyday situations
- investigational work'

(Cockcroft 1982: paragraph 243)

Problem-solving was to 'relate to both the application of mathematics to everyday situations within the pupils' experience, and also to situations which are unfamiliar' (Cockcroft 1982: paragraph 249). 'Investigations' were not presented as equivalent to 'projects', i.e. as being necessarily an extended piece of work, but rather as concerning a willingness to ask 'what if?' questions generally in lessons (Cockcroft 1982: paragraph 250).

A subsequent document from Her Majesty's Inspectorate (1985), *Mathematics from 5 to 16*, recommended that 'appropriate practical work', 'problem-solving' and 'investigative work' should all form part of classroom approaches. Problem-solving and investigative work were seen as not clearly distinguishable, but it was suggested that the former involved relatively convergent tasks and the latter more divergent ones. It was argued:

> It is worth stressing to pupils that, in real life, mathematical solutions to problems have often to be judged by criteria of a non-mathematical nature, some of which may be political, moral or social. For example, the most direct route for a proposed new stretch of motorway might be unacceptable as it would cut across a heavily built-up area.
>
> (HMI 1985: 41)

There is a certain irony in all these reactions to the consequences of the 'modern mathematics' movement. As it happens, in contrast with the European and US versions of 'modern mathematics', the varieties produced in England, at least for adolescent children, had been compromises reflecting both the abstract algebraic preferences of some pure mathematicians and the newer applications of mathematics favoured by other interest groups (Cooper 1985a). Throughout the debate in the late 1950s and 1960s there had been voices arguing for a more 'realistic' approach in mathematics alongside those arguing for more abstract algebraic elements. One such key actor was Hammersley, an applied mathematician later to attack 'modern mathematics', who had claimed at a meeting, which arguably started the process of reform in England:

> Mathematical examination problems are usually considered unfair if insoluble or improperly described; whereas the mathematical problems of real life are almost invariably insoluble and badly stated, at least in the first instance. In real life, the mathematician's main task is to formulate problems by building an abstract mathematical model consisting of equations, which shall be simple enough to solve without being so crude that they fail to mirror reality.
>
> (Abbreviated Proceedings 1957: 10)

Mathematics educators will recognize in these remarks a comparison of well and ill-structured problems (Pandey 1990). We shall see below that there remains considerable confusion about which of these types of supposedly 'realistic' problem it is that children should study and be able to solve.

Children and 'realistic' mathematics problems

It is not just in England that the 'realistic' aspects of mathematics education have been a central concern (NCTM 1991). Indeed, it has been argued that 'how children transfer knowledge between school and the outside world may be the central problem in education' (Baranes *et al.* 1989: 287). Not surprisingly therefore, in recent years there has been a considerable body of research and writing across the world addressing a set of interconnected issues concerning 'realistic' contexts and school mathematics (Boaler 1993a, 1993b; Davis and Maher 1993). Much of this work is concerned with the possible beneficial effects of using 'realistic' contexts in the teaching of mathematics, both for children's motivation and learning and for user groups such as employers outside the school (Cockcroft 1982). Another strand of it reports research showing that both children and adults can calculate and use numerical reasoning successfully in 'real' contexts, often employing situational resources, without recourse to school-taught algorithms (Scribner 1984; Nunes *et al.* 1993). This strand might be said to focus broadly on individuals' 'successful' numerical activities-in-context. Yet another strand in the work, however, concerns children's 'failure' to apply their knowledge of school-taught algorithms 'appropriately' to textual representations of supposedly 'real' problem contexts (e.g. Baranes *et al.* 1989; Greer 1993; Silver *et al.* 1993; Verschaffel *et al.* 1994). Because of its apparent relevance to the focus in our research on performance on 'realistic' test items, it is this latter work we discuss in this chapter.

This particular body of research looks in some detail at children's relative performance, written and/or oral, on mathematics items that contextualize numerical operations in different ways. For example, in the work by Baranes and her colleagues, problems range through what are described as 'symbolic computations', 'word problems' and 'simulated store situations' (Baranes *et al.* 1989). Examples from her work, where the dashes are replaced by given numbers in actual testing, are:

Symbolic computation: 12×50
Word problem: John had ____ marbles. He played with Paul and won ____ marbles. How many marbles does he have now?
Store problem: The pen costs $____. I'm paying you with $____. How much is my change?

Baranes *et al.* (1989) were interested, amongst other things, in differences in children's performance between items where the numbers matched the problem content (e.g. 100 divided by four in the context of US money – quarters) and where they did not. They found that children were more likely to access their everyday knowledge of money, for example, when 'numbers matched the problem content'. A key type of problem in this work, however, is what has been termed (by Silver *et al.* 1993) 'augmented quotient' problems. For example, Silver *et al.* recall the US child's frequent failure, in the context of testing, to respond 'realistically' to the now infamous item 'An army bus holds 36 soldiers. If 1,128 soldiers are being bussed to their training site, how many buses are needed?' Children commonly gave non-whole number answers. Such answers were seen by the test designers as inappropriate for counting buses.

Much of this body of research on 'realistic' problem-solving has several typical characteristics, which we list here before discussing them in greater detail.

1 The 'realistic' problems discussed are usually *textual representations* of problem situations rather than actual problems situated in everyday contexts (e.g. Baranes *et al.* 1989; Greer 1993; Verschaffel *et al.* 1994). Occasionally the use of simulation moves the problem a step further away from this textual focus (e.g. work by Curcio and DeFranco reported by Silver *et al.* 1993). The problems are also very stereotyped, often unintentionally under-specified, and superficially look just like traditional word problems.

2 The accounts of the research are often characterized by an assumption that children *ought* to be able and willing to apply school-taught algorithms 'realistically' to *textual representations* of 'everyday' problems. Verschaffel *et al.*, for example, having shown that Flemish children 'fail' to take 'realistic' considerations into account in solving a certain range of problems then go on to discuss how these 'undesirable learning outcomes' arise and might be remedied (Verschaffel *et al.* 1994: 291–3).

3 The mathematics educators' own discussions of these problems and their solutions suggest that a rather peculiar set of conventions about the 'real' are being drawn on in this research literature.

4 The favoured explanations for children's failure to import 'realistic' considerations into their solution processes refer to what might be described as 'internalist' cultural accounts. It is children's experience of a particular pedagogic approach in school that is seen to produce their defective responses, and it is in pedagogic reform that the remedy is seen to lie (e.g. Verschaffel *et al.* 1994). What children bring from non-school settings is not generally discussed (though, ironically, such settings are the key focus of attention in the well-known work of Lave 1988 and Nunes *et al.* 1993).

5 Linked to the previous point there is a tendency in this research literature to treat children as an undifferentiated group. Perhaps because the locus of explanation is seen as internal to the school, the findings are not typically broken down by, for example, social class, gender or ethnicity. There is no recourse, for example, to the sociology of culture as practised by Bernstein (1996) or Bourdieu (1986) as a possible source of explanations for *differences* between children in their mode of response.

We now discuss some examples of this work in more detail in order to develop some of these points. We then consider features of some English NC test items in the light of the discussion.

An example

We take as our first example the work of Verschaffel, De Corte and Lasure (1994). In this work, 75 Flemish 10–11-year-olds from three schools 'composed of middle class children' were asked to solve two broad categories of ten questions each:

> pupils were collectively administered a word problem solving test in a regular classroom context. Besides problems that are simple and straightforward from the mathematical modelling point of view, the tests contained parallel versions in which the mathematical model-ling assumptions were deliberately made problematic, *at least if one seriously takes into account the realities of the context in which the mathem-atical problem is embedded.*
>
> (Verschaffel *et al.*: 274, their italics)

They describe the difference between the items in each pair as follows:

> a standard problem (S problem) asking for the straightforward application of one or more arithmetic operations with the given num-bers (e.g., 'Steve has bought 5 planks of 2 m each. How many planks of 1 m can he saw out of these planks?'), and

> a parallel problem (P problem) in which the mathematical model-ling assumptions are problematic, at least if one seriously takes into account the realities of the context called up by the problem state-ment (e.g., 'Steve has bought 4 planks of 2.5 m each. How many planks of 1 m can he saw out of these planks?').
>
> (Verschaffel *et al.* 1994: 275)

In the second case, for the child who takes 'the realities of the context' into account, the correct answer is said to be eight planks, not ten. On the other hand, ten is presented as the correct response to the first of the plank problems. But consider the child's situation. Both these problems are paper and pencil problems in a school context. However, in *both* cases there are 'realistic' considerations that might be taken into account. In the first planks problem, if it were to treated as representing the real, there would be loss of material due to sawing. This would result in very slightly short 'one metre' planks. Yet, perhaps for reasons of convention, the authors disregard this. They seem to assume that *approximately* one metre will do, and that the child will recognize this. On the other hand, they do not disregard the apparent assault on the real represented by giving the answer ten to the second plank problem. One might argue that if a child sees the need to introduce 'realistic' considerations at all then he or she ought to do so in both cases. However, what the authors seem to be doing is drawing on some tacit assumptions – their 'feel for the game' – to recognize the S and the P items as different.

In fact, it is more complicated than this. What if a child does act in the way they would like to see. He or she 'decides' to treat the P problem as requiring reference to 'realistic' considerations and/or 'common-sense' knowledge? Look at the problem again. Steve has four planks of 2.5 metres. He needs one metre planks. But what does he need them for? If it is shelves that he is building then perhaps the model of the real situation traded on by Verschaffel *et al.* is appropriate. It would be very difficult, though not impossible, to suspend two (approximately) half-metre planks between two supports set at, say, 80 cm apart. However, what if the task is to cover a floor with floorboards? Does it matter now that we have half-planks? Presumably not, assuming the underlying frame is suitably arranged.

What this shows is that the child who wanted to take seriously the 'realistic' considerations required by the authors would find him or herself with a rather ill-defined problem space to negotiate. It seems that both the right answers, of ten and eight respectively, are contestable; one because the levels of accuracy required are unclear, and one because the 'real' context is under-specified, being left to the child's imagination.

This discussion suggests that the P problem here might rationally be read by the child in the same way as the S problem. In both cases 'realistic' considerations could be seen as relevant. On the other hand, given the school context and the lack of adequate specification of the 'real' problem context, it might be a good bet to treat both as stereotypical school word problems where no reference to the 'real' is expected. This would seem to be the approach taken by one child in a second phase of this Flemish work in which some children were encouraged ('scaffolded') to reconsider their 'non-realistic' answers (De Corte *et al.* 1995). Here is the transcript, described as 'typical' (I = interviewer; P = pupil):

I: Can you read aloud this problem as well as what you have written in response to it on your answer sheet?

P: Steve has bought 4 planks of 2.5 meter each. How many planks of 1 meter can he get out of these planks? Answer: $2.5 \times 4 = 10$; Steve can saw 10 planks of 1 meter.

I: One of your friends responded in this way: '$4 \times 2 = 8$; Steve can saw 8 planks'. Who is right? (= scaffold 1)

P: I am right. That other pupil thought the problem was about '4 planks of 2 meter each' instead of '4 planks of 2.5 meter each'.

> I: Can you draw what happened with these planks according to the story and show on this drawing how many planks of 1 meter Steve can saw out of these 4 planks? (= scaffold 2)
>
> P: (The pupil draws one long and small rectangle consisting of four planks that are joined together tightly.)
>
> I: How many planks of 1 meter can Steve saw out of these 4 planks?
>
> P: 10.
>
> I: Can you draw one plank of 2.5 meter.
>
> P: (The pupil draws one small rectangle with a length of 1/4 of the long rectangle.)
>
> I: How many planks of 1 meter can Steve saw out of this plank?
>
> P: 2.
>
> I: And how many planks of 1 meter can he saw out of 4 such planks?
>
> P: 10, because he ends up with 4 planks of 0.5 meter and . . . two halves make one whole.
>
> (De Corte *et al.* 1995: 13)

De Corte and his co-authors see this as confirming 'pupils' tendency to exclude common-sense knowledge and realistic considerations from their understanding and solution of school arithmetic word problems' (1995: 14). The use of 'exclude' perhaps suggests too positive and conscious a choice on the part of the pupil, but the point we wish to discuss here is a different one. It concerns the asymmetry of the views presented by the authors of the children on the one hand and themselves on the other. We can grant that the children have 'excluded' 'realistic' considerations (unless, of course, it is argued that the children's responses are 'realistic' given their previous experience of school word problems and their asso-ciated 'right answers'). However, we can also point to the authors' own 'failure' to take 'realistic' considerations seriously enough in their design of the items. To reiterate, the 'realistic' problem is underspecified. Who 'really' saws wood into planks without knowing what they are to be for? Furthermore, there are other potentially variable features of the problem that are apparently assumed to be non-variable. For example, an unchan-ging width for the planks is just taken for granted by the researchers. We could always saw the planks in two dimensions, generating an enormous number of solutions, which do or do not take 'realistic' considerations into account. Given all this, it is perhaps a little harsh to describe the children's strategies for the P problems as 'mindless and non-realistic' (De Corte *et al.* 1995).

Since some readers are likely to find this discussion strange, and may be worried that we have selected a particular example to make a point, we will also consider the most famous item template in this literature, the one concerning soldiers and buses. Here is one instantiation of the template, referring to a real baseball team in Pittsburgh, and taken from Silver *et al.* (1993: 121):

> The Clearview Little League is going to a Pirates' game. There are 540 people, including players, coaches and parents. They will travel by bus, and each bus holds 40 people. How many buses will they need to get to the game.

The required answer is not 540 divided by 40, giving a result of 13.5, which is seen as an 'inappropriate interpretation', but rather 14. Buses, we must assume, come as wholes not as decimal fractions. However, drawing on the same reasoning as we applied to the planks problem, it is not difficult to conjure up problem situations where 13.5 buses, or thirteen-and-a-half buses, would be a 'realistic' term in a child's reasoning and/or solution. A simple, and arguably not unrealistic, problem that would generate 13.5, would be one in which several 'Little Leagues' are going to the game and have decided to share costs and buses. Consider the 540 people from Clearview as given and add another 180 from the Foggyview Little League, giving a total of 720 people to be bused. We will assume that there are no bench seats, in order that the relative size of children and adults does not become a relevant matter. Now, in all, we need 18 buses. But is it unrealistic and/or inappropriate to say that we need thirteen-and-a-half of these buses for the Clearview people? We think not. As with the planks problem, it is as if there is an unexamined convention underlying the researchers' preferred solution. It appears to be something like, 'the particular and perhaps restricted model of the "real" in the mind of the researcher can be assumed to be the only one'.

Now, although the focus in all this work has been on the child's 'failure' to access their 'common-sense', 'realistic' or 'everyday' knowledge in responding to these types of questions, there are some reasons for suspecting that the published results overestimate the tendency of children to 'exclude' the 'real'. Verschaffel *et al.* (1994) themselves note that, in written tests, even where children are asked to comment on their own answers, there are several reasons why researchers can not be sure that children have 'excluded' the 'real'. First, in some cases some children may just lack the relevant 'realistic' knowledge. The problem here, as they say, then becomes one of the absence rather than the non-application of knowledge. This seems to have been the case in one of their items concerning the physics of mixing two amounts of water at different temperatures. Second, in the first phase of their work, the collection of data by a 'collective paper-and-pencil test' may have hidden from view those cases where children did 'activate' 'real-world knowledge' at some point during their solution process but where it was not reflected in their written response 'simply because they finally decided to respond and react in a "conformist" rather than a "realist" way in line with their beliefs and conceptions about "the rules of the game" of school arithmetic problems' (1994: 291). Their subsequent work, involving a small number of interviews, attempts to address this methodological issue (De Corte *et al.* 1995).

Given these points, it is valuable to note several things about children's responses in both the Flemish and the US work. First of all, as Verschaffel *et al.* emphasize, there was an apparent effect of item. Some items were much more likely to produce evidence of 'realistic' responses than others. Of their ten parallel (P) items two in particular produced a 'considerable number' of 'realistic' adjustments of responses. One was an instantiation of the bus template: *450 soldiers must be bussed to their training site. Each army bus can hold 36 soldiers. How many buses are needed?* The other was this: *Grandfather gives his four grandchildren a box containing 18 balloons, which they share equally. How many balloons does each grandchild get?* Note this problem is presented as requiring 'realistic' considerations, and yet 'realistic' considerations might rule it out as a meaningfully soluble problem! In fact, one child wrote, having made an arithmetical error, '18 divided by 4 is 4.2. But 4.2 balloons is meaningless, so I really do not know how to handle this problem'. Another seems to have opted instead for a humorous response to the difficulty. Having written the answer, 'they get 4.5 balloons each', he or she added as a comment, '18 divided by 4 is 4.5. But I am afraid that they will have a hard time blowing up the balloons that were cut in half'.

The authors note what they regard as an 'important difference' between the balloon problem and the buses problem: 'for the buses problem the appropriate situation-bound interpretation involves rounding up the outcome of the division; in contrast, the quotient of the balloons problem needs to be rounded down' (Verschaffel *et al.* 1994: 286). It might actually be more important, however, from a 'realistic' considerations point of view, to note that it is less easy to give a 'realistic' gloss to half a balloon than to half a bus! Perhaps that is why 59 per cent of children made some 'realistic' reference in answering the balloon question, but only 49 per cent for the bus problem?

These were the two P items that elicited evidence of 'realistic' considerations from around half the 75 children in the study. Of the remaining eight P items, another three produced 'realistic' responses from 13 per cent, 17 per cent and 20 per cent of the children, and the remaining five produced very few. Interestingly, there were a few 'realistic' references in responses to the standard (S) items. One of these items was: *A shopkeeper has two containers of apples. In the first container there are 60 apples and in the other 90. He puts all apples into a new, bigger container. How many apples are there in that new container?* One child replied: If the new, bigger container was empty, then the answer is 170 apples; but if this bigger container was not empty at the outset of the story, then the problem is unsolvable (both '170' and 'unsolvable' appear in the original: Verschaffel *et al*. 1994: 280). Interestingly, these rare 'realistic' references to S items came from the children who gave most 'realistic' responses to the P items, suggesting that, alongside item effects, an individual predisposition of some sort might be operating here.

In the work by Silver *et al*. on the Little League buses item there was also some evidence of children's capacity to bring 'realistic' considerations to bear on word problems. The sample here comprised 195 sixth, seventh and eight graders from a large urban middle school in the USA. The school population was 'approximately 40 per cent Caucasian and 60 per cent African-American of all ability levels' (Silver *et al*. 1993: 121). Typically, for this research literature, we read 'since neither grade level nor ethnic differences were of particular interest in this study, results are reported for the aggregated sample' (Silver *et al*. 1993: 122). Here is how the authors describe some of their results:

> Appropriate interpretations. About one-third of the students gave responses that were classified as appropriate interpretations. Examples of interpretations considered appropriate include one student who wrote, 'You'll need 13 and a third buses. Since buses don't come in thirds, you get a whole other bus,' and another student who wrote, '14 to hold everyone, and you would have empty seats for more people who decided to come.' Some appropriate explanations were provided for final answers other than 14. For example, one student who gave a final answer of 13 1/2, wrote: '520 people are riding a big bus, and you'd have to get a van for the other 20 [people].' Some students who provided final answers of 13 1/2 gave interpretations such as, 'You need 13 buses and 1 van [cab or minibus].'
>
> (Silver *et al*. 1993: 124)

It is interesting to see some children giving a 'realistic' meaning to half a bus, including one who goes beyond the data given to discuss 'more people who decided to come'. It is also interesting to note that, outside the confines of the 'task format and administration conditions' (as a written test item during a regular class session) more children seem to have introduced various 'realistic' considerations:

> The task format and administration conditions also appeared to influence the tendency of students to provide explanations and interpretations of non-whole-number answers. Anecdotal evidence from our discussions with teachers whose students participated in the study indicated that, during the discussions that followed the problem-solving activity in some classes, many students argued vigorously for alternative solutions using a variety of interpretations for the remainder and explanations of how to represent their interpretation numerically. Some students apparently argued that an extra bus was

not needed because some students would be absent and would not attend the game. Others were reported to say that some kids could walk to the baseball game because the school is close to the stadium (the school our students attended is located less than one mile from the baseball stadium mentioned in the problem). These rich, situation-based comments about possible problem solutions are reminiscent of the kinds of reasoning exhibited by some students in the Smith and Silver (1991) interview study, yet they were rarely found in the children's written responses in this study. Children's perception of this task as a school mathematics problem, rather than a task about which to be thoughtful, may have negatively influenced their per-formance.[2] The task was administered by their mathematics teacher as part of a regular mathematics class; hence students probably viewed it as a formal classroom exercise and therefore responded in a manner that they believed to be both 'mathematically correct' and acceptable to their teacher. The formality of writing a response rather than giving it orally in a class discussion may also have contributed to the tendency of students not to reveal all of their informal thinking and reasoning about the problem.

(Silver et al. 1993: 130–1)

We have here considerable, if anecdotal, evidence that these children at least are possibly quite predisposed to introduce 'realistic' considerations, including ones not given in the question but derived from their everyday experience. They might not, however, demonstrate this predisposition in the regular classroom context of answering what might seem to be, superficially, stereotypical word problems.

Explaining the findings

We now move to the issue of explanation. As we have said earlier, explana-tions are sought most often amongst factors internal to the school. Here is a typical example from the Flemish work:

While the present study yields further confirmation that pupils do not tend to properly consider the assumptions and appropriateness of the mathematical model underlying their solutions of school arith-metic word problems, it does not provide a deeper insight into the instructional factors that are responsible for the development of this tendency and its underlying beliefs and conceptions. As said before, these undesirable learning outcomes are generally considered the result of the interplay between (1) the stereotyped and straightfor-ward nature of the large majority of the word problems given in the mathematics lessons, and (2) the nature of the teaching and learning activities with these problems. From these aspects of the current classroom practice and culture, pupils gradually construct the belief that making realistic considerations and elaborations about the situation described in a school arithmetic word problem may be more harm than help to solve such problems.

(Verschaffel *et al.* 1994: 291)

It is not our intention to argue that these factors are not important ones in accounting for the findings of the research. However, it is a feature of this research in general, as was mentioned earlier, that the variables discussed are restricted to, on the one hand, the nature of questions (e.g. the S versus the P items, along with variations in the P items themselves, in the Flemish work) and, on the other, a taken-for-granted account of 'classroom culture' concerning teaching, learning and assessment. What is *not* discussed is equally interesting. In particular, up to now this particular tradition of research has not paid much attention to possible differences between children in their predisposition to make reference (or not) to everyday, common-sense knowledge when operating in school problem contexts, whether mathematical or otherwise. This possible focus is not entirely absent from the work. As we have noted, Verschaffel *et al.* (1994) comment in passing that the rare 'realistic' references to S items came from the children who gave most 'realistic' responses to the P items. Furthermore, they entertain the notion of a 'disposition' in suggesting elsewhere that reformed teaching can 'develop in pupils a disposition towards realistic mathematical modelling' (De Corte *et al.* 1995). But what we do not find is any discussion of the possibility that, for example, social class or gender might be associated with differentiated prior dispositions to bring everyday experience and knowledge into the classroom, either 'appropriately' or 'inappropriately'. Ironically, given the point we are making here, the authors go on to argue the need to investigate 'the influence on children's problem-solving processes of the broader sociocultural context in which their mathematical modelling skills are analysed' (De Corte *et al.* 1995: 17). However, the reference to 'socio-cultural' here is not to possible cultural differences between social groups outside of school but rather to different contexts for problem-solving (such as other school subjects, and 'even' out-of-school contexts). Again it is the situation that is being prioritized at the expense of what is brought to it by the problem-solver. It is as if the only significant learning experiences relevant to numerical problem-solving that the children have had are those in school classrooms. But we know, of course, from the work of Nunes *et al.* (1993) and Walkerdine (1988, 1990), as well as everyday observation, that this is not the case.

This 'internalist' focus reflects much recent constructivist discussion in mathematics education circles. Culture is often reduced to what a particular teacher and his or her pupils share as a result of their 'negotiations' (communities of practice, intellectual communities, etc.). Clearly this aspect of 'culture' is important if we wish to understand children's mathematical behaviour in school. Yet a socio-cultural perspective ought to be concerned with more than this. Classrooms are nested within broader social structures or, if the reader prefers, communities of practice (Lemke 1997). For young children in particular, it seems quite likely that experience of these other settings, such as the family, will at least mediate, if not dominate, responses to some tasks in school (De Abreu 1995). Not all of the factors operating in a situation are products of its own boundaried local history. As Bourdieu puts it, in discussing analogous problems characteristic of the 'situational' approach of conversational analysis in the sociology of language:

> Let me take the example of communication between settlers and natives in a colonial or postcolonial context . . . Let us turn now to the situation, which in fact is by far the most frequent one, where it is the dominated who is obliged to adopt the language of the dominant – and here the relation between standard, white English and the black American vernacular provides a good illustration. In this case, the dominated speaks a broken language, as William Labov (1973) has shown, and his linguistic capital is more or less completely devalued, be it in school, at work, or in social encounters with the dominant. What conversation analysis leaves out too easily, in this case, is that every linguistic interaction between whites and blacks is constrained by the encompassing structural relation between their respective appropriations of English, and by the power imbalance which sustains it and gives the arbitrary imposition of middle-class, 'white' English its air of naturalness. To push this analysis further, one would need to introduce all kinds of positional co-ordinates, such as gender, level of education, class origins, residence, etc. All these variables intervene at every moment in the determination of the objective structure of 'communicative action,' and the form taken by linguistic interaction will hinge substantially upon this structure, which is unconscious and works almost wholly 'behinds the backs' of locutors.
>
> (Bourdieu and Wacquant 1992: 143–4)

Bourdieu reminds us in these remarks that interaction takes place in settings structured, though not determined, by factors outside of the setting itself. The same point surely needs to be applied to our understanding of mathematics classrooms and mathematical problem solving. Considering problem-solving strategies in particular we have a range of work claiming that both social class (Holland 1981; Morais *et al.* 1992) and gender (Gilligan 1982; Belenky 1986; Boaler 1997) are associated with different typical approaches to tackling problems, and some of this work at least is directly relevant to the issue of responses to 'realistic' mathematics questions. Having noted the absence of this perspective in the mathematics education literature discussed earlier, we will turn now to a discussion of the nature of 'realistic' items in the English NC tests.

National Curriculum assessment items

A possible way of summarizing one aspect of our earlier discussion would be to say that Verschaffel *et al.* and other similarly motivated researchers have not taken their thinking concerning 'realistic' considerations to its logical conclusions. They are worried by children's 'failure' to introduce 'realistic' considerations but they only seem to want what might be described as homeopathic doses of such realism. Hence the difficulties we discussed in the case of the underspecified planks problem. Similar potential problems can be discerned in several English NC mathematics items, which we will now discuss.

The lift item

The NC tests have contained items, at both KS2 and KS3, which are relatives of the 'buses and soldiers' template discussed earlier. One such item from KS3 allows us to develop a number of points concerning the 'esoteric'/'realistic' boundary that children have to negotiate in answering such questions. The lift item in Figure 3.1 is recognizably derived from the template. The SoA is given as *Solve number problems with the aid of a calculator, interpreting the display* (2/4d).[3] The Marking Scheme (SEAC 1992: Band 1–4, Paper 1) specifies as 'appropriate evidence' of achievement: 'Gives the answer to the division of 269 by 14 as 20, indicating that they have interpreted the calculator display to select the most appropriate whole number in this context. Do not accept 19 or 19.2'. The key point is that the child's answer must not be fractional. The lift cannot go up (and down) 19.2 times. The child is required therefore to introduce a 'realistic' consideration into his or her response. In Silver *et al.*'s terms (1993: 129), the child, having carried out the correctly chosen arithmetical operation, needs 'to exit from the mathematical space in order to return to the story situation and interpret their numerical answer'. In fact, the child must manage something apparently rather complex in doing this (cf. Säljö 1991; Cooper 1992). He or she must introduce only a small dose of realism – 'just about enough'. The child must not reflect that the lift might not always be full; or that some people might get impatient and use the stairs; or that some people require more than the average space, e.g. for a wheelchair. Such considerations – 'too much realism' – will lead

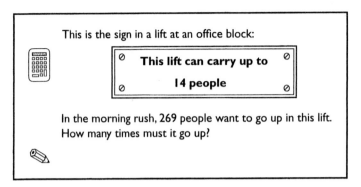

This is the sign in a lift at an office block:

> **This lift can carry up to**
>
> **14 people**

In the morning rush, 269 people want to go up in this lift. How many times must it go up?

Figure 3.1   'Realistic' items and ambiguity: an illustration (SEAC 1992)

to a problem without a single answer, and no mark will be gained. The 'story space' must be assumed to be a very simple one. There is a certain irony here. Many reformers have argued for the use of 'ill-structured' items in mathematics teaching, learning and assessment contexts (e.g. Pandey 1990). This lift item, however, like the planks item discussed earlier, is apparently *unintentionally* ill structured. Children's and schools' interests now hinge on managing the resulting ambiguities in a 'legitimate' manner.

In the case of this lift item, the child is asked to exercise some 'realistic' judgement and, in doing so, might be presumed to be undertaking a 'realistic' application of some mathematical (or at least arithmetical) knowledge. But on whose account of 'applying'? The lift item essentially concerns queuing behaviour. A mathematics of queuing exists. We might turn for some insight to an 'élite' disciplinary source: *Newer Uses of Mathematics*, edited in 1978 by Sir James Lighthill, FRS, then Lucasian Professor of Applied Mathematics at Cambridge. (Other holders of this post have included Sir Isaac Newton and Stephen Hawking.) In the preface, Lighthill writes, 'we want to outline some of the many ways of using mathematics for significant practical purposes . . .' (Lighthill 1978: 12). This edited collection includes a paper on methods of operational analysis by Hollingdale (former Head of the Mathematics Department at the Royal Aircraft Establishment), which discusses queuing. An edited extract follows:

> Everyone, nowadays, is only too familiar with queues – at the supermarket, the post office, the doctor's waiting room, the airport, or on the factory floor. Queues occur when the service required by customers is not immediately available. Customers do not arrive regularly and some take longer to serve than others, so queues are likely to fluctuate in length – even to disappear for a time if there is a lull in demand . . . The shopper leaving the supermarket, for example,

desires service; the store manager wants to see his cashiers busy most of the time. If customers have to wait too long, some will decide to shop elsewhere; . . . The essential feature of a queuing situation, then, is that the number of customers (or units) that can be served at a time is limited so there may be congestion . . . Queuing problems lend themselves to mathematical treatment and the theory has been extensively developed during the last seventy years . . . The raw materials of queuing theory are mathematical models of queue-generating systems of various kinds. The objective is to predict how the system would respond to changes in the demands made on it; in the resources provided to meet those demands; and in the rules of the game, or queue discipline as it is usually called. Examples of such rules are: 'first come, first served'; 'last come, first served', as with papers in an office 'in-tray'; service in an arbitrary order; or priority for VIPs or disabled persons. To analyse queuing problems, we need information about the input (the rate and pattern of arrival of customers), the service (the rate at which customers are dealt with either singly or in multiple channels), and the queue discipline. . . . One of the simplest queuing models postulates an input of identical units (e.g., customers), an unlimited queue that is served in order of arrival and a single service channel, with the patterns of arrival and service times specified by probability distributions.

(Hollingdale 1978: 244–5)

The question that arises is whether a model incorporating all or some of the variables listed by Hollingdale (e.g. the nature of the 'service') would deliver the correct answer according to the producers of marking schemes for NC tests.[4] If not, why not, and what approach does? Can the 'required' approach be specified via teachable 'rules of engagement' for such items? If not, why not? Should they be?

Various writers have employed the notion of ground rules to capture what is demanded of children in cases like that of the lift item (Bernstein, 1973; Edwards and Mercer 1987). There is clearly some affinity between this concept and those of recognition and realization rules employed later by Bernstein (1996) (see Chapter 4). However, it can be seen that it would be quite difficult – if not impossible – to write a set of rules that would enable the child to respond as required to the lift question. Certainly, the rule – in the sense of a mandated instruction – to employ 'realistic' considerations would not do, since 'how much' realism is required remains a discretionary issue. It is this problem that has led to a range of attacks on the use of rules to model human activities (e.g. Taylor 1993) and, in particular, has led Bourdieu to reject a rule-based account of cultural competence (see Bourdieu 1990a). Bourdieu's concept of *habitus* aims to capture the idea of a durable socialized predisposition without reducing behaviour to strict rule-following (Bourdieu 1990b). Bourdieu sometimes describes what *habitus* captures as 'a feel for the game' and we can see that this describes fairly well what is required by the lift problem and others like it. Both Bernstein and Bourdieu have shown that members of the working class are more likely to respond to test-like situations by drawing on 'local and/or 'functional' rather than 'esoteric' and/or 'formal' perspectives (for examples of such research, see Holland (1981), discussed in Bernstein (1990, 1996); and Bourdieu (1986)). It can be seen why the neglect of socio-cultural background by much of the mathematics education research literature might matter. The children who, in the work of Silver *et al.* (1993) referred to their local baseball stadium when discussing the Little League busing problem might well have tended to come from some social backgrounds rather than others. We return to this possibility in later chapters, when we explore how English children vary in their responses to 'realistic' items. We turn now to another 'realistic' NC test item.

The basketball problem

So far all of the problems discussed have been relatively stereotyped. Indeed several of them are variants of just one problem template (buses and soldiers). However, a feature of the English NC tests in mathematics has been a wider range of problem types set for children than in the research contexts that we have been discussing in this chapter. Some of these raise further interesting issues concerning the relevance or otherwise of 'realistic' considerations. Consider the item in Figure 3.2 concerning basketball team selection. This is another apparently 'real life' problem. The statement of attainment (SoA) here is *Use the mean and range of a set of data* (5/4c). 'Appropriate evidence' of achievement is 'Shows an understanding of both mean and range in their reason for their choice of player'. It is not enough to say, for example, 'I would choose Karen because her mean is 12 and her range is only 4'. An 'appropriate' answer would be: 'I would choose Karen because her mean score is quite high and her range shows that she always scores about the same' or 'I would choose Jo because her mean score is quite high and her range shows she fluctuates between very high and low so it would be more exciting'.

Here we have reference to an emotionally charged area of children's lives. We also have reference to an area where choice is difficult, having to take into account, in the real 'real world' such features of the context as: (1) who are we playing; (2) what are the strengths of the other players in our team; (3) is this a knock-out match or one played for points in a league; (4) how and why did these distributions of scores arise (for example, were Karen and Jo playing together in six matches, or were there more than six, or have either of the players had temporary fitness

The school basketball team has an important match next week. The captain can choose Karen or Jo to be in the team.

This term Karen and Jo have both played in 6 matches.

The following list shows their scores:

Karen: 12 10 12 14 12 12
   Jo: 10   2   4 30   2 24

Karen's mean or average score is 12.
Karen's range (her highest score − her lowest score) is 4.

Jo's mean or average score is 12.
Jo's range is 28.

Use the mean and the range of Karen's scores and Jo's scores to choose who you would pick to play in the next match.

It doesn't matter which player you choose but you must use the mean **as well as** the range to **explain** which player is better.

Figure 3.2 The basketball problem (SEAC 1992, Band 1–4, Paper 3)

problems, or were they playing against teams of different strengths)?; and (5) what might be the effect of one choice or another on personal relationships.

But the child must bracket all of these potentially relevant issues out of his or her thinking about the problem. It is the mean and range of the two sets of scores that are to be considered. And, as in other problems in these tests, although they are being asked to make a choice, they are also told 'It doesn't matter which player you choose but you must use the mean as well as the range to explain which player is better.' One is better – though we have not got enough information to decide who it is – but it does not matter which player is chosen. A strange 'real' world! The child has to know, and be willing to accept, the ground rules associated with this strange 'real' world to be able to succeed. One of these rules may be 'Do not ask any unnecessary questions.' In particular, do not import *too many* 'realistic' considerations. But how is a child to determine just how many are too many? We will see in Chapter 4 that some children seem more ready than others to make this judgement in a 'legitimate' manner.

A **drink** and a **box of popcorn** together cost **90p**.

2 drinks and a **box of popcorn** together cost **£1.45**.

What does a **box of popcorn** cost?

Explain how you got your answer:

Figure 3.3 The shopping item (SCAA 1996)

The shopping item

However, before providing in Chapter 4 an in-depth illustrative discussion of two children's responses to these types of items, we want to give one more example of what 'a feel for the game' can require of children taking the national tests. Consider Figure 3.3, which bases mathematics on shopping – a fairly common 'relevant' topic in school mathematics for younger children.

This problem, for those socialized into 'esoteric' mathematics, reduces to the solution of the pair of simultaneous linear equations set out below (in pence).

$$C + P = 90$$
$$2C + P = 145$$

One way of solving the problem – legitimately from the point of view of the marking scheme – would be to see this embedded structure and apply whatever technique has been taught for solving such equations. Alternatively, the embedded equations might be solved in a more 'intuitive' manner by some approach involving trial and error. However, what the child must not do (note the 'rule'-like formulation!) is to read the item as an invitation to draw on what they know about and from everyday shopping contexts. This would be to construct an 'inappropriate' goal for the problem (Newman *et al.* 1989) or, under another description, to engage in an 'inappropriate' discursive practice (Walkerdine 1990). Here is an example of what can happen if the child makes this 'mistake':

Response of a working-class girl (taken exactly as written in her national test paper in May 1996):

I said to myself that in a sweetshop a can of coke is normally 40p so I thought of a number and the number was 50p so I add 40p and 50p and it equalled 90p.

This response, instead of recognizing the hidden structure of the problem – the pair of simultaneous equations – uses just the first 'equation' plus knowledge of the price of cola gained from shopping in everyday life to generate a solution. In some respects this solution, which includes correctly worked arithmetic, is efficient – if one is rushing through a timed test – but it is, nevertheless, 'incorrect' given the total information available and the context of a school mathematics test. We are left not knowing whether the child has the 'competence' required to solve the pair of equations taken together. What is it that the child has 'failed' to do? Has she failed to read the whole question? Or to solve the equations? Or to bracket out her everyday knowledge? It may be that, in Bourdieu's (1990a: 64) terms, this child lacks the required 'feel for the game'. To answer this question, of course, one would need to examine her responses across a range of items. This is exactly what we do, for two children, in Chapter 4.

Summary

In this chapter we have first considered some examples of previous research concerning 'realistic' problem-solving in mathematics. Such work has produced a variety of interesting findings. In particular, it has shown that many children attempt to solve 'realistic' problems *of a certain type* as if they are not 'realistic' at all. They seem to treat them as merely differently presented exemplars of standard arithmetic problems and, as a consequence, produce answers that are perceived by the test designers as not meaningful in the context of the 'real world'. This behaviour is typically explained by reference to pupils' classroom experience of a restricted range of 'non-realistic' problems in the context of a pedagogy based on the learning of standard algorithms. We have argued that this research programme has several limitations. The work sometimes appears to trade on a number of taken-for-granted and conventional assumptions. It is sometimes too readily assumed that the boundary between problems demanding or not demanding 'realistic' solutions is easy to specify. It is also too readily assumed that explanations should be sought within classrooms, without reference to 'culture' in a broader sense than the 'culture' of the classroom (Davis 1989). We then discussed three 'realistic' NC items, showing that two of these, if taken as serious injunctions to think 'realistically', would become very ill-structured problems indeed. Their marking schemes, however, show that they are not intended to be taken as properly realistic problems of the type that might occur in everyday life, but rather as examples of the severely restricted type of 'realistic' problem that has traditionally inhabited mathematics texts and tests. Since the child does not have access to these marking schemes he or she needs to be able to decode the requirements of the test designers by other means, via a 'feel for the game' in fact.

In the next chapter we examine in detail two children's responses to a range of NC items. We see that one of these children seems to have perceived the items, at least in the context of an interview, as invitations to refer to the 'everyday' and, furthermore, that he refers to the 'everyday' in mainly 'inappropriate' ways. The other child understood that such responses were 'inappropriate'. Since these two children had attended the same school, and shared many teachers, this finding will be seen to beg the question of what else might explain their different response styles. Notwithstanding the attacks in recent years on the concept of transfer (e.g. Lave 1988), it seems likely that the answer to this question might require reference to some sort of predisposition, which a child carries from situation to situation, and whose origins may not be entirely in his or her own school experience.

Notes

1 The Mathematical Association was an organization of teachers mainly based, at the time, in selective secondary schools and universities.
2 Actually, if the children had introduced some of the locality-specific knowledge mentioned here, this might have 'negatively influenced their performance', unless the marking scheme were to be changed to accommodate it. Perhaps they were being more 'thoughtful' than the researchers allowed?
3 The 2/4d refers to a mapping of the National Curriculum in mathematics by attainment target and level. Here we have a level 4 item from AT2.
4 These producers of the items and marking schemes exist in a field distinct from that of Hollingdale, of course.

4 | Key Stage 2 'realistic' items: two children, two cultural competences?

Introduction

We have two main purposes in this chapter. We wish to illustrate one particular threat to the validity of assessment that arises from the increasing stress put in mathematics education circles on the embedding of mathematics in supposedly 'realistic' contexts (Cockcroft 1982; National Council of Teachers of Mathematics 1991). We also wish to show that this threat may operate differently for children with different styles of response to 'realistic' items, and partly independently of children's knowledge of mathematical operations *per se*. In particular we discuss some sociological ideas (Bernstein 1996; Bourdieu 1986), which suggest that some types of 'realistic' items, when used in the context of testing children, might be expected to be 'differentially valid' (Gipps and Murphy 1994), in the sense of favouring some social groups over others, and hence that their use might introduce unfairness into the tests. To do this we draw on qualitative pilot work undertaken in the summer of 1994 to explore the ways in which children understand and respond to different types of test item in mathematics. We focus on one issue that arose from this work – the problems some children have when negotiating the boundary between esoteric mathematical knowledge and their everyday knowledge.

As we saw in Chapter 3, there has been considerable work drawing attention to children's failure to access their everyday knowledge where it is 'appropriate' to do so (e.g. De Corte *et al.* 1995). Here the concern is with the inverse problem – some children's tendency to import their everyday knowledge when it is 'inappropriate' to do so. We have chosen to do this by presenting in some detail responses from two children: Diane – a girl of high measured 'ability' from a professional middle-class background, and Mike – a boy of average measured 'ability' from a working-class background. Obviously, no general conclusions can be drawn from the differences in these two children's responses to test items, which embed mathematics in 'realistic' contexts. However, by presenting alongside the data some general ideas developed over many years by Bernstein in England and Bourdieu in France concerning the relation between socio-economic status, culture and cognition we hope to show why it is worth exploring in more detail the possibility that such items may systematically underestimate the mathematical capacities of children from certain social backgrounds. We end the chapter by presenting a working model of the relationship between cultural orientations and test validity.

The pilot work

The data to which we will refer in this chapter derive from small-scale pilot work carried out in the summer of 1994 in one primary school in the south of England (School A in Table 2.1, see p. 13). The school has an annual entry of 60–70 children, most of whom come from families positioned in the middle range of the socio-economic structure. Fifteen clinical interviews were carried out with Year 6 children (10–11-year-olds) selected to provide some coverage of the range of measured 'ability' and socio-economic status in the school. The children (eight boys and seven girls) worked through a booklet of items taken from the NC tests designed for use in 1993 and 1994. Teachers in this school previously had boycotted the tests as part of a widespread dispute between teachers and the State over workload and other issues. As a consequence the children had received no experience of any of these particular items. The children were told that the researcher wanted their help in deciding which items were suitable for children of their age and that they were therefore to 'do their best' to solve the items. They seemed, in general, to find the experience interesting and not highly threatening. Others not in the sample requested to be involved. The interviews were tape-recorded and transcribed in full.

The data, though based on a small sample, threw up many problems with the tests and the associated marking schemes. Some of these concerned Messick's first principle for construct validity, i.e. 'minimal construct under-representation' (Messick 1994). We do not focus on these problems here, though we briefly illustrate their nature in the context of a probability item concerning a traffic survey (for further discussion see Cooper 1998a). Our focus instead is on problems concerning Messick's second principle, i.e. the avoidance of 'construct-irrelevant variance', and especially those that seem to have resulted from the embedding of mathematics in 'real' contexts in conjunction with children's ways of reading and responding to such items.

We present qualitative data from two children whose response styles are markedly different. The working-class child will be seen to respond 'inappropriately' to 'realistic' items. It will be shown how, in the case of a particular variety of item, this might lead to the underestimation of his mathematical understanding and skills. In parallel we will discuss some sociological work which suggests that such differences in response style might be non-randomly distributed across the socio-economic structure. If the latter were to be the case then we would have good reason for concern that certain types of item might be differentially valid by social class and hence implicated in the generation of less than fair assessment outcomes. However, we must stress again that the two cases to be looked at in this chapter are being used merely to illustrate two apparently distinct response styles. It is not being claimed that they prove any case. They should be seen as representing and illustrating hypotheses to be explored in more detail in later chapters. Of course, were these differences in response styles not to be related to socio-economic background that would still leave the problem of validity *per se*, and its relation to item type, on the table. Only the issue of differential validity by socio-economic status would have receded.

Responses to the socks item

Consider Figure 4.1, which derives from the 1994 tests. It can be seen to have the potential to draw children into error, especially as pupils are often taught to aim to compare 'like with like', via the use of percentages. Its purpose was to assess the children against the SoA *Interpret statistical diagrams* (5/5c). The marking scheme states:

a, b, c

One mark for each of the following categories of explanations, without repeats, to a maximum of three marks.

For the award of a), a mention of the number of boys and girls: 'There are 5 extra girls,' OR 'They had more girls.'   1 mark

For the award of a) and b), a mention of the same percentage for boys and girls: 'Because they are both 20%'   2 marks

For the award of a), b) and c) a mention of the same percentage and the number of boys and girls: 'Because there are 35 girls and 20% of 35 is more than 20% of 30'   3 marks

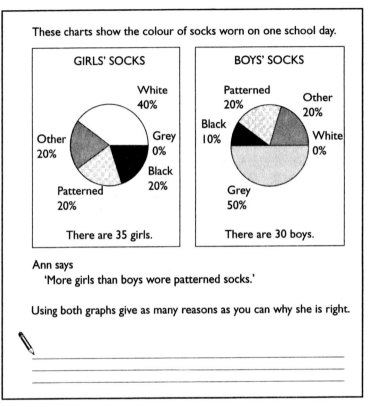

These charts show the colour of socks worn on one school day.

GIRLS' SOCKS

White 40%
Grey 0%
Black 20%
Patterned 20%
Other 20%

There are 35 girls.

BOYS' SOCKS

Patterned 20%
Other 20%
Black 10%
White 0%
Grey 50%

There are 30 boys.

Ann says
'More girls than boys wore patterned socks.'

Using both graphs give as many reasons as you can why she is right.

Figure 4.1 The socks item: interpreting statistical diagrams (SCAA 1994)

How did Diane and Mike respond to the challenges of this item? Here is what they had to say (BC: Barry Cooper):

Diane: Socks

Diane: [reads the question] But it says, why she's right, but she's wrong. Cos they're identical! [animatedly]

BC: Are they? Have you read it all, carefully?

Diane: Oh, drat! Oh, there are 30.

BC: A tricky question.

Diane: Usually, in schools, it's more boys than girls though.

BC: In this school?

Diane: In most schools, I'm saying, that I've visited.

BC: There are more?

Diane: Boys than girls.

BC: Are there? More boys than girls? Ah. [pause]

Diane: [muttering to herself] It's quite hard to (explain?).

BC: What, to explain?

Diane: Um, just to work out whether, I mean, whether she is right.
BC: Ah, do you think she's right?
Diane: Yes.
BC: Right, so why do you think she's right?
Diane: Because, although it's the same proportion, there are more girls.
BC: That's it. Same proportion but there are more girls.

Mike: Socks
BC: How about this one?
Mike: These charts show the colour of socks worn on one school
day. [pause] That says that they, the girls, wore more
patterned socks than the boys, but it says they both, they
both had the same [sounding puzzled].
BC: So what do you think then? What do you want to say? [pause]
Mike: Is it – I think, really, boys just wear, like, plain old sporty
socks, white socks – unless they're, like, teachers' pets – with
the socks up here, and things – socks all the way up to their
knees. [pointing to his knees during this] But the girls, the
girls seem to have more pattern on their socks – they're
white and they've got patterns on all of them. The boys have
just got the old sporty things with something like sport
written down them. Not much of a pattern.
BC: So you want – you don't agree with that then?
Mike: No.
BC: OK. What about this bit here? [Interviewer points to the
35/30 statements.] There are 35 girls. There are 30 boys.
Does that make a difference?
Mike: It might do [pause] in one way. Or another. But [pause] I
mean, really, you've got [pause] five more girls than boys
and, like, they're just going for it.

There is a clear difference between the two responses. Diane manages to
avoid inappropriate use of her real world experience (though she does
refer to this) while Mike fails to avoid this trap. We will look at the
children's responses to several more items, but first, is there any evidence from other work to suggest such differences in response may be
widespread and/or social class linked?

Bernstein's pedagogic codes thesis

Holland (1981), working with Bernstein, and drawing on the approach
of Luria (1976), presented primary age children with a set of 24 coloured
photographs of food items. These were organized in terms of a set of
'context-independent principles':

- animal: roast beef, pork chop, sausages, hamburgers, sardines, fish fingers
- vegetable: lettuce, green beans, peas, boiled potatoes, chips, baked beans
- animal products: milk, butter, cheese, ice-cream, boiled egg, fried egg
- cereal: bread, cakes, biscuits, rice, rice crispies, spaghetti rings

As part of the work, children were asked to group the items and give reasons for their grouping. It was found that there were social class differences in the initial responses of children. The instruction was: 'Here are some pictures of food. What we would like you to do with them is put the ones together you think go together. You can use all of them or you can use only some of them' (Bernstein 1996: 33). Middle-class children were more likely to use general principles of classification, e.g. 'The same kind of thing, both made from milk' or 'Those two you get from the sea'. Working-class children were more likely to refer to their everyday life, e.g. 'That's what we have for Sunday dinner'. Given a second chance to classify the pictures the middle-class children often switched to an everyday life classification, while the working-class children remained in this mode of response.

Bernstein's understanding of these findings is constructed within the terms of his constantly developing general theory of pedagogic codes, which, on the one hand, describes the organization of educational knowledge on the side of the pedagogic transmitter in terms of particular values of classification and framing (translating power and control relations) and, on the other hand, describes the learner, i.e. the acquirer, in terms of access to recognition and realization rules (Bernstein 1996). Very briefly, and crudely, classification refers to the degree of insulation between categories – discourses, practices, agents, etc. Framing refers to the balance of control over pedagogic communication in local interactional contexts. 'Classification refers to what, framing refers to how meanings are to be put together, the forms by which they are to be made public, and the nature of the social relationships that go with it' (Bernstein 1996: 27). Recognition rules, 'at the level of the acquirer', are the means by 'which individuals are able to recognise the speciality of the context that they are in' (Bernstein 1996: 31). Realization rules allow the production of 'legitimate text'. 'The recognition rule, essentially, enables appropriate realisations to be put together. The realisation rule determines how we put meanings together and how we make them public' (Bernstein 1996: 32). These rules are potentially independent of one another, e.g. 'many children of the marginal classes may indeed have a recognition rule, that is, they can recognise the power relations in which they are involved, and their position in them, but they may not possess the realisation rule. If they do not possess the realisation rule, they cannot then speak the expected legitimate text' (1996: 32).

Because Holland's findings concerning children's classifying strategies are of crucial relevance to the issues in this chapter we want to
quote Bernstein's recently published discussion of them at some length.
He argues:

> The difference between these reasons should not be seen as just simply
> that of abstract/concrete. To do this would be to lose sight of the social
> basis of the difference. One classification refers to a principle which
> had a direct relation to a specific material base. The reason is embedded
> in a local context, in a local experience. The other type of reason refer-
> ences an indirect relation to a specific material base. In sociological
> terms we are looking at a selection of classifying principles, each of
> which has a different relation to a material base. What we found
> initially was that the middle-class children were much more likely to
> offer reasons which had an indirect relation to a specific material
> base and that the working-class children were much more likely to
> offer reasons which had a direct relation to a specific material base.
>
> (Bernstein 1996: 34)

He then turns to the finding that middle-class children, given a second
chance, changed their mode of grouping:

> we concluded that the middle-class children had two principles of
> classification, which stood in a hierarchic relation to each other. One
> was privileged and came first. The questions which then arose were:
> why did the middle-class children select one type of reason first, and
> why did the working-class children offer only one type of reason? In
> the case of the working-class children, I suggest the coding instruction
> is taken at its face value ... The children, from their point of view,
> select a non-specialised recognition rule which, in turn, regulates the
> selection of non-specialised contexts. From the children's perspect-
> ive, these are domestic or peer group contexts. This contrasts with
> the middle-class children, who initially recognised the context as
> specialised. Thus, for the middle-class children ... this context is a
> specialised context and must be treated in a particular way. In other
> words, the recognition rule marks the context as having an intrinsic
> speciality ... Thus ... 'talk about the grouping in any way you want
> to', is transformed into a realisation rule which selects a very par-
> ticular orientation to meanings on the basis of the recognition
> rule ... But the recognition by the middle-class 7-year-old of the
> strong classification between home and school is itself based on the
> dominance of the official pedagogic practice and meanings over
> local pedagogic practice and meanings in this child's home. Such a
> dominance creates a position of relative power and privilege for the
> middle-class child and much less so for the working-class child.
>
> (Bernstein 1996: 34–5, some algebraically notated material removed)

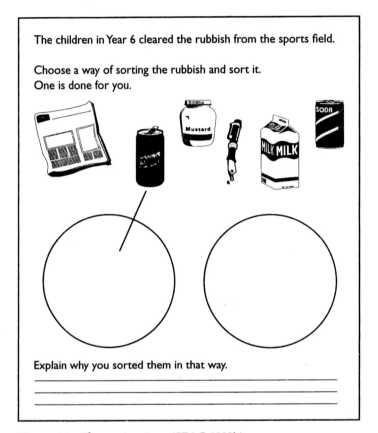

The children in Year 6 cleared the rubbish from the sports field.

Choose a way of sorting the rubbish and sort it.
One is done for you.

Explain why you sorted them in that way.

Figure 4.2 The sorting item (SEAC 1993b)

Responses to the sort item

One item covered by the pilot work made similar demands of the children to that of Holland's task (see Figure 4.2). The SoA is *Sort a set of objects describing criteria chosen* (5/1a). The marking scheme for this level 1 item states:

> There are a number of ways of sorting these items – by shape of container, by being edible or drinkable, and so on.

> If the lines drawn to the circles seem to be consistent, award the marks, one mark for the line(s) to the left hand circle and one mark for the line(s) to the right hand circle. Not all the items need be included. Drawings in the circles can be accepted also.

> The third mark is for the explanation of the sort, and should be consistent with the lines drawn.

The respective responses of Diane and Mike will be seen to have paralleled those of Holland's sample from their respective socio-economic backgrounds.

Diane: Sort

Diane: We did this! Clearing rubbish off the sports field. [laughs]
[works] Is that paper?

BC: Yea, newspaper, I think.

Diane: [writes, laughing every so often] Could I, um, like, put an
A in one circle and a B in the other circle. So that I can
refer to them?

BC: Uh, uh [signifying yes]. [she works] OK. Easy? Hard?

Diane: Um, quite easy, because there are so many ways you can
do it.

She had drawn lines putting just the newspaper into the right-hand
circle, labelled B, and everything else into the left-hand circle, labelled A.
She wrote:

I sorted the things this way for two reasons. 1. The things I put in
circle A were all 3d, and the one I put in circle B was 2d. 2. The
things I put in circle A were all containers of some sort. The one I
put in circle B, was not.

Mike: Sort

Mike: The children in Year 6.
[He continues reading silently. He writes the words meatle
(sic) and glass in the left-hand circle, and the words paper
and card in the right-hand circle. He then draws lines linking
the mustard pot, pen, and soda can to the LH circle, and the
newspaper and milk carton to the RH circle. He mutters:]
Metal. And glass. Metal and glass.

BC: OK. Easy? Hard? Right. How did you do it then?

Mike: Easy, 'cos, 'cos this stuff can get crushed and things, but this
stuff is more loosely – I mean, that stuff, you'd have to take,
like, to bottle banks and things 'cos if you left it out for the
dustman, it would just get crushed, and glass would fly
everywhere, and you'd get – you'd cut all your fingers and
everything on it.

BC: Right, OK. Next one then?

Mike: We got – Where we live we used to have some dopey man
living next door to us. He seemed alright – and then he
started digging up this wall – to build like a wall there –
and he found all these flints and stuff in there. Puts it all in
Sainsbury's [a major grocery chain] carrier bags and leaves
it out for the dustman [laughs].

These responses demonstrate the *potential* relevance of Bernstein's work to NC assessment via such items. Diane illustrates well the typical middle-class response discussed by Holland. She does make a reference out to her previous everyday experience but, in spite of this, answers in terms of the rubbish-independent property of dimensionality. In Bernstein's terms she seems to have a priority rule that privileges such responses in this type of 'realistic' testing context. She seems to recognize the context as one requiring a response in terms of esoteric mathematical knowledge. Mike, on the other hand, answers in terms more tied to a material base – though some reference is made to a general property of the materials. In this case, the marking scheme allowed both children to receive full marks.

Before discussing other examples, including one where Mike's particular response style seems to have resulted in less than valid assessment of his mathematical capacities, it is worth looking at some evidence which suggests that Diane knew explicitly, i.e. at a metacognitive level, what she needed to do – and what she needed to censor – in order to produce 'legitimate text'. In Bernstein's terms she recognized the power relations in which she is embedded in her schooling.

Responses to the tree measuring item

Consider Figure 4.3, which was the second part of an item in 1993. The first part concerned constructing a formula concerning the tree's height. The SoA is given as *Use units in context* (2/5d). The marking scheme states:

21.5 m

Other ways of writing it are acceptable, e.g. 21.5 metres, $21\frac{1}{2}$ m, $21\frac{1}{2}$ metres, but no other unit is sufficiently appropriate. It is acceptable to have just the number in the second box if the first box has 'metres'. Otherwise, the first box can be ignored.

Diane: Tree measuring
   [She writes metres in the first box.]
Diane: I can never remember how you. [She mutters under her breath. There is a longish pause.]
BC: Not sure how many millimetres in a metre?
Diane: Well, a thousand, I think. [pause] But you'd have to take off three noughts and I've only got two.
BC: You'd have to take off three noughts and you've only got two.
Diane: Um. [pause]

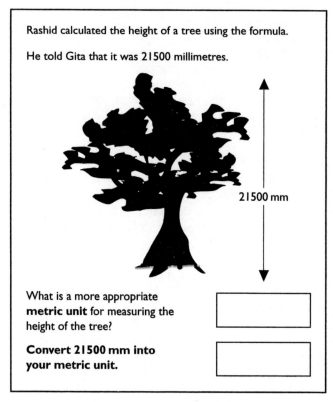

Rashid calculated the height of a tree using the formula.

He told Gita that it was 21500 millimetres.

21500 mm

What is a more appropriate **metric unit** for measuring the height of the tree?

Convert 21500 mm into your metric unit.

Figure 4.3   Measuring a tree's height (SEAC 1993b)

BC: Yes, well that rule doesn't always work. That's one of the places where it doesn't work.

Diane: I know! [laughing] [pause] Well, we haven't done very much if there aren't enough noughts, if you know what I mean [laughing].

BC: Yes. [pause]

Diane: Can't do it, really.

BC: OK. Well, you haven't done it yet, but let's just think for a minute. What does this mean? Twenty-one thousand, five hundred. Yes? [Interviewer points to 21500.]

Diane: So there's twenty-one thousands.

BC: Does that help, if you think about how many thousands in it? Does that help you think how many metres there would be? [pause]

Diane: Twenty-one?

BC: Yep, twenty-one, and then [pause] what's left?

Diane: Five centimetres, fifty centimetres?
[She writes 21 m 50 cm in the second box.]

BC: Right. [pause] Now, before you turn over, did you – was anything strange about that question?

Diane: How, how on earth would he get it in millimetres?

BC: How on earth would he get it in millimetres. Did that worry you at all? Or are you only thinking about it now I've mentioned it? Did you think about it before I mentioned it?

Diane: Um, a bit, I was just, I was thinking, oh, it's a bit unreal really, because you wouldn't measure something in millimetres if the tree was swaying in the wind [laughing]. You'd get it a few centimetres out [laughing].

BC: Yes, but you still did the question. You didn't stop and tell me that or . . .

Diane: No. Because – well, we've been told to just do what it says.

BC: You've been told to do just what it says. What, by the teachers you mean?

Diane: Um [apparently signifying assent].

BC: OK.

Diane: Like you know, if we question, um, like, the reasoning of the questions, sort of 'Get on with your work, it doesn't matter'. [She drops the pitch of her voice here, and simulates a fierce-sounding teacher.]

It is clear that Diane is able to refer, at a metacognitive level, to her role position in the school's transmission of knowledge. This enables her to engage in an appropriate or legitimate manner with the test item. She knows, in Bernstein's terms, the recognition and realization rules for this context and, furthermore, she knows them explicitly.

Responses to the traffic item

We will see Diane's understanding of these rules operating again in the case of the next item to be considered (Figure 4.4). This is organized around a survey of the traffic flow past a school. It is a level 3 item from 1993 concerning likelihood. The associated SoA is *Use appropriate language to justify decisions when placing events in order of 'likelihood'* (5/3c). The item refers to a common topic in school mathematics – the traffic survey – and therefore refers to an area in which children are likely to have some previous school experience as well as their experience of traffic in everyday life. The marking scheme gives the acceptable answers as follows, with one mark for each:

The children in Year 6 conduct a traffic survey outside the school for 1 hour.

Type	Number that passed in one hour
car	75
bus	8
lorry	13
van	26

When waiting outside the school they try to decide on the likelihood that a **lorry** will go by in the next minute.

Put a ring round how likely it is that a **lorry** will go by in the next minute.

| certain | very likely | likely | unlikely | impossible |

They also try to decide on the likelihood that a **car** will go by in the next minute.

Put a ring round how likely it is that a **car** will go by in the next minute.

| certain | very likely | likely | unlikely | impossible |

Figure 4.4   The traffic item (SEAC 1993b)

Lorry – Unlikely

Car – Likely or Very Likely

We have much more to say about children's responses to this item in Chapter 6. It is therefore worth noting several problematic aspects of this item and the provided marking scheme.

1 It is not clear that the item operationalizes the SoA – which refers to using language to *justify* a decision (our italics). In Messick's (1994) terms, the construct being measured is not adequately represented in the item.

2 Although the data presented are quantitative, the terms which the children are asked to use are qualitative. These qualitative terms do

comprise an ordered scale. However, on what authority is the frequency of 13 lorries associated with the term unlikely? It may be *less likely* that a lorry will appear than will a car, but it surely cannot be said to be *unlikely* rather than *likely*.

3 There is an apparent lack of symmetry in the answers allowed by the marking scheme. While two options are acceptable for the case of a car, only one is for the lorry. No account is provided of this decision and given the qualitative nature of the terms being used it is not clear that such an account is available.

4 Strangely, while there is a mark for each of the two likelihoods, there is not one allowed for preserving the order of the two likelihoods. It might have been useful, if children's understanding is being judged, to have provided a mark for labelling the car as more likely than the lorry (perhaps by one point of the scale), especially so as the SoA refers to ordering likelihoods.

5 The particular context employed in the operationalization of the SoA might be expected to cause interference for children between the given survey data and their own (variable) everyday experience, given the centrality of cars and roads in children's everyday lives.

What did Diane and Mike make of its demands?

> *Diane – refers to given data – both marks awarded*
> *Responses: lorry – unlikely; car – very likely*
> BC: Right, why have you chosen those two?
> Diane: Well, because in an hour, if there were, if there were
>   60 minutes in an hour, then if there were only thirteen
>   lorries in one hour, it's not very likely that, um, you're
>   going to get a lorry just in one minute. And the cars –
>   cos there were 75 cars, more than one a minute, so
>   it's more likely that you'd [pauses, stops].
> BC: It's not certain though?
> Diane: It's not certain but there's, I mean, – I don't know, there
>   could be a traffic jam [laughing].

In spite of the last reference to a traffic jam, this response was coded during the pilot work as solely referring to the given data for several reasons. First, the interviewer had elicited this additional response after Diane apparently had completed what she had to say. Second, it was clearly intended as humour (which Diane used throughout the interview in a similar way). Third, it could be taken as referring to the given data framework (though not perhaps in the appropriately required manner). There was no evidence to counter this interpretation. Diane's performance again seems to be related to an underlying competence, which includes the capacity to bracket out 'irrelevant' everyday knowledge.

Mike – refers to everyday experience – no marks
Responses: lorry – impossible; car – certain

Mike: A traffic survey outside the school. One hour. [He mutters;
         he reads under his breath.]
         Impossible. Cos it would probably take him a minute just to
         get past.
BC: Right, why have you put those two then?
Mike: Cos, lorries, you don't come across lorries very often, only if
         they've been delivered (sic) somewhere, or something like
         that. But cars, people use them all the time and things.

Again it can be seen that while Diane does not allow her everyday experience to take precedence over the given data, Mike refers immediately to his experience of life outside of school. For Mike, this experience seems to take priority over the given data. We see in Chapter 6 that, in the case of this item, such a response style does not rule out the gaining of marks. In Mike's particular case, however, he fails to gain any marks as a result of his selection of 'certain' and 'impossible' as answers.

Responses to the tennis item

We want to present one more pair of responses to an item and, in this case, to suggest that the response style demonstrated by Mike produces an initial false negative in validity terms (Wood and Power 1987). In fact, we show that this seems to have been the case for several of the sample of 15 children for this item. The item was a level 6 item concerning a tennis tournament (see Figure 4.5). It should be stressed that level 6 items were only intended for the most 'able' children and, in presenting them to children of all 'abilities', the item was not being used as intended. It had been decided, however, to mix item level and measured 'ability' in a fairly free manner given the exploratory nature of the work – and also because of a decision to bracket out assumptions about what children of various 'abilities' can and cannot do. The issue to be explored here is whether the item was assessing the mathematical SoA itself or, rather, the child's access to the appropriate recognition and realization rules for the context – or, of course, both simultaneously. We shall see that Mike constructs an 'incorrect' goal for the problem (Newman *et al.* 1989). The given SoA is *Identify all the outcomes of combining two independent events* (5/6c). The marking scheme for the item states:

Rob & Katy
Rob & Ann
Rob & Gita
Rashid & Katy

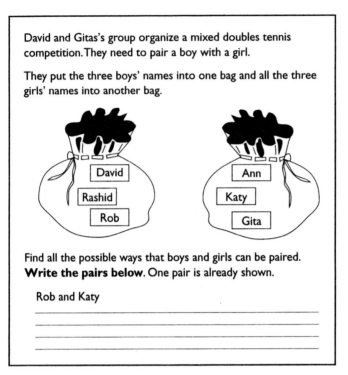

David and Gitas's group organize a mixed doubles tennis competition. They need to pair a boy with a girl.

They put the three boys' names into one bag and all the three girls' names into another bag.

David	Ann
Rashid	Katy
Rob	Gita

Find all the possible ways that boys and girls can be paired. **Write the pairs below.** One pair is already shown.

Rob and Katy
_____
_____
_____
_____

Figure 4.5 The tennis tournament item (SEAC 1993b)

Rashid & Ann
Rashid & Gita
David & Katy
David & Ann
David & Gita

There should be exactly nine pairings, all different. One way to check is as follows:

Are there 3 with Bob? Are they all different?
Are there 3 with Rashid? Are they all different?
Are there 3 with David? Are they all different?

It is interesting to note the particular way in which the pairs are set out here. The arrangement of the names seems to bear no relation to the tennis context. We return to this point in Chapter 6. Here we wish to concentrate on a different issue. In an earlier paper, before interviewing the pilot children, it had been argued:

This item seems to be based on the assumption that the children will not be misled by acting in a common-sense way – by imagining, for example, that they might be acting physically on the 'names' on the cards in the context of an imagined 'realistic' competition. On the contrary, in order to be successful, they are expected, having abstracted the mathematical problem from its pictorial setting, to approach this in a Piagetian 'formal operational' mode. The problem is that, even where children are capable of undertaking the abstracted combinatorial act, they might not demonstrate it in this case. After all, objects put in such bags are normally there to be taken out (as, for example, in televised draws for the Football Association Cup). If children were to operate on this assumption they would have, in their imagination, to put the 'names' back in order to generate all the possibilities. (In an empirical case, it could, in principle, given a run of bad luck, take a very long time to generate the nine possible pairs by this means.) It seems clear, therefore, that to achieve level 6, the child must treat this as a mental exercise in combining names and must be able to avoid being side-tracked by any element of the device used to test the Statement of Attainment. The bags must not be taken to signify the request for the 'empirical' three pairs that might seem implicit in the physical act of removing names without replacement (as in the case of real draws for knock-out competitions), when a step into mathematical discourse with replacement can allow the production of nine.

(Cooper 1994b)

It will be seen below from Mike's response that, if anything, this preliminary analysis underestimated the problems this question would cause, since there was also a basic ambiguity in its wording.

Diane: Tennis pairs
She wrote, with an accelerating use of ditto marks:

Rob and Katy
Rob and Ann
Rob and Gita
David and Ann
David and Katy
  "   and Gita
Rashid and Ann
  "   and Katy
  "   and Gita

BC: How many have you got? Nine. Now, were you sure? Did you know immediately you were going to get nine? When you started.

Diane: No, I didn't even think about it, really.

BC: Did you think at all about stopping after three, or . . .

Diane: Um, no, because I knew that each boy had a chance of three girls, and each girl had a chance of three boys, so, um, if you write both down you get the same answer [laughing].

Mike: Tennis pairs

Mike's case is very interesting. The transcript is worth quoting at length, especially as the interviewer may have encouraged him in his initial 'incorrect' interpretation of the question, which seems to have focused on 'ways' as much as 'pairs'. He began by reading under his breath:

Mike: Find all the possible ways that the boys and girls can be paired. [pause] There's – is it – I won't, I won't write it down here, I suppose. Is it because they put their hand, they go, they put their hand in there first, so they pull out Rob, cos they go right to the bottom first. Then second in the girls they go half way down, so they pick out Katy. Then the boys, they go to the top and pick out David. And they go right to the bottom of the other one to pick out Gita, and you should, you should end up with Rashid and [pause] Ann. [stops]

BC: OK, write those down then.

Mike: Shall I just write who they're going to go with?

BC: Yep.

Mike: Rob and Katy [pause] David and Gita [pause] Rashid and Ann.

BC: Now, before you go on, look at it again. Find all the possible ways that the boys and girls can be paired. All the possible ways. Do you think you've found all the possible ways that boys and girls can be paired?

Mike: There's only one other one. There's only one other way. It's just, just to be lucky who you go with really. That's it just about . . .

BC: There's only one other way, just to be lucky who you go with?

Mike: Yea, 'cos they just, they just dip their hand in. They'd probably shake the bag around while they put their hand in, and pick out whoever.

BC: OK, so do you think there are some other ways?

Mike: Only the one I've just said. And that's about it. There's no other possible way unless you took them out – oh, David can go with Gita – and just do that, Rob can go with Ann, and Rashid can go with Katy.

BC: Alright, if you did that though, how many different pairs do you think you could possibly get? If you, if I said, here, write down all the pairs you think you could get, of boys

and girls – all the possible ones – do you think there are
more than three? Or just three?

Mike: There'd be nine.

BC: There'd be nine? Can you write those nine down, on this
page here?

He writes:

David + Ann
Rashid + Katy
Rob + Gita
David + Gita
Rashid + Ann
Rob + Katy
David + Katy
Rashid + Gita
Rob + Ann

BC: Right, how did you know there'd be nine before you started
then?

Mike: Because there's three boys and three girls, plus you've got to
add another three because – you'll be going David and Ann,
Rashid and Katy, Rob and Gita. Put Gita to Ann, Ann to
Katy, and Katy to Gita. And then you keep doing that, the
same method. So they'd be going, um, from there [pause]
from there she'd go to there [he draws linking lines between
the names on the diagram of the bag containing girls'
names]. She'd go to there, then she'd go to there, then she'd
go back up to there, and she'd go down to there, and so on.
Nine ti . . . , three times.

BC: Right, so why do you think, when you first did it, you
stopped at three then? What was it about the question, do
you think?

Mike: Um, it [pause] just said, um, find the possible ways, of the
boys and girls, were paired. Just says one pair – um – the
way – the way that they're going to be paired, not who
they're going to be paired with.

It seems possible that Mike's initial 'incorrect' response reflected his general tendency to respond to these test items within an everyday frame of reference, though clearly the potential confusion between process ('ways') and product ('pairs') is also a relevant consideration here. However, in his responses to these 'realistic' items, there is no evidence that he was metacognitively aware of his choices in the way Diane was of many of hers. In the case of the tennis item, he seems to have had access to an

Table 4.1 Children's production of pairs on the tennis item: first and second attempts

	Nine correct pairs	*Fewer than nine but more than three pairs*	*Three pairs (using all six names)*	*Other*	*Total*
After initial attempt	7	0	7	1	15
After subsequent attempt	11	2	1	1	15

appropriate realization rule and the required 'mathematical' operation but not initially to have recognized the context as one that required their use. The interview brings this out; a test presumably would not do so.

Table 4.1 shows the initial and subsequent responses of all 15 children in the pilot study to this item. The procedure was simply to allow those who had not produced nine pairs initially a second chance once it was clear that they had finished their initial attempt. It can be seen that the success rate has risen from 7 to 11 of the 15, which suggests a not very reliable or valid test item. In this case we have tried to show what difference might be made to our account of what children can do by the particular way a piece of mathematics is embedded in a pseudo-narrative context (Edwards and Mercer 1987).

Bourdieu

Although it may initially appear to be an irrelevant digression we want, before presenting a working model of the culture/validity relation, to discuss some work by Bourdieu on adults' comments on works of art and then to relate it to Mike's responses. We do not wish to engage here in the dispute over the correct metatheoretical reading of Bourdieu's work (e.g. Bourdieu 1990a; Harker and May 1993; Alexander 1995; Mouzelis 1995; Bernstein 1996) but rather to point to its substantive usefulness for discussions of fairness in testing. We will draw on his work in *Distinction: A Social Critique of the Judgement of Taste* concerning the relation between social class and the nature of individuals' responses to a photograph of an old woman's hands (Bourdieu 1986: 45). We have two reasons for doing this. First of all, there is obviously a potential case to be made that the response style demonstrated by Mike will tend towards that of Diane as he progresses through school because of his eventual learning of the required recognition rule. It is therefore of interest to look at similar work to Bernstein's but with adults. Second, Bourdieu's work is in fact directly relevant to our research. It concerns a social situation not unlike the clinical interviews undertaken with the 15 children. In both his work and ours a researcher who is a stranger to the subjects asks questions in a test-like way. In his work, as in ours, a particular concern is with the boundary between 'everyday' and 'esoteric' concerns and frames of reference.

Bourdieu, rather than using the notion of rule, prefers to employ his concept of *habitus* to describe the tendencies people have to respond to certain contexts in certain ways. *Habitus* is rooted in individuals' socio-economic and cultural experience: 'The conditionings associated with a particular class of conditions of existence produce *habitus*, systems of durable, transposable dispositions' (Bourdieu 1990b). In his terms, individuals' behaviours (or strategies) can be accounted for but certainly not mechanistically predicted. As he is careful to say elsewhere, 'the *habitus* goes hand in hand with vagueness and indeterminacy' (Bourdieu 1990a). *Habitus* sets boundaries within which actors are able to generate behaviours of considerable variety – resulting in improvization within a set of predispositions that have 'generative capacities'.

In his work, Bourdieu develops, in the context of a relational theory of types of capital and their distribution, a discussion of the differences between the cognitive and aesthetic frameworks of individuals from different social class backgrounds, and between what he terms different 'cultural competences'. These originate in the family, itself situated in the social division of labour, but are further developed within the educational system. A pair of long quotes will illustrate his position. The crucial point here concerns whether respondents concentrate on form or function, or on the abstract or the everyday – and on the relation of their aesthetic responses to their previous socialization.

> When faced with legitimate works of art, people most lacking the specific competence apply to them the perceptual schemes of their own ethos, the very ones which structure their everyday perception of everyday existence. These schemes, giving rise to products of an unwilled, unselfconscious systematicity, are opposed to the more or less fully stated principles of an aesthetic. The result is a systematic 'reduction' of the things of art to the things of life, a bracketing of form in favour of 'human' content, which is barbarism par excellence from the standpoint of the pure aesthetic. Everything takes place as if the emphasis on form could only be achieved by means of a neutralisation of any kind of affective or ethical interest in the object of representation which accompanies . . . mastery of the means of grasping the distinctive properties which this particular form takes on in its relations with other forms (i.e., through reference to the universe of works of art and its history).
>
> (Bourdieu 1986: 44)

The aesthetic disposition which tends to bracket off the nature and function of the object represented and to exclude any 'naive' reaction – horror at the horrible, desire for the desirable, pious reverence for the sacred – along with all purely ethical responses, in order to concentrate solely upon the mode of representation, the style, perceived and appreciated by comparison with other styles, is one dimension of a total relation to the world and to others, a life-style, in which the effects of particular conditions of existence are expressed in a 'misrecognizable' form. These conditions of existence, which are the precondition for all learning of legitimate culture, whether implicit and diffuse, as domestic cultural training generally is, or explicit and specific, as in scholastic training, are characterised by the suspension and removal of economic necessity and by objective and subjective distance from practical urgencies, which is the basis of objective and subjective distance from groups subjected to those determinisms.

(Bourdieu 1986: 54)

The sorts of differences in response Bourdieu has in mind can be illustrated by what several individuals from different social backgrounds said in response to a photograph of an old woman's hands. His reference in presenting these data to 'cultural deprivation' should be understood in the context of his relational theory of culture and social class (see Bourdieu and Wacquant 1992). What people are 'deprived' of, in this view, is not 'culture' in any general sense – which would obviously be a nonsensical claim – but of access to field-dependent 'privileged' ways of discussing the photograph. He reports:

Confronted with a photograph of an old woman's hands, the culturally most deprived express a more or less conventional emotion or an ethical complicity but never a specifically aesthetic judgement (other than a negative one): 'Oh, she's got terribly deformed hands! . . . There's one thing I don't get (the left hand) – it's as if her left thumb was about to come away from her hand. Funny way of taking a photo. The old girl must've worked hard. Looks like she's got arthritis. She's definitely crippled, unless she's holding her hands like that (imitates gesture)? Yes, that's it, she's got her hand bent like that. Not like a duchess's hands or even a typist's! . . . I really feel sorry seeing that poor old woman's hands, they're all knotted you might say' (**manual worker, Paris**). With the lower middle classes, exaltation of ethical virtues comes to the forefront ('hands worn out by toil'), sometimes tinged with populist sentimentality ('Poor old thing! Her hands must really hurt her. It really gives a sense of pain'); and sometimes even concern for aesthetic properties and references to painting make their appearance: 'It's as if it was a painting that had been photographed . . . Must be really beautiful as a painting' (**clerical worker, Paris**). 'That reminds me of a picture I saw in an exhibition of Spanish paintings, a monk with his hands clasped in front of him and deformed fingers' (**technician, Paris**). 'The sort of hands you see in early Van Goghs, an old peasant woman or people eating potatoes' (**junior executive, Paris**). At higher levels in the social hierarchy, the remarks become increasingly abstract, with (other people's) hands, labour and old age functioning as allegories or symbols which serve as pretexts for general reflections on general problems: 'Those are the hands of someone who has worked too much, doing very hard manual work . . . As a matter of fact it's very unusual to see hands like that' (**engineer, Paris**). 'These two hands unquestionably evoke a poor and unhappy old age' (**teacher, provinces**). An aestheticizing reference to painting, sculpture or literature, more frequent, more varied and more subtly handled, resorts to the neutralisation and distancing which bourgeois discourse about the social world requires and performs. 'I find this a very beautiful photograph. It's the very symbol of toil. It puts me in mind of Flaubert's old servant-woman. . . . That woman's gesture, at once very humble. . . . It's terrible that work and poverty are so deforming' (**engineer, Paris**).

(Bourdieu 1986: 44–5)

It seems to us that aspects of Mike's response to the tennis item, and to other items, are open to description in Bourdieu's terms. The tennis item exactly requires a concern with pure form – as opposed to any easily imaginable everyday practice – and Mike's initial response appears to miss this. Similarly, his response to the sorting task, which included telling a story drawn from his everyday life, also suggests a reduction of the 'things of art' – here mathematics – to the 'things of life'. It should, of course, be pointed out that Bourdieu's (1986) discussion is based on data from the 1960s. It is clearly an empirical question whether cultural change since then would result in different patterns of response by social class today, whether in France or elsewhere. However, it is important to add that both Bernstein and Bourdieu are concerned with the level of the forms of organizing common sense and esoteric knowledge (and their interrelations) rather than their specific content (Apple 1995a: 74). Cultural change on this level is likely to be relatively slow.

A working model of the assessment process in relation to culture

There are obviously other sources to which we could refer to justify our concern with the socio-cultural aspects of test validity (e.g. Eco 1995).

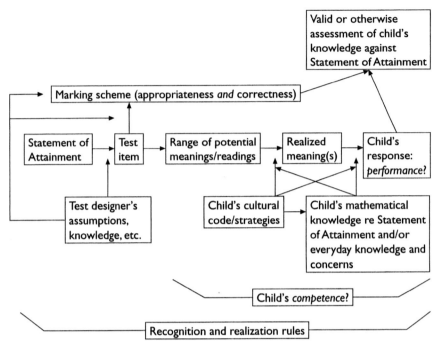

Figure 4.6 A working model relating some aspects of culture and assessment

What the work of Bourdieu and Bernstein suggests, however, is that the appropriate reading of contexts and items is a necessary though not sufficient condition for success in tests and that such readings may not be distributed randomly across the social structure. The model in Figure 4.6 tries to capture this. The model was developed to show how the issues discussed in this chapter might be brought to bear on our understanding of test validity. The model as constructed does not claim to cover all relevant variables and relationships. What it does is pick out some of those which we have examined in our research. It addresses one of the 'assessment questions in relation to equity' raised by Gipps (1995: 273), following Apple (1989): 'How does cultural knowledge mediate individuals' responses to assessment in ways which alter the construct being assessed.' The diagram shows *some* of the sources of threats to valid assessment. In particular, it allows a place for the mediating effects of cultural background. Some readers will recognize that the central core derives from long-standing literary-theoretical ideas about texts and readers' relationships to them. This core has been related to Bernstein's formulation of the ways in which acquirers differ in their possession of recognition and realization rules. The model currently is drawn to refer to the Statements of Attainment that characterized the English National

Curriculum at the time of the pilot research. However, the reference to an SoA can be replaced by any member of the family of behavioural objectives in general. A possible further addition to the model would be that of the marker who has to judge whether the child's response has met the criteria set out in the marking scheme. There are also various places where the researcher might be inserted. He or she also has to read texts and make judgements about them.

The references in the model to competence and performance invite further discussion. First, if we are to work with any notion of underlying competence it will have to be, as Hymes (1971) argued many years ago, a differentiated one – not one which, like Chomsky's in the context of linguistics, assumes some ideal speaker-hearer – but rather one which recognizes socio-cultural factors. Bernstein's and Bourdieu's work offers obvious ways forward here. Second, it is clearly not possible to do more than infer an underlying competence from a range of performances in context.[1] If the reader prefers, the research reported here can be read as concerned not with the demonstration that underlying competences may not express themselves in certain assessment situations but as another demonstration of the ways in which context constrains and/or facilitates individuals' mathematical productions (Lave 1988; Nunes *et al.* 1993) and the implications of this for fairness and validity in testing.

Summary

In this chapter we have used data from two children to illustrate one way in which sociological ideas on social class and culture might be applied in the context of research on mathematics assessment. We saw that there were major differences in the way that the middle-class girl and the working-class boy responded to 'realistic' items and, furthermore, that these differences were as might have been predicted on the basis of both Bernstein's and Bourdieu's accounts of social class differences in cultural competences. The middle-class girl negotiated the 'everyday'/'esoteric' boundary 'appropriately' – that is as required by those who designed the NC tests and their marking schemes. The working-class boy did not and, as a result, failed in the case of the tennis item to demonstrate initially his combinatorial competence. As we have stressed several times, no general conclusions can be drawn from just these two cases.

In Chapter 6 we consider just two of the items that have appeared here, the traffic survey and the tennis competition, in more detail and on the basis of data from more than one hundred children. Before that, however, we wish to consider, in Chapter 5 employing a more quantitative approach, the ways in which performance on NC items in general, and 'esoteric' and 'realistic' items in particular, varies by social class and sex within this larger sample.

Note

1 Knowing something through its effects has never, of course, held back physical scientists (cf. 'gravity'). For a general discussion of this point and its implications for the human sciences, see Bhaskar (1978, 1979).

Social class, sex, contextualization
and performance: a quantitative
analysis at Key Stage 2

Introduction

In this chapter we discuss the overall performance of our Key Stage 2
sample of children on national mathematics test items. Initially, after a
brief discussion of some problems associated with measuring achievement by 'levels' of attainment we discuss children's performance in the
statutory tests taken in May 1996, with particular reference to social class
and sex. However, the account set out in the last two chapters of the
ways in which 'realistic' items might cause problems of interpretation for
children provides us with a reason to be particularly interested in the
ways in which children perform on 'realistic' and 'esoteric' items taken
separately. We therefore analyse in some detail these children's performance on the sub-groups of 'realistic' and 'esoteric' items and, for that part
of the chapter, we also draw on the data from the February 1996 tests.

When the results of the statutory May 1996 tests became publicly available both the national and the local media paid them considerable attention. Comparisons were made between years, between local authorities,
and between individual schools. The latter comparisons, between individual schools, were not confined to the local press and media. The
Financial Times, for example, under the headline, 'Primary school tests
show gulf in standards', reported the comparative performance of two
named schools in the London Borough of Hackney, as well as the performance of the 'worst school' of all, where only eight per cent 'passed'
English (11/03/98: 20). This semantic slippage, by the way, from the
officially promoted language of 'expected levels' of performance (level 4
or above at KS2) to that of 'pass' and 'fail' was common across the
media, both in their reporting of the 1996 and the 1995 results. Even in
the case of supposedly 'quality' newspapers, comment on the distribution
of tests results left much to be desired. *The Guardian*, for example, in a

comment on the 1995 results, wrote, 'ministers need to highlight the reasons why some schools in disadvantaged areas still do well – and why others, in prosperous areas like Avon, Dorset and East Sussex, have been doing badly' (27/08/96). Such comments show a curious lack of awareness of the ways in which individual schools within 'prosperous areas' differ in the social composition of their intake – a matter that perhaps needs to be addressed before such comments can be directed justifiably against poorer performing schools in these 'prosperous areas'.

Preliminaries

First of all, what was the range of achievement by NC level amongst these children, from our three primary schools, in their May 1996 tests? Table 5.1 shows the distribution of level achieved for the 125 children whose results, broken down by sex, we analyse in this chapter.[1] Of these children, 76 per cent achieve the officially 'expected' level 4 or better. This is a higher figure than the national average (*Times Educational Supplement* 14/03/97).

It would be possible to begin immediately to analyse further these achieved levels employing social class, sex, 'ability', etc., as independent variables. However, these levels' are produced by a set of rules that operate on children's raw marks. As a consequence the 'levels' are yet one further step away from children's mathematical understanding and skills than these raw marks themselves. We will therefore begin by describing the official procedure whereby marks on the two main papers taken in May 1996 were turned into levels (SCAA, no date a) and by considering its consequences for our purposes here. According to SCAA (no date a) marks awarded on the two papers A and B were added together and the ranges set out in Table 5.2 were used to generate a 'level' for the two tests taken together.

Table 5.1 NC levels awarded in the May 1996 tests in three schools, by sex

| Level | Female | | Male | | All | |
	Count	Col %	Count	Col %	Count	Col %
No level awarded	1	1.9	1	1.4	2	1.6
3	11	20.4	17	23.9	28	22.4
4	29	53.7	31	43.7	60	48.0
5	13	24.1	22	31.0	35	28.0
Total	54	100.1	71	100.0	125	100.0

Table 5.2   Relation between NC level and raw mark
(maximum 80) for the May 1996 tests (SCAA, no date a)

Level	Mark range
2	17–19
3	20–40
4	41–60
5	61+

Table 5.3   Children falling around the 3–4 level boundary in May 1996 tests

Mark achieved	35	36	37	38	39	40	41	42	43	44	45
Level awarded	3	3	3	3	3	3	4	4	4	4	4
Number of children	5	0	2	3	3	2	2	2	1	7	2

Table 5.4   Children falling around the 4–5 level boundary in May 1996 tests

Mark achieved	55	56	57	58	59	60	61	62	63	64	65
Level awarded	4	4	4	4	4	4	5	5	5	5	5
Number of children	2	4	0	2	0	3	8	1	4	1	2

Such a procedure has one obvious and well-known disadvantage. Children falling just above or below a boundary will receive different levels. In cases of pairs of children where one scores just above and one just below a boundary a small quantitative difference will become a qualitative one. In large national samples this is not likely to lead to problems if data are being used to present overall descriptions of levels achieved. For such purposes the decisions concerning the placing of the boundaries themselves are likely to produce the greatest difficulties of interpretation. This would be the case, for example, when performances from year to year are compared. However, once the issue becomes one of comparing individual schools or using data from small samples for research purposes, the problem becomes rather more significant. We can illustrate this by looking at the boundary between levels 3 and 4, and levels 4 and 5. The total marks and the levels awarded for children scoring 35–45 in our data are shown in Table 5.3, and those for children scoring 55–65 are shown in Table 5.4.

Table 5.5 Children falling around 3–4 level boundary by sex in May 1996 tests

Mark achieved	38	39	40	41	42	43
Level awarded	3	3	3	4	4	4
Number of boys	2	2	2	0	0	1
Number of girls	1	1	0	2	2	0

We can see in the second case that three children have scored 60 and eight have scored 61. If some of the latter children had dropped just one mark they would have received a level 4 rather than a 5. This suggests that, in research work with small samples, the use wherever possible of the raw marks (or percentages based upon them) is likely to lead to less error in interpreting children's comparative performance than the use of levels. A little more detail might make this clearer. Consider sex. Table 5.5 shows how the 13 children gaining marks in the 38–43 range break down by sex. As it happens, the sexes are not spread similarly over the two sides of the key boundary, which falls between marks of 40 and 41. Boys tend to be just below this boundary, while girls tend to be just above. This illustrates why analyses based on levels that employ small samples might be particularly subject to random error due to boundary effects.

It is possible to simulate what this distribution around the boundary might have looked like had each child gained slightly higher or lower marks. To do this we have added to each child's total raw score for May 1996 a number in the range –2 to +2 selected randomly (using Microsoft Excel). The rationale for this is simply that it seems likely that children's performances might vary randomly day by day within this small range. In the very first run of this simulation (chosen to avoid the danger of selection) three children find themselves with scores that result in new NC levels. The correlation between the actual raw score and this simulated raw score total is 0.9949, indicating that, even where a very high correlation exists at the level of raw scores, children can still shift across boundaries. In this case each of the three children has moved from level 3 to level 4. The new distribution of marks around the boundary after the simulation is shown in Table 5.6. Three children change their achieved level as a result of this simulated re-testing. Many more, of course, change their mark, but with no consequence for their level.

Now three may not seem a very large number. However, in this chapter we wish to analyse children's performances, both overall and on certain types of item, using such variables as social class, gender, and school. If we look at how the three moving children distribute themselves across

Table 5.6 Children falling around 3–4 level boundary by sex after the simulation of random error

Mark achieved	38	39	40	41	42	43
Level awarded	3	3	3	4	4	4
Number of boys	1	1	0	2	2	0
Number of girls	0	1	2	1	3	2

Table 5.7 NC levels awarded in the May 1996 tests by sex after the simulation of random error

Post-simulation level	Female		Male		All	
	Count	Col %	Count	Col %	Count	Col %
No level awarded	1	1.9	1	1.4	2	1.6
3	11	20.4	14	19.7	25	20.0
4	29	53.7	34	47.9	63	50.4
5	13	24.1	22	31.0	35	28.0
Total	54	100.1	71	100.0	125	100.0

Table 5.8 Percentage achieving 'expected' NC level pre- and post-simulation of random error

Percentage achieving level 4 or above	Females	Males	All
Actual marks	77.8	74.6	76.0
Simulated marks	77.8	78.9	78.4

these variables, we can see that using levels may not be the best way to proceed. While one child came from each of our three social class categories (though it will be seen later that these are not equally represented in our sample), all three of the movers were boys and all came from just one school (School A). The new simulated distribution of levels by sex is shown in Table 5.7. We can now compare the proportions of children gaining the 'expected' levels by sex prior to and post the simulation (Table 5.8). We can observe that, while the overall percentage achieving at least the 'expected' level has changed only a little, the boundary effects we have been discussing have operated to move boys from being slightly behind to slightly ahead of girls in the proportion gaining the 'expected' level, though both differences are non-significant statistically.

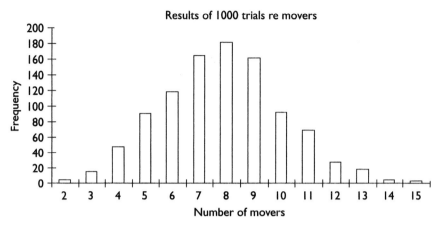

Figure 5.1 Results of 1000 trials of the simulation of random error in measuring performance

In fact, we have been very conservative in using the first run of our simulation as the basis for this discussion. If we run the simulation a number of times, it is possible to produce a distribution of the number of children who change levels each time as a result of our randomly changing their mark by a small amount (−2, −1, 0, +1, or +2). Figure 5.1 shows the results of 1000 runs of the simulation. The most common result is that eight children change levels. In 55.8 per cent of the 1000 runs eight or more children change their level. It turns out that the result of three discussed above is actually atypically low for a simulation employing our assumptions. If we consider how moving just three children across level boundaries was able to move boys' results ahead of those of girls, then, similarly, it is easy to see how the use of levels, in conjunction with the small samples involved in the comparison of primary schools, is likely to lead to a considerable amount of misrepresentation of a school's relative strengths and weaknesses at a local level. As we saw earlier, this will not prevent the media reporting comparative performance at the level of the individual school.

These boundary problems present us with a minor dilemma. As far as the children, parents, teachers, the media and government are concerned the levels are the official measure of children's progress. On the other hand, our eventual purpose in this chapter is to try to understand how different item types interact with characteristics of children to produce differences in performance. We have shown that the representation of children's performance by levels would introduce another, and unhelpful, type of potential error into our analyses, especially in respect of any analyses by school. We will therefore employ raw marks or percentages based on them in this chapter. We are also aware that the use of levels might compromise the anonymity of our sample schools, and it is for this reason that we have used sex differences rather than school differences in our discussion of levels in these preliminary remarks.

Performance in the May 1996 tests: social class, gender, 'ability' and school

We have shown why we use raw marks and percentages based on them in most of this chapter. For the record, however, we begin by describing how the levels achieved by our sample varied by social class (see p. 18). We have already presented the case of sex in Table 5.1. The results for social class are shown in Table 5.9 as counts and percentages within each social class grouping. In order to protect the anonymity of our sample schools, we will omit any discussion of school differences until we move to the use of raw marks and percentages in the next section. Table 5.9 shows that 85 per cent of service-class children, 80 per cent of intermediate-class children and almost 58 per cent of working-class children achieve at least the 'expected' level of 4. Within this distribution it is also clear that as we move from the working class through the intermediate class to the service class an increasing percentage of children achieve level 5. We move now to consider children's achievements in the May tests in terms of the underlying marks gained, rather than levels achieved. The basic distribution of test scores is shown in Figure 5.2. A maximum total of 80 marks was achievable. From this point, we will treat children's performances as percentages of these maximum marks.

Table 5.9   NC levels awarded in the May 1996 tests by social class (two cases missing)

Level	Service class		Intermediate class		Working class		All	
	Count	Col %	Count	Col %	Count	Col %	Count	Col %
No level awarded	1	1.7	0	0.0	1	3.0	2	1.6
3	8	13.3	6	20.0	13	39.4	27	22.0
4	27	45.0	17	56.7	15	45.5	59	48.0
5	24	40.0	7	23.3	4	12.1	35	28.5
Total	60	100.0	30	100.0	33	100.0	123	100.1

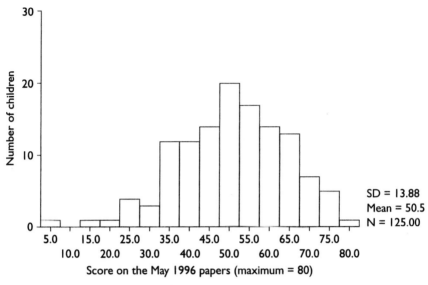

Figure 5.2 Distribution of Key Stage 2 marks

Table 5.10 Percentage of available marks achieved on May 1996 tests by social class and sex

Social class	Female		Male		Total	
	Mean	Count	Mean	Count	Mean	Count
Service class	67.12	26	68.64	34	67.98	60
Intermediate class	62.12	13	63.68	17	63.00	30
Working class	53.65	13	56.69	20	55.49	33
Total	62.50	52	64.08	71	63.41	123

The mean *percentages* of the total marks available achieved on the two tests taken together, broken down by social class (see Table 2.2 for definitions of the categories) and sex, are shown in Table 5.10. In this sample, boys achieve slightly higher scores than girls (non-significant by an analysis of variance of achievement by social class and sex). Social class differences are more substantial, with the mean percentage achieved running from 55.49 per cent to 67.98 per cent as we move from the working class through the intermediate class to the service class children (significant by analysis of variance). This pattern of achievement by social class holds for both boys and girls.

Table 5.11 Percentage of available marks achieved on May 1996 tests by social class and school

Social class	School C		School B		School A		Total	
	Mean	Count	Mean	Count	Mean	Count	Mean	Count
Service class	68.13	2	75.28	22	63.51	36	67.98	60
Intermediate class	64.64	7	59.00	5	63.47	18	63.00	30
Working class	62.00	15	45.73	12	58.75	6	55.49	33
Total	63.28	24	64.10	39	63.02	60	63.41	123

The distribution of achievement by social class and school is shown in Table 5.11, where the reader should note some cell sizes are very small. The overall differences between the schools themselves are small (non-significant by an analysis of variance of score by social class and school), though, as in the previous table, no attempt has yet been made to take account of measured 'ability' (an issue to which we will return below). Within each school the rising gradient of achievement from the working class to the service class is preserved (overall social class differences are significant by analysis of variance). However, what is most noticeable about the distribution of scores in Table 5.11 is the difference between service- and working-class scores in School B (interaction of school and social class is significant by analysis of variance). It would be easy to suggest that this is a 'school effect', perhaps reflecting in particular the skills of the children's most recent teachers. But we must not jump too hastily to this conclusion, simply because it is possible that the working-class children in School B are different from those in School C in some relevant way not picked out by the three-way social class division employed here. The same point applies to the service-class samples in School B and School A. Eighty-five of the 123 children fall into the shaded eight cells of Table 5.11, four appearing in the lower left and four in the upper right sections. It can be seen that the mean working-class score in School B is very low in comparison with that in School C (45.73 per cent versus 62.00 per cent), while the service-class mean score in School B is high in comparison with that in School A (75.28 per cent versus 63.51 per cent). Is the large service/working difference within School B due to some school effect operating within this school or, alternatively, might it be due to some other relevant differences between the working-class samples in School C and School B on the one hand, and the service-class samples in School B and School A on the other? In other words, might the 'school' effect be explicable not in terms of school policy and practice differences, but in terms of the ways in which other relevant differences within our broad social classes are distributed across the schools? This

Table 5.12 Percentage of available marks achieved on May 1996 tests by underlying social class categories and school

	School C		School B		School A		Total	
	Mean	*Count*	*Mean*	*Count*	*Mean*	*Count*	*Mean*	*Count*
Service class, higher grade	90.00	1	78.96	12	68.00	15	73.48	28
Service class, lower grade	46.25	1	70.88	10	60.30	21	63.16	32
Routine non-manual employees	68.54	6	68.75	1	60.00	6	64.62	13
Personal service workers	–	0	–	0	55.00	3	55.00	3
Small proprietors with employees	–	0	–	0	86.88	2	86.88	2
Small proprietors without employees	41.25	1	53.33	3	63.54	6	58.25	10
Foremen and technicians	–	0	66.25	1	62.50	1	64.38	2
Skilled manual workers	65.63	4	40.75	5	64.06	4	55.58	13
Semi- and unskilled manual workers	60.68	11	49.29	7	48.13	2	55.44	20
Group Total	63.28	24	64.10	39	63.02	60	63.41	123

decision problem is inherent in all survey analyses (Lieberson 1985) and is certainly a serious problem in the context of locating effects due to schooling. As we collapse data into a smaller number of categories to generate adequate cell sizes we inevitably run the risk of losing access to finer relevant differences within these broader groups.

To begin to gain a better idea of what might be happening here we can examine a more detailed breakdown of performance by social class and schooling. Table 5.12 shows how the underlying categories of our social class schema (see Table 2.2) are distributed by school. Again the cells containing the 85 children are shaded. These data show that the service-class sample in School B has a greater proportion of 'higher grade' occupations (12/22 = 55 per cent) in its total than does School A (15/36 = 42 per cent). In each case, the children from the 'higher grade' occupations score above the children from the 'lower grade' section of the service class (School B: 78.96 per cent versus 70.88 per cent; School A: 68.00 per cent versus 60.30 per cent), suggesting social class matters. It can be seen, however, that, for both 'higher grade' and 'lower grade' sections, School B children have higher scores than School A children (higher grade: 78.96 per cent versus 68.00 per cent; lower grade: 70.88 per cent versus 60.30 per cent). This pattern of results would appear to offer support for both social class and school effects.

What about the working-class comparison between School B and School C? In this case the proportion of the working-class sample who are categorized as 'skilled' is higher in School B (5/12 = 42 per cent) than in

Table 5.13 Percentage of available marks achieved on May 1996 tests by sex and school

| Sex | School C | | School B | | School A | | Total | |
	Mean	Count	Mean	Count	Mean	Count	Mean	Count
Female	60.83	12	62.06	17	62.05	25	61.78	54
Male	65.73	12	65.43	23	62.67	36	64.08	71
Total	63.28	24	64.00	40	62.42	61	63.09	125

School C (4/15 = 27 per cent), but the total working-class scores achieved run in the opposite direction (45.73 per cent versus 62.00 per cent). In School C the four children from 'skilled' backgrounds outscore the 11 children from 'unskilled' backgrounds (65.63 per cent versus 60.68 per cent). In School B, on the contrary, the five children from 'skilled' backgrounds underscore the seven children from 'unskilled' backgrounds (40.75 per cent versus 49.29 per cent). In the cases of children from both 'skilled' and 'unskilled' backgrounds School C outscores School B. Compared with the other two schools, School B seems to produce better scores for service-class children and worse scores for working-class children. There does remain therefore evidence of a school effect when we move to finer social class categories. Our attempt to remove the effects of variation within the categories of the three-way division into social classes has not threatened the suggestion of a school effect. Of course, the division of the working class by 'skill' is difficult for a variety of reasons (Blackburn and Mann 1979). Furthermore, the numbers in the working-class case become very small when we move to the finer categories. Nevertheless, this exercise indicates the need for further analysis. One way forward involves the use of children's measured 'ability', but first we will consider achievement by sex and school.

In Table 5.10 we saw that boys achieved slightly higher scores than girls in all social class groups (non-significant by an analysis of variance of achievement by sex and social class), with the largest difference being found in the working class. Table 5.13 shows that boys achieve higher scores than girls in each school, but most especially so in School C, the school with the highest proportion of working-class children. Neither the school or the sex differences are statistically significant (analysis of variance). Neither is the interaction of school and sex. Nevertheless, the sex difference is greater in School C. We can explore further the relations between social class, sex and school by using an analysis of variance that employs the three variables simultaneously, with achievement as the dependent variable. This finds the main effect due to social class approaching significance ($p = 0.12$), but not that due to either sex or school.

The two-way interaction for school and social class is significant ($p = 0.008$), while that for sex and school approaches significance ($p = 0.098$). The three-way interaction of social class, sex and school approaches significance ($p = 0.079$), and again this begs the question of why. For example, is the greater sex difference in School C due to some 'school effect' or more to something about the social class distribution of children in this school? To help us answer this question, we will now consider measured 'ability'. We have previously discussed, in Chapter 2, the way in which we wish our use of 'ability' scores to be understood (see p. 14). Summarizing what we said there, we see these scores as 'predictors' of likely academic success rather than as culture-free measures of some unchanging set of cognitive powers. With this proviso in mind, we will return to the issue of the relatively greater differentiation by social class that we found in School B and by sex in School C.

We shall consider how the introduction of 'ability' scores can illuminate the differences we have pointed to between the schools, social classes and sexes. Table 5.14 shows the distribution of quantitative Cognitive Ability Test (CAT) scores across the schools by social class. (Note that two children, for whom we have no quantitative CAT scores, are lost from the 123 in Table 5.11.) We can see immediately that, in terms of this 'predictor of academic achievement', it is indeed the case that service-class children are predicted to do better in quantitative activities in School B as compared with School A (115.85 versus 103.25) and, similarly, working-class children are predicted to do better in quantitative activities in School C than School B (102.40 versus 97.83). In Table 5.15 we have employed a simple procedure to assess whether these differences in CAT scores can 'account' for (in the purely statistical sense) the large social class differences in achievement that we found in School B. We have divided each child's percentage achievement by his or her quantitative CAT score, and then multiplied by the inverse of the mean of this variable for the whole sample in order to construct a final variable with a convenient mean of one.[2] In Table 5.15, therefore, scores higher than one suggest children are, relative to others, achieving ahead of what the CAT score might have predicted, and children with scores lower than one are achieving less well than the prediction. We can see that the result we discussed initially (see Table 5.11) survives this treatment. School B still appears to produce a greater differentiation by social class than the other two schools. Not only is the range of means by social class greatest in this school, but also the comparisons of the service-class children across School B and School A (1.10 versus 1.01) and of working-class children across School C and School B (1.00 versus 0.77) still suggest something noteworthy is happening in this school (though bear in mind the original proviso concerning unmeasured or incorrectly measured aspects of 'social class', which still applies).

Table 5.14 Quantitative 'ability' by social class and school

Social class	School C		School B		School A		Total	
	Mean	Count	Mean	Count	Mean	Count	Mean	Count
Service class	111.50	2	115.85	20	103.25	36	107.88	58
Intermediate class	107.00	7	106.00	5	99.89	18	102.57	30
Working class	102.40	15	97.83	12	97.00	6	99.76	33
Total	104.50	24	108.68	37	101.62	60	104.35	121

Table 5.15 Performance, adjusted for quantitative 'ability', in the May 1996 tests by social class and school

Social class	School C		School B		School A		Total	
	Mean	Count	Mean	Count	Mean	Count	Mean	Count
Service class	0.99	2	1.10	20	1.01	36	1.04	58
Intermediate class	1.00	7	0.92	5	1.05	18	1.02	30
Working class	1.00	15	0.77	12	0.98	6	0.91	33
Group Total	1.00	24	0.97	37	1.02	60	1.00	121

Returning to Table 5.15, there is another key point to note. While, with quantitative 'ability' taken into account, there remains a social class difference in achievement in the overall sample (1.04, 1.02, 0.91), it can be seen that most of this is due to the results of School B. However, it would not be very sensible to take the findings concerning social class in Schools A and C too seriously. There are only two service-class children in School C, and only six working-class children in School A. Lastly, looking at the overall achievement on this 'ability'-adjusted measure by school, it can be seen that the schools fall in a narrow range (1.00, 0.97, 1.02). There is a reminder here that the study of school effects needs to take into account the effects of school policies and practices on particular groups as well as overall means. It is of little use to the working-class children in School B that the school's overall achievement is much the same, if a little lower, than the others. Their achievement, measured against the quantitative 'ability' criterion, is 0.77 versus 1.00 for the overall sample including themselves. If, of course, the quantitative 'ability' scores are to any degree biased against working-class children, as we suggested in Chapter 2 that they might be, this underestimates these children's plight. Similarly, service-class children in School A seem to underscore on the 'ability'-adjusted measure relative to both service-class children in School B and to intermediate-class children in School A itself.

Table 5.16 Performance, adjusted for quantitative 'ability', in the May 1996 tests by underlying categories of social class and school

School	School C		School B		School A		Total	
	Mean	Count	Mean	Count	Mean	Count	Mean	Count
Service class, higher grade	1.15	1	1.13	11	1.10	15	1.11	27
Service class, lower grade	0.84	1	1.07	9	0.95	21	0.98	31
Routine non-manual employees	1.04	6	1.01	1	1.03	6	1.03	13
Personal service workers	–	0	–	0	0.99	3	0.99	3
Small proprietors with employees	–	0	–	0	1.27	2	1.27	2
Small proprietors without employees	0.73	1	0.85	3	1.03	6	0.94	10
Foremen and technicians	–	0	1.02	1	1.11	1	1.07	2
Skilled manual workers	1.08	4	0.72	5	1.04	4	0.93	13
Semi- and unskilled manual workers	0.98	11	0.80	7	0.88	2	0.91	20
Group Total	1.00	24	0.97	37	1.02	60	1.00	121

We can also look anew at the comparisons (now involving 83 children) between sections of the service class and working class across the three schools. Again, in Table 5.16, the relevant cells are shaded. In the upper right-hand corner, we can see an apparent social class effect, with children from 'higher grade' service-class backgrounds outscoring those from 'lower grade' service-class backgrounds in both schools on the 'ability'-adjusted measure. There is also an apparent school effect, with School B children outscoring School A children in both 'higher grade' and 'lower grade' comparisons, though the effect is clearly much greater in the 'lower grade' case (1.07 versus 0.95). In the lower left-hand corner, looking at the two working-class groups, we can see that, in both cases, School C outscores School B in both cases on the adjusted measure.

What about achievement scores in relation to sex, school and measured 'ability'? Table 5.17 jumps straight to the 'ability'-adjusted measure used in Table 5.15. We see straightaway that the sex difference in School C largely disappears once quantitative 'ability' score is taken into account. Here, in fact, it is, as in the case of social class, School B which appears as the most differentiating school by sex. Barring interaction effects, this would suggest that School B is not, *relatively* speaking, the best place to be for a working-class girl.[3] In fact, if we look in more detail at the adjusted achievement score we find that of all the possible social class/sex/school combinations ($3 \times 2 \times 3 = 18$) it is indeed the group of five working-class girls in School B who have the lowest adjusted score (0.64 versus 1.00 for the whole sample) and by a long way (Table 5.18).

Table 5.17   Performance, adjusted for quantitative 'ability', in the May 1996 tests by sex and school

Sex	School C		School B		School A		Total	
	Mean	Count	Mean	Count	Mean	Count	Mean	Count
Female	0.99	12	0.91	15	1.02	25	0.98	52
Male	1.01	12	1.01	22	1.01	36	1.01	70
Total	1.00	24	0.97	37	1.01	61	1.00	122

Table 5.18   Performance, adjusted for quantitative 'ability', in the May 1996 tests by social class, sex and school

School	School C		School B		School A		Total	
	Mean	Count	Mean	Count	Mean	Count	Mean	Count
Service class, girls	0.84	1	1.10	7	1.02	17	1.04	25
Service class, boys	1.15	1	1.11	13	1.00	19	1.05	33
Intermediate class, girls	1.00	4	0.91	3	1.06	6	1.01	13
Intermediate class, boys	0.99	3	0.93	2	1.05	12	1.02	17
Working class, girls	1.01	7	0.64	5	1.31	1	0.89	13
Working class, boys	1.00	8	0.86	7	0.92	5	0.93	20
Group Total	1.00	24	0.97	37	1.02	60	1.00	121

Of course, we are now running up against problems of cell size, and we have shaded those cells which have at least five cases to emphasize this.

We can employ an analysis of variance of the 'ability'-adjusted achievement score by three-category social class, sex and school to increase our understanding of what is occurring here. Of the main effects only school is statistically significant ($p = 0.047$). However, the interaction of school with social class is significant ($p = 0.002$) and that of school with sex approaches significance ($p = 0.084$). The introduction of a measured 'ability' variable has reduced the statistical importance of social class. Whether this reduction reflects the actual importance of social class hinges, as we explained in Chapter 2, on one's view of 'ability' tests and, in particular, the relation of what they measure to cognitive and cultural differences between social classes. What is particularly interesting is the very significant interaction between social class and school. This is precisely what our discussion has brought out. In this sample, it does seem to matter what school you attend and, furthermore, it matters differently for service- and working-class children. But, as we have repeatedly stressed, this conclusion is subject to a proviso concerning 'selective' effects resulting from aspects of what the children bring with them to school, which are not picked up by our measures. We turn now to the comparison of performance on 'esoteric' and 'realistic' items.

Relative performance on 'realistic' and 'esoteric' items: an overview

In this section we will draw on the data from all three tests taken by the Key Stage 2 children. These include the two tests taken in May 1996, but also the test taken in February 1996, which comprised a selection of national test items from previous years.

Each separately marked item or sub-item of the three tests taken by 10–11-year-olds was coded on a variety of dimensions, including a twofold division into what we have termed 'realistic' or 'esoteric' items using a rule that is simple to state though not always easy to operationalize.[4] An item has been categorized as 'realistic' if it contains either persons or non-mathematical objects from 'everyday' settings. Otherwise it is coded as 'esoteric'. Given that in some cases a person appeared just to introduce the item we experimented initially with a threefold category system, putting such items into a category we termed 'ritualistically realistic'. However, in the end, we decided not to pursue this distinction within the 'realistic' category as we felt unable to judge, when coding items prior to the analysis of data, whether what to us might seem 'ritualistic' might seem the same to a child. Clearly, it is also possible to raise questions here about whose 'everyday' and whose 'esoteric' it is that we are referring to. We wish 'everyday' here to refer to such activities as shopping, sport, etc. of which we can assume most children have some personal knowledge and experience. Solving $x^2 - 3 = 6$ might well be describable as 'everyday' by reference to some group's behaviour in some setting, but we assume here that such items are recognizably different from those that embed mathematics in shopping, etc. The purpose of our distinction is not to legislate on what ultimately counts, in some universalistic way, as 'everyday' or 'esoteric', but to enable empirical analysis of important issues to get off the ground. Examples of 'realistic' items have already been discussed in Chapters 3 and 4 (e.g. Figures 3.1– 3.3). Two illustrative 'esoteric' items are shown in Figures 5.3 and 5.4. In each case it can be seen that there are no references to an 'everyday' context as we have defined it.

For each child the percentages of total marks scored on the two categories of items taken separately were calculated, giving a 'realistic' and an 'esoteric' percentage for each individual. The final handful of items from our 'mock' test of February 1996 was omitted from this analysis in order to only include items that all or very nearly all children had definitely attempted. One hundred and ten separate items or part-items entered

---

n stands for a number.

n + 7 = 13

What is the value of **n + 10?** ✎ _____

Figure 5.3 The algebra item (SCAA, 1996)

Here is a row of numbers.

✎ 1 2 3 4 5 6 7 8 9 10 11 12 13 14 15 16 17 18

Find **three numbers <u>next to each other</u>** which add up to **39**. Draw a ring round them.

Figure 5.4 The numbers item (SCAA, 1996)

Table 5.19 Percentage score achieved on KS2 'realistic' items on the three tests by social class and sex

Social class	Female		Male		Total	
	Mean	Count	Mean	Count	Mean	Count
Service class	57.74	26	60.33	34	59.21	60
Intermediate class	55.68	13	55.04	17	55.32	30
Working class	47.34	13	51.07	20	49.60	33
Total	54.62	52	56.46	71	55.68	123

the analysis. It should also be noted that two-thirds of the items come from the May 1996 tests and only a third from earlier incarnations of the NC tests. For each child a ratio was created by dividing the 'realistic' by the 'esoteric' percentage' achieved. Tables 5.19–5.21 show the distribution by social class and sex of the two percentages and the resulting ratio for the primary school children for whom we have full relevant information.[5]

Ratios such as these have properties that can make them difficult to interpret. In particular, a ratio of percentages will have an upper bound set by the size of its denominator. If, for example, a child scores 50 per cent as their 'esoteric' subtotal then their highest possible 'realistic'/'esoteric' (r/e) ratio will be 100/50 or 2. If another child, on the other hand, scores 40 per cent as their 'esoteric' subtotal their highest possible ratio

Table 5.20 Percentage score achieved on KS2 'esoteric' items on the three tests by social class and sex

Social class	Female		Male		Total	
	Mean	Count	Mean	Count	Mean	Count
Service class	71.07	26	70.10	34	70.52	60
Intermediate class	70.35	13	69.98	17	70.14	30
Working class	65.71	13	64.69	20	65.09	33
Total	69.55	52	68.54	71	68.97	123

Table 5.21 Ratio of KS2 'realistic' percentage to 'esoteric' percentage by social class and sex

Social class	Female		Male		Total	
	Mean	Count	Mean	Count	Mean	Count
Service class	0.81	26	0.88	34	0.85	60
Intermediate class	0.79	13	0.79	17	0.79	30
Working class	0.71	13	0.79	20	0.76	33
Total	0.78	52	0.83	71	0.81	123

will be 100/40 or 2.5. Since service-class children, on average, do better than others on the 'esoteric' subsection of the tests their potential maximum r/e ratio is lower than that for the working-class children who score lower on the 'esoteric' subsection. Notwithstanding this, Table 5.21 shows that the service-class children have the highest ratios of any group.[6]

There is a clear relation of this ratio to social class background, with its value ranging from 0.85 for the service class, through 0.79 for the intermediate grouping, to 0.76 for the working class for boys and girls taken together.[7] Service-class children as a whole have a better performance on 'realistic' items in relation to 'esoteric' items than do working-class children. The relation of the ratio to social class is particularly clear in the case of girls. Looking at sex, the r/e ratio is higher for boys in both the service- and working-class groups, though it is identical for girls and boys in the intermediate grouping.[8] The social class effect is illustrated in Figure 5.5, where two linear regression lines have been fitted to capture the 'realistic'–'esoteric' relation for these two social class groupings.[9] What this finding suggests is that, all other things being equal, the higher the proportion of 'realistic' items in a test, the greater will be the difference in outcome between service- and working-class children.

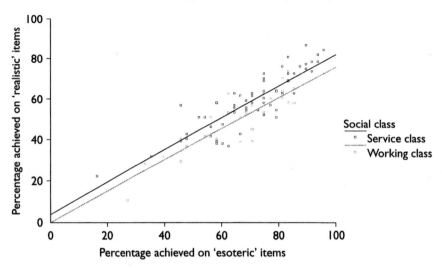

Figure 5.5 The distribution of KS2 'realistic' percentages by 'esoteric' percentages by child (service class and working class only)

It is important to stress that these social class differences are not ones of kind. There is much overlap in the distribution of these ratios across our three social class groupings. The differences in Table 5.21 appear to be differences 'on average' not of kind. The charts in Figure 5.6 demonstrate this clearly. However, it is also worth noting that, given the many other dimensions on which these test items differ within the categories 'realistic' and 'esoteric', it is also possible that these results underestimate the importance of the effect of 'realistic' versus 'esoteric' contextualization. It is perhaps surprising that the effect appears at all amidst all this 'noise'.[10]

It is important to consider other possible explanations of this pattern of differences. It might be the case, for example, that 'ability', or attainment, or some concomitant of school attended such as curriculum coverage, or systematic differences in the easiness of the 'realistic' versus 'esoteric' items are the real underlying causes of the results in Table 5.21. We have tried to approach these problems from several directions. First, we have examined whether the relation of the r/e ratio varies by performance on the esoteric items considered alone (treating the latter performance as a proxy for attainment). The results can be seen in Table 5.22. It can be seen that the r/e ratio varies by social class in the same way within each of three categories of achievement on 'esoteric' items.[11] In each case, the ratio falls as we move from service- through intermediate- to working-class groups. Second, we have used logistic regression to examine the associations between school, 'ability', sex, social class and the ratio. This

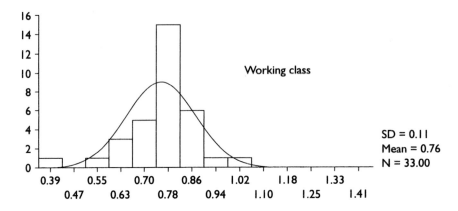

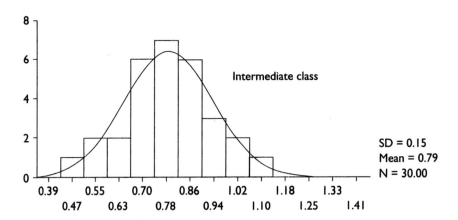

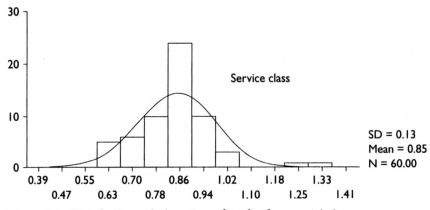

Figure 5.6 Distributions of r/e ratio within the three social class groups (numbers of children)

Table 5.22 Ratio of KS2 'realistic' percentage to 'esoteric' percentage by social class and performance on 'esoteric' items (grouped into three categories)

Social class	Lowest achieving third of sample on the 'esoteric' items		Middle achieving third of sample on the 'esoteric' items		Highest achieving third of sample on the 'esoteric' items	
	Mean	Count	Mean	Count	Mean	Count
Service class	0.88	18	0.85	20	0.83	22
Intermediate class	0.81	9	0.78	10	0.78	11
Working class	0.78	13	0.72	10	0.77	10

regression analysis (Cooper *et al.* 1997) with our 'realistic'/'esoteric' ratio as dependent variable and social class, sex, school and non-verbal 'ability' as independent variables, suggests that social class and sex are statistically significant here and that school and non-verbal 'ability' are not.[12] Third, concerning curriculum topic/area we have looked at how the ratio varies within attainment targets. Details of this analysis by attainment target are set out in the following section.

The differences within attainment targets

Early versions of the English National Curriculum assumed that each test item could be associated with one statement of attainment – a form of behavioural objective within each of the attainment targets of 'number', etc. We are not convinced believers in the idea that an item can assess just one statement of attainment from within an attainment target. However, we are following the early 'official' practice of the National Curriculum assessors in coding each item (or part-item) as belonging to one AT. Clearly, any item is likely actually to demand a cluster of skills and understandings for its solution. More recently, the National Curriculum test papers have dropped the labelling of each item by one statement of attainment. We have taken the 'official' coding where it exists and have attempted to reproduce it in the case of more recent items where it does not (by close examination of items against previous officially labelled ones). Some of these codings are difficult for the very reason mentioned above. How, then, do the social class and gender differences in the r/e ratio behave within attainment targets, i.e. in relation to broad topic areas within mathematics. In fact, Tables 5.23–5.25 show that the social class and gender differences continue to appear within 'number', 'algebra' and 'shape and space'.

The patterns are less clear than they were in Table 5.21 but are nevertheless there. In particular, in each case an overall service-/working-class comparison of the r/e ratio favours the service class against the working

Table 5.23   Ratio of 'realistic' percentage to 'esoteric' percentage by social class and sex (*number* only)

	Female		Male		Total	
	Mean	*Count*	*Mean*	*Count*	*Mean*	*Count*
Service class	0.79	26	0.83	34	0.81	60
Intermediate class	0.82	13	0.81	17	0.81	30
Working class	0.78	13	0.79	20	0.78	33
Total	0.79	52	0.81	71	0.80	123

Table 5.24   Ratio of 'realistic' percentage to 'esoteric' percentage by social class and sex (*algebra* only)

	Female		Male		Total	
	Mean	*Count*	*Mean*	*Count*	*Mean*	*Count*
Service class	0.69	26	0.88	34	0.80	60
Intermediate class	0.66	13	0.71	17	0.69	30
Working class	0.57	13	0.56	20	0.56	33
Total	0.66	52	0.75	71	0.71	123

Table 5.25   Ratio of 'realistic' percentage to 'esoteric' percentage by social class and sex (*shape and space* only)

	Female		Male		Total	
	Mean	*Count*	*Mean*	*Count*	*Mean*	*Count*
Service class	1.17	26	1.17	34	1.17	60
Intermediate class	1.04	13	1.13	17	1.09	30
Working class	1.04	13	1.19	20	1.13	33
Total	1.10	52	1.17	71	1.14	123

class. In parallel with this, an overall male/female comparison of the r/e ratio consistently favours the boys. These differences are particularly marked in the case of algebra. It is also interesting to note that, in the case of 'shape and space', the children found the 'realistic' items generally easier than the 'esoteric' ones. Nevertheless, the r/e ratio remains highest in the case of the service class taken as a whole, and boys have a higher ratio than girls. We are not able to present a table for the case of data handling since all of the items under this heading have been coded as 'realistic'. However, some idea can be gained of the 'behaviour' of the data handling items in relation to social class by examining their position in Table 5.26. Here we show how children from each social class group performed on each of the seven attainment target – context coding combinations. Table 5.27 shows comparable calculations for boys and girls. Comparing the service class with the working class, and boys with girls, there appear to be similar social class and gender effects across attainment targets, suggesting that the differences in the r/e ratio in Table 5.21 are not merely 'spurious' topic effects.

Another possibility which needs to be addressed is that it is because the 'esoteric' items are, in general, found easier in this data set, coupled with social class related differences in typical educational achievement, that the r/e ratio patterns by social class are as they are. Perhaps working-class children just perform less well on harder items? In fact, however, statistical analyses employing items rather than the child as the case have shown that broad social class differences in a relative of this r/e ratio remain (though are reduced in importance) when examined within four categories of items ordered by average difficulty levels. The means in Table 5.28 derive from a variable constructed by dividing, for each item, the service-class mean score by the working-class mean score. Differences in measured 'ability' are automatically controlled for in this approach, as in the use of the realistic/esoteric ratio earlier. It can be seen that, within each category of items, from the most easy to the most difficult, the service-class children perform relatively better than working-class children on 'realistic' items as compared to 'esoteric' items.[13] Similarly, the previously discussed findings also hold when the 'wordiness' of items is controlled by the simple measure of words counted in each item or sub-item, as can be seen from Table 5.29.

The social class effects we have been discussing may appear small, and it must be stressed that they are not, as has been seen from Tables 5.23– 5.27, equally important across the four ATs addressed here. Table 5.26, reporting the comparative performance of service-class and working-class children across seven combinations of attainment target and contextualization, showed that it is in the cases of 'realistic' algebra items and, to a lesser extent, 'realistic' data handling items that the largest social class differences appear. Furthermore, it is clearly possible that the items in these categories happen to have been the least *well-designed* amongst our particular sample of items.[14] It would obviously be premature to decide on the basis of our work with a particular set of items, and sample sizes constrained by our decision to focus our data collection energies on the interview context, that 'realistic' items *necessarily* must favour service-class children over working-class children. On the other hand, there are, as we argued in Chapter 4, sociological accounts of social class and culture, which provide some grounds for the expectation that they might, relative to their 'esoteric' companions. Our wish in presenting the analysis in this

Table 5.26 Mean percentage scores by social class for each existing attainment target/context combination

	Service class	Intermediate class	Working class	Total	Service class mean divided by the working class mean	Number of separately coded items and sub-items
Number – 'esoteric'	78.81	77.94	75.61	77.74	1.04	21
Number – 'realistic'	64.05	63.57	59.96	62.83	1.07	22
Algebra – 'esoteric'	68.46	66.92	61.54	66.23	1.11	10
Algebra – 'realistic'	50.60	44.05	30.74	43.67	1.65	11
Shape and space – 'esoteric'	66.79	66.19	57.58	64.17	1.16	11
Shape and space – 'realistic'	72.50	66.33	60.00	67.64	1.21	9
Handling data – 'esoteric'	n/a	n/a	n/a	n/a	n/a	0
Handling data – 'realistic'	62.86	55.42	49.34	57.42	1.27	26
n (children)	60	30	33	123		110

Table 5.27 Mean percentage scores by sex for each existing attainment target/context combination

	Girls	Boys	Total	Boys' mean divided by the girls' mean	Number of separately coded items and sub-items
Number – 'esoteric'	76.63	78.27	77.56	1.02	21
Number – 'realistic'	60.71	63.88	62.51	1.05	22
Algebra – 'esoteric'	68.23	64.36	66.03	0.94	10
Algebra – 'realistic'	42.06	44.37	43.37	1.05	11
Shape and space – 'esoteric'	63.49	64.08	63.89	1.01	11
Shape and space – 'realistic'	65.19	68.87	67.28	1.06	9
Handling data – 'esoteric'	n/a	n/a	n/a	n/a	0
Handling data – 'realistic'	55.67	58.19	57.10	1.05	26
n (children)	54	71	125		110

Table 5.28 Ratios of service-class mean score to working-class mean score for an item by observed item difficulty and nature of item (count is of items)

Item difficulty levels	Realistic items		Esoteric items		Total items	
	Mean	Count	Mean	Count	Mean	Count
1 Most difficult quartile	1.62	21	1.37	6	1.56	27
2 Second quartile	1.42	18	1.20	9	1.35	27
3 Third quartile	1.21	14	1.10	12	1.16	26
4 Most easy quartile	1.06	15	1.03	15	1.04	30
Totals	1.35	68	1.14	42	1.27	110

Table 5.29 Ratios of service-class mean score to working-class mean score for an item by 'wordage' and nature of item (count is of items)

Word count	Realistic items		Esoteric items		Total items	
	Mean	Count	Mean	Count	Mean	Count
1 Up to 12 words	1.34	13	1.15	14	1.24	27
2 13 to 20 words	1.40	11	1.10	16	1.22	27
3 21 to 32 words	1.25	19	1.22	7	1.24	26
4 32 words and above	1.41	25	1.11	5	1.36	30
Totals	1.35	68	1.14	42	1.27	110

chapter is certainly not to provide ammunition to those individuals favouring, on the basis of preference alone, a 'back to basics' approach; though, inevitably, some individuals probably will make such use of selective accounts of our analysis. Our wish is rather to ensure that the assessment products of those favouring approaches other than 'back to basics' in mathematics education, and in particular any unintended consequences of these products, are subjected to ongoing examination via research evidence. In carrying out such research, we have to face the fact that the unintended consequences of our work may not always be to our own taste.

We have noted that some of the effects we report are small. However, in the world of educational practice, where decisions are often taken on the basis of thresholds being achieved or not by children, differences of this size can have large effects. To illustrate this, we have developed a simulation of what would happen to children from different social class backgrounds if a selection process were to occur on the basis of three differently composed tests: one comprising items that behave like our 'esoteric' items, one of items that behave like our 'realistic' items, and one comprising an equal mixture of the two.[15] This process might be realized as a selection examination for secondary school or for 'ability' group placement within the first year of secondary school. A summary of the results is shown in Table 5.30 and Figure 5.7. It can be seen that, using our results as the basis for predicting outcomes, the proportion of working-class children in this sample who would be selected by an 'esoteric' test is double that which would be selected by a 'realistic' test. The two tests lead to quite different outcomes, mainly for intermediate- and working-class children. While about 24 per cent of working-class children are selected on the basis of the 'esoteric' test, only about 12 per cent are selected on the basis of the 'realistic' test. Clearly, these findings would also have implications for any comparison of socially differentiated schools via league tables based on the three simulated tests discussed here. It should, of course, be remembered that topics in mathematics are not spread evenly over the 'esoteric' and 'realistic' sub-tests whose results we are employing here. In particular, data handling items only appear in the 'realistic' test. The simulation therefore should be seen as exploratory in intent – as illustrative of the type of effect small differences can lead to in selection contexts – and as an argument in favour of further research into the ways items and social background interact to produce performance. It is also the case that there may be other educational values which, for some readers, will override any worries that 'realistic' items might be more social class differentiating with respect to performance. An overriding belief in other merits of the teaching, learning and assessing of mathematics in the context of supposedly realistic applications would be one obvious example.

Table 5.30 Percentage outflow selected from social classes under three simulated testing regimes (KS2)

Percentage of class selected	Esoteric test (26% selected in total)	Mixed test ($^1/_2$ and $^1/_2$) (26.8% selected in total)	Realistic test (27.6% selected in total)
Service class	30.0	33.3	33.3
Intermediate class	20.0	23.3	33.3
Working class	24.2	18.2	12.1

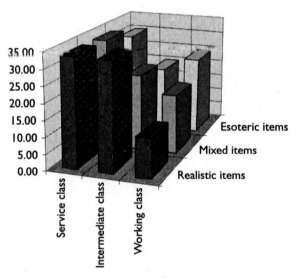

Figure 5.7 Percentage of children selected from each social class under three simulated testing regimes (KS2)

A similar simulation for sex does not show such large effects, reflecting the smaller differences in the realistic/esoteric ratio in Table 5.21. While in the case of social class, a move from 'realistic' through mixed to 'esoteric' test composition linearly increases the proportion of working-class children selected, any pattern for sex is less clear (see Table 5.31 and Figure 5.8), though it is the case that, relative to boys, the highest proportion of girls are selected under the 'esoteric' regime.

Considering the apparent social class effect, a key issue begs to be explored. Is there any evidence that 'realistic' items, for various reasons,

Table 5.31 Percentage outflow selected from sexes under three simulated testing regimes (KS2)

Percentage of sex selected	Esoteric test (26% selected in total)	Mixed test ($\frac{1}{2}$ and $\frac{1}{2}$) (26.8% selected in total)	Realistic test (27.6% selected in total)
Girls	22.2	18.5	22.2
Boys	28.2	32.4	31.0

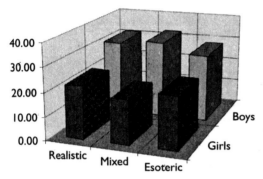

Figure 5.8 Percentage of boys and girls selected under three simulated testing regimes

are underestimating working-class capacities relatively more than those of children from other social class backgrounds? Might they be differentially valid in general? Or is it simply the case that 'realistic' items happen to demand 'legitimately' some mathematical capacities which are more social class-related than those required by 'esoteric' items? We have evidence suggesting that a *part* of the social class effect found is due to the social class distribution of children's 'choice' of an 'illegitimate' and 'inappropriate' 'everyday' response mode rather than to their lack of mathematical capacity *per se* (Cooper 1996, 1998a, 1998b; Cooper *et al.* 1997; Cooper and Dunne 1998). We consider this possibility in the next chapter. In particular we examine in some detail the responses of these 125 children to two previously discussed items, the traffic survey and the tennis competition, in relation to social class and, to a lesser extent, sex. We will show that, in the case of both items, there is some social class patterning to the nature of children's responses, and we will consider the implications of these patterns for the validity of such items.

Table 5.32   Ratio of KS2 'realistic' percentage to 'esoteric' percentage by social class and sex (definite finishers)

Social class	Female		Male		Total	
	Mean	*Count*	*Mean*	*Count*	*Mean*	*Count*
Service class	0.81	18	0.87	24	0.84	42
Intermediate class	0.79	9	0.77	14	0.78	23
Working class	0.76	5	0.78	14	0.77	19
Total	0.80	32	0.82	52	0.81	84

Notes

1 These 125 are the children from amongst the 136 in Table 2.1 for whom we have complete or near-complete sets of data.

2 This variable has a mean of one, a standard deviation of 0.21, and ranges from 0.19 to 1.47. It is defined for 122 of the 125 children. In the other three cases, we have no quantitative CAT score. In one of these three cases, we also lack social class data. There is one other case for whom we also lack social class data among the 125 children who form the sample for this chapter.

3 The '*relatively*' is important here. A school may be 'better' or 'worse' than another without being 'good' or 'bad'.

4 In a few cases there is some dependency of one sub-item on another but most sub-items are independent of one another.

5 We are providing tests of significance mainly in note form for the remainder of this chapter, though we have some doubts about their value. Our samples are not the sort of simple random samples that the mathematics of significance testing generally assumes (e.g. Hoel 1971). Neither are the members of our samples selected independently of one another, given the decision (the only practical one) to select schools as our basic unit. We tend to see the relationships discussed as features of these particular groups of Year 6 and Year 9 children. Whether the relationships are likely to generalize to larger populations is, for us, as much a matter of theoretical plausibility as of the application of significance testing to the data. These comments apply equally to our use of significance testing earlier in the chapter.

6 There will be some children in the analysis of the r/e ratio in this chapter who did not attempt all of the final items in each of their three tests, though it is difficult to be sure whether a child reached an item but wrote nothing or did not reach it at all. In the case of the February 1996 test, we already have omitted the last few questions from our analyses because we were aware that this test had been a little too long for some of the children. We have subsequently repeated the analysis in Table 5.21 for a smaller sample of children who had written something in responses to the last item on each of their papers. (In the case of the February 1996 test, this refers to the last item in the truncated version used in the analyses in this chapter.) Table 5.32 shows how the r/e ratio was distributed by social class and sex for these 84 children. The

pattern by social class can be seen to be broadly as it was in Table 5.21. Again the service-class children have a markedly higher ratio than the working-class. The intermediate-class children, however, appear here as more similar to the working-class than they did in Table 5.21.

7 An analysis of variance of the r/e ratio by social class finds the differences between social classes to be statistically significant ($p = 0.005$).

8 An analysis of variance of the r/e ratio by sex finds the differences between sexes to be statistically significant ($p = 0.027$). A further analysis of variance including both social class and sex finds both independent variables significantly related to the r/e ratio (social class: $p = 0.003$; sex: $p = 0.048$) and finds the social class/sex interaction to be non-significant. R-squared is 13.7 per cent (adjusted R-squared ten per cent).

9 The line for the intermediate class falls between these two lines, and has a similar slope.

10 Furthermore, it is a common error of empiricism to move from the absence of an effect, or the small size of it, to the absence of a mechanism, forgetting that the effects of a real mechanism may be hidden by other factors at work. See, for example, Bhaskar (1979).

11 The corresponding table for the 84 children who definitely reached the end of each of the three tests shows the same patterns.

12 Logistic regression, employing backward elimination. It should be noted, however, that statistical significance is difficult to interpret when procedures such as logistic regression are applied to samples, such as ours, which are not simply random. See, e.g., Gilbert (1993: 77–78). The result holds, by the way, if quantitative 'ability' is used in place of non-verbal 'ability'.

13 An analysis of variance of this ratio of mean service class to mean working class performance for each item by difficulty level and nature of the item ('realistic' versus 'esoteric') finds both independent variables significant (difficulty: $p = 0.001$; nature of item: $p = 0.051$), with the interaction term non-significant. R-squared is 25.7 per cent (adjusted R-squared is 20.5 per cent).

14 We will see in the next chapter that poor item design is a relevant issue where these items are concerned, but that it is not likely to be the whole story.

15 Because of ties in the data, it has been necessary to select very slightly different overall proportions of children in the three cases: 26 per cent for the 'esoteric' simulation, 27.6 per cent for the 'realistic' simulation, and 26.8 per cent for the mixed test. These are small differences in relation to the size of the resulting effects.

6 'Realistic' items, social class and sex: two examples from Key Stage 2

Introduction

The idea that children (and adults) experience difficulty in understanding and meeting the demands of formal educational tasks – and that these difficulties are not randomly distributed across the social structure – is hardly a recent one (Holland 1981; Edwards and Mercer 1987). Neither is it an idea particular to sociologists (e.g. Cole *et al.* 1971; Cole 1996). However, it is sociologists who have been mainly associated with particular versions of the claim in the post-war period (Bernstein 1973, 1990, 1996; Bourdieu and Passeron 1977; Bourdieu 1986). Early versions of Bernstein's thesis of a cultural discontinuity between the lower working-class home and the school attracted considerable critical debate, with the claim being made by various critics that his thesis was flawed by an attachment to a 'deficit' model of the working-class child and family. Bernstein has, of course, employed considerable energy in attempting to answer these critics (Bernstein 1990, 1996) and, perhaps more importantly, has revised his ideas substantially over a period of almost 40 years. The resulting theoretical account (Bernstein 1996), which we have summarized in Chapter 4, seems primarily to be a relational account of cultural differences and their consequences within organized educational systems akin to that Bourdieu has developed over a similar period in France. While there are important differences between the two (especially with respect to their use of the concept of rules: Bourdieu 1990a, 1990b) both are arguing that subordinate groups within society lack access, relatively speaking, to the cultural resources that schools demand of children and which, in their nature, reflect the ways of life of dominant social groups. Bernstein captures this via his concept of code; Bourdieu via his concept of *habitus*. While, notwithstanding their expressed intentions, it may in both cases be possible to detect a residual tendency for 'academic', 'abstract' forms of thought to be favoured over alternatives (e.g. Bourdieu and Wacquant 1992: 83–9), this is hardly the central thrust of their relational sociologies of education and culture. To the extent that such a 'preference' remains visible in their work this probably reflects the partial dependence of both thinkers on Durkheim's analyses of the relation of cognition to the form of the division of labour in society and an associated realist claim that 'minds' and mental processes do differ across social orders characterized by qualitatively different degrees of complexity of the division of labour. The debate on the latter claim continues, closely connected with debates about the effects of literacy and methods of testing human capacities (e.g. Spradley 1972; Keddie 1973; Gould 1984; Street 1984; Lave 1988; Nunes *et al.* 1993; De Abreu 1995; Cole 1996).

In this chapter we show how the ideas of Bernstein and Bourdieu can be used to make *partial* sense of the ways in which the 125 children discussed in Chapter 5 respond to two particular 'realistic' items, the traffic survey and the tennis item (see Figures 4.4 and 4.5). These items have been chosen to contrast with one another. In the case of one of the items, children responding 'inappropriately', that is in 'everyday' terms, can nevertheless gain marks, while in the case of the other item, it becomes unlikely that they will do so. In both cases, however, we will see that what appears to be obvious to test designers is not always so obvious to children. In both cases we show that working- and intermediate-class children seem to be more predisposed than service-class children, at age 11, to employ initially their everyday knowledge in answering mathematics test items and, in the case of one of the items, that this can lead to the underestimation of their actual 'mathematical' capacities. We therefore use the idea of cultural difference in a critical examination of the differential validity of test items.

It is often argued that what characterizes formal educational knowledge above all else is its disconnectedness from everyday life and concerns (Neisser 1976; Edwards and Mercer 1987). Sociologically speaking, such a description can be improved by a reference to whose supposed concerns the knowledge is disconnected from (Young 1971). In the case of the items to be discussed here, we can see that in both cases the child is required to disconnect their reasoning from their own knowledge and experience of 'everyday' matters. In the case of the traffic item, they seem to be expected to draw on the given data, rather than on their own knowledge of the behaviour of traffic in the proximity of schools. In the case of the tennis item they are required to engage in an abstracted process of formal combination of names rather than consider the requirements of any imagined, recalled or actual tennis competition. We might expect knowledge and experience of traffic flows around schools to be more generally shared than knowledge of setting up tennis competitions.

In the remainder of the chapter, we describe in some detail the patterns of response to these two 'realistic' test items by social class and sex, showing that there does seem to be a stronger predisposition among working- and intermediate-class than service-class 11-year-olds to draw 'inappropriately' on their everyday knowledge in the context of mathematics testing. In the second case – the tennis item – we demonstrate that this leads to an under-estimation of what children are actually able to do – and hence raises potential equity issues with respect to these tests.

The traffic item: the production of false positives?

As we showed in Chapter 4, this item (Figure 4.4) can be criticized severely on 'mathematical' grounds (see p. 55). Here, however, our concern is with children's responses to it. The marking scheme asymmetrically allowed a mark for 'likely' or 'very likely' in the case of the car, and for 'unlikely' in the case of the lorry. The SoA being assessed is, supposedly, *Use appropriate language to justify decisions when placing events in order of likelihood*. In the test of which it was a part, there was little apparent sign of any strong social class patterning to the marks awarded (see Table 6.1). It does not seem therefore that this data handling item will have contributed greatly to the social class differences in the r/e ratio discussed in Chapter 5, though it is the case that service class scores are higher than those of other children.[1]

What the test results do not tell us, however, is anything about the children's response strategy and, in particular, whether they utilized the given data or drew on their everyday knowledge (presumably an 'incorrect' response from the perspective of the test designers, though the method of solution was not addressed in the marking scheme). In the context of the interview we can address this issue. Children were asked, after they had circled two choices, why they had chosen these. Two examples follow:

Table 6.1 Marks obtained on the traffic item in the February 1996 test by social class and sex (2 marks available)

	Female		Male		Total	
	Mean	Count	Mean	Count	Mean	Count
Service class	1.08	26	1.09	34	1.08	60
Intermediate class	0.85	13	1.12	17	1.00	30
Working class	1.15	13	0.90	20	1.00	33
Total	1.04	52	1.04	71	1.04	123

A working-class girl – response 'esoteric'

M: I don't like this one.

BC: Don't you? Why don't you like it?

M: I don't know, I just don't like it – too hard for me.
   [She laughs. She circles likely for lorry – no mark, very likely for car – one mark.]

BC: OK, how did you decide on those two?

M: That one, you look at that, and there was only 13 that went past in an hour, so it was not pretty like-, it might have happened but it wasn't that likely it would happen, and the car, because there's 75 went past in an hour, it's very likely but you can't be certain.

BC: Right, why can't you be certain?

M: Just in – don't know – you just can't be certain.

BC: You can't be certain. OK. I thought you – why didn't you like that one then? You seemed to do it quite quickly.

M: Yeah, but, I don't like trying to figure which one's which.

BC: Well it's fine. OK, number 14 next.

A working-class boy – response 'realistic'

   [He circles unlikely for lorry – one mark, very likely for car – one mark.]

BC: Now how did you decide on those two?

R: 'Cos, because the lorry, there's not as many lorries around as there is cars.

BC: What were you thinking of, whereabouts?

R: Outside of school, more parents would come to like collect a child in a car than they would in a lorry.

BC: That's true, right, OK, did you look at these numbers at all here? Did you read that part?

R: No.

BC: OK so you did the question without looking at that part?

R: Yep.

BC: Right, why do you think you didn't bother to read that then, because you knew already?

R: Yep.

We have coded each of the children's responses to our request to explain why they choose what they chose for lorry and car (taken together) according to whether they employed the given data (the 'esoteric' response here) or their everyday knowledge of vehicles and roads (the 'realistic' response here). Ironically, of the two cases quoted, it is the child responding 'realistically' who, in spite of ignoring the given data, gains full marks. Table 6.2 shows the social class distribution of responses on a three category scale, which includes a mixed response. It can be seen that

Table 6.2 Distribution of response strategies by social class (traffic item in the interview context)

	Uses given data alone	Uses everyday knowledge and given data	Uses everyday knowledge alone	Totals
Service class	38	10	11	59
Percentage	64.4	16.9	18.6	
Intermediate class	16	10	4	30
Percentage	53.3	33.3	13.3	
Working class	16	6	10	32
Percentage	50.0	18.8	31.3	
Totals	70	26	25	121
Percentage	57.9	21.5	20.7	

Table 6.3 Distribution of response strategies by sex (traffic item in the interview context)

	Uses given data alone	Uses everyday knowledge and given data	Uses everyday knowledge alone	Totals
Girls	26	16	10	52
Percentage	50.0	30.8	19.2	
Boys	44	11	16	71
Percentage	62.0	15.5	22.5	
Totals	70	27	26	123
Percentage	56.9	22.0	21.1	

working-class children are almost twice as likely as service-class children to refer only to their everyday knowledge in answering our enquiry (and, we might assume, the original question itself). The parallel Table 6.3, on the other hand, shows less sign of any simple gender effect, with similar percentages of boys and girls using only everyday knowledge – though the fact that girls are twice as likely to use both given and everyday data may deserve further study.

Table 6.4 draws on the interview data to show the relationship between social class, response strategy and mark achieved for the question in the interview context. The relations with sex are shown in Table 6.5. There is no clear relation in Table 6.4 between social class and success – though there was a relation between social class and strategy (Table 6.2). An analysis of variance – though this statistical approach is not perfectly

Table 6.4 Mean marks obtained on the traffic item in the interview context by social class and response strategy (2 marks available, n in brackets)

	Uses given data alone	Uses everyday knowledge and given data	Uses everyday knowledge alone	Totals
Service class	1.21 (38)	1.20 (10)	0.91 (11)	1.15 (59)
Intermediate class	0.88 (16)	1.40 (10)	1.50 (4)	1.13 (30)
Working class	1.25 (16)	0.83 (6)	1.10 (10)	1.13 (32)
Totals	1.14 (70)	1.19 (26)	1.08 (25)	1.14 (121)

Table 6.5 Mean marks obtained on the traffic item in the interview context by sex and response strategy (2 marks available, n in brackets)

	Uses given data alone	Uses everyday knowledge and given data	Uses everyday knowledge alone	Totals
Girls	0.96 (26)	1.38 (16)	1.00 (10)	1.10 (52)
Boys	1.25 (44)	1.00 (11)	1.06 (16)	1.17 (71)
Totals	1.14 (70)	1.22 (27)	1.04 (26)	1.14 (123)

suited here – supports this initial reading. Neither social class nor response strategy are statistically significant predictors of the mark achieved. Why, in spite of the relation between social class and strategy, is there no relation between social class and mark? This is possibly because the design of this particular question allowed an 'inappropriate' 'everyday' response – one that ignored the given data in some cases completely – to gain marks. Had the item employed given data that conflicted with what children have experienced in their everyday lives rather than paralleled it, then we might have seen a stronger relation between mark and social class. It is worth stressing this counterfactual point – the associations reported here result from, amongst other unexamined factors, the relation between what children bring to the context as a result of their academic and general socialization (in and out of school) and the particular nature of the items. The lack of an association between social class, response style and mark here can be seen as an example of how a really existing predisposition of a person may or may not, depending on context, lead to 'predicted' associations in a data set. The distribution of the required 'recognition rule' does seem to be related to social class, with the result that working-class children are more likely to 'misrecognize' the demands of the problem background (Table 6.2). However, coupled with the particular choice of the given survey data by the test designers, this results in an item that does not measure validly whether children can produce the required probabilistic reasoning about the *given* data.

In the case of the traffic item, therefore, we have a clear case of a question that seems to generate 'false positives' in assessment terms (Wood and Power 1987). Children are being awarded marks for 'non-mathematical' behaviour – as judged by 'esoteric' criteria. However, in the light of the findings discussed in the next section concerning the tennis problem (Figure 4.5), it will be seen that the children who used their everyday experience to decide on likelihoods perhaps could have used the given survey data to the same end – had they been asked to do so more explicitly – rather than having been left to recognize for themselves that given data should have priority over their own experience in most cases in these tests.

The tennis item: the production of false negatives?

The Statement of Attainment for the 'tennis' item shown in Figure 4.5 is given as *Identify all the outcomes of combining two independent events*. The (very!) esoteric mathematical 'equivalent' of the tennis item is: Find the Cartesian product of the sets {a, b, c} & {d, e, f}. The item is intended to be difficult, being judged by the test designers to be a level 6 item suitable only for higher attaining children. Why, however, should it be difficult? We have already discussed some possible reasons in Chapter 4. There we concentrated on why this item might invite an 'everyday' response of three pairs rather than an esoteric one of nine pairs. However, it is worth discussing this item further, in the light of the analysis of similar combinatorial tasks by Newman, Griffin and Cole (1989).

The latter authors compared children's responses to several tasks. These included one task in which children had to produce, working with the experimenter, all the possible pairs from a set of cards picturing movie stars, and in which the children were 'trained' by the experimenter to answer the question. Here the 'problem' of finding pairs was made explicit to the children. They did not have to discover it for themselves. Then, in a subsequent 'isomorphic' task, children were given four household chemicals and had to explore, in small groups, what happened when pairs of these chemicals were mixed. Here they needed to discover the 'problem', that of finding all the possible pairs, for themselves, 'as they began to run out of pairs of chemicals to mix' (Newman *et al.* 1989: 33). The authors describe the contrasting situations in these terms:

> In the laboratory setting, we expect the task to be presented clearly to the subject. It is part of the experimenter's job. We conduct pilot

studies to find out how to do this effectively; we arrange training on the task and choose criterion measures that let us know whether the subject "understands" the task that we have constructed. These procedures are certainly socially constructed. In everyday situations people are not always presented with clearly stated goals. They often have to figure out what the problem is, what the constraints are, as well as how to solve the problem once they have formulated it. In other words, in everyday situations people are confronted with the "whole" task. There is no experimenter responsible for doing the presentation part.

This broader conception of the whole task is important to our analyses of the transformation of a task when it is embedded in different social settings. When we look for the "same task" happening outside of the laboratory, we have to look for how the work of specifying and constraining the task is getting done and who is doing it. This kind of analysis provides us with the basis for arguing that the practical methods of maintaining control in the laboratory veil a crucial process: formulating the task and forming the goal.

(Newman *et al.* 1989: 33–34)

The key point here concerning test items is that there is no one problem embedded in any text, but rather a whole range of possible problems that might be constructed by children. In Chapter 4, we discussed various items in the terms of Bernstein's theory, employing his concept of recognition rules to make sense of children's use or otherwise of 'everyday' knowledge in responding to these questions. However, these remarks of Newman *et al.* serve to remind us that, within the choice of an 'everyday' or 'esoteric' response mode discussed in Chapter 4, there are yet further issues for the child to confront. In the case of the tennis item, for example, there are several. Is the item about 'methods' of producing pairs or the pairs themselves, or both? Why is the given pair, **Rob and Katy**, in bold ink? Can this pair nevertheless be 'disturbed' in order to be rearranged? Given these probable interpretative problems it seems quite likely that children may fail to construct for themselves the same goal as the test designers' intended one.

Returning to the broader issue, we showed, via a discussion of the cases of Diane and Mike in Chapter 4, that this item seems likely to be a candidate for confusion about what is relevant knowledge to bring to bear. Notwithstanding all the public rhetoric of recent years concerning 'realistic' mathematics, what might be seen as 'appropriate' in the context of real sports competitions will not be seen as 'appropriate' or 'legitimate' in the context of a mathematics test. In Bourdieu's terms, given what the marking scheme (see pp. 57–8) states, the item requires a 'scholastic' rather than a 'practical' response (Bourdieu and Wacquant 1992). There is a potentially confusing boundary to negotiate. That children find this a difficult boundary can be illustrated by the fact that several children took the apparent national origins of the competitors into account in making their decisions. Two of the following three illustrative cases initially produced three pairs, and one did so after some elaboration by the interviewer of the test item's demands.

Service-class girl

MD: Have you finished? OK, explain to me how you worked that out then.

Child: Well, Rob and Katy, they're like normal names, and they'll be OK together, and they sound like different country names.

MD: What Rashid and Gita?

Child: Yeah, and so, they would be quite happy as a pair because they come from a different country and they've got those names and just put them together.

Intermediate-class boy

Child: Done.

MD: OK, so how did you work that out?

Child: Well, Rob and Ann's sound like not really, um, [indecipherable phrase, possibly 'brother and sister',] so I'll come back to them. Rashid and Gita are like, sort of the same names from a different country.

MD: Mm.

Child: So it might be them two pairs, and Rob and Ann.

MD: David and Ann do you mean?

Child: I mean David and Ann.

MD: OK, so you worked it out because of where the country, is that what you're saying?

Child: Yeah.

Working-class boy

MD: OK, what have you done then – Rashid and Ann.

Child: Rashid and Gita, sound like different country names so that it wouldn't exactly be fair if Rashid and Gita got together, because you've got to give them a chance to meet other people.

Clearly, from the perspective of 'esoteric' mathematics the children's national origins are not a relevant consideration, though they might well be in the everyday life of school children. Yet another child referred to male and female sexual organs in her test answer and subsequently wrote 'pink and blue' in her interview response, again demonstrating how non-obvious the intended goal of this item could be for some children.

Table 6.6   Mean marks achieved on tennis item in the February 1996 test context (1 mark available)

	Female		Male		Total	
	Mean	Count	Mean	Count	Mean	Count
Service class	0.62	26	0.56	34	0.58	60
Intermediate class	0.54	13	0.41	17	0.47	30
Working class	0.38	13	0.40	20	0.39	33
Total	0.54	52	0.48	71	0.50	123

Table 6.7   Marks achieved on tennis item for child's initial response in the interview context (1 mark available)

	Female		Male		Total	
	Mean	Count	Mean	Count	Mean	Count
Service class	0.81	26	0.85	34	0.83	60
Intermediate class	0.77	13	0.82	17	0.80	30
Working class	0.69	13	0.60	20	0.64	33
Total	0.77	52	0.77	71	0.77	123

What does the full data set suggest about children's reading of this question? In fact, in the February 1996 test, 28 of the 125 children produced three pairs as their answer rather than the required nine, suggesting, since these three pairs could serve as an adequate response to the goal of choosing pairs to play tennis, that for these children 'everyday' concerns may have dominated esoteric ones. How did success on this item relate to social class and gender? Tables 6.6 and 6.7 show that, in both the test and the interview the working-class children do considerably less well on this item, for which one mark was available, than the service-class children.[2] The boys do slightly less well as a group than the girls in the test but the difference disappears in the interview. We will concentrate on social class in this rest of this section.

Turning to children's strategies for responding to the item, in this case, since in contrast with the traffic item, we do have relevant written text available to us, we have coded the written text produced in the interview setting – as opposed to the children's oral responses to our questions. The marking scheme allows a mark only for nine distinct pairs. Children therefore respond 'appropriately' to this item by setting out nine pairs. However, if they do so, it is possible to code the nine pairs as 'esoteric' or 'realistic' by reference to the way they have been grouped. Here is what we would term an 'esoteric' set:

Rob and Katy
Rob and Ann
Rob and Gita

Rashid and Katy
Rashid and Ann
Rashid and Gita

David and Katy
David and Ann
David and Gita

Here, by contrast, is a 'realistic' set:

Rob and Katy
David and Gita
Rashid and Ann

David and Ann
Rashid and Katy
Rob and Gita

David and Katy
Rashid and Gita
Rob and Ann

In the second case the pairs, taken in groups of three at a time, might engage, two pairs at a time, in games of tennis – hence our coding of the set as 'realistic'. In the first case, on the other hand, each group of three pairs could not 'realistically' play tennis, given the repeated use of one child's name. Now it might be argued that the second set of nine pairs above is a 'better' response than the first – as far as tennis is concerned – but it is arguably not from the point of view of 'esoteric' mathematics. The first set of pairs, from the latter point of view, is more 'abstract', more obviously 'mathematical' in its 'systematicity' (and so, interestingly, is the pattern of the exemplar set out in the marking scheme: see pp. 57–8). Turning to those cases where children produced just three pairs, in both the test and the interview, they were typically a 'realistic' three pairs, using each child just once, and have been coded as such. We can now consider the distribution by social class of children's response styles in the tennis case. Table 6.8, in fact, shows that response style is strongly related to social class. In particular, service-class children are most likely to produce some form of 'esoteric' response, while working-class children are most likely to produce some form of 'realistic' response.

Table 6.9 breaks down the marks achieved in the interview by social class and response style. Given the apparent relation between response style and mark – though remember that we have coded responses of

Table 6.8   Response strategy on the tennis item in the interview context by social class

	'Esoteric' pairings	Other (typically mixed)	'Realistic' pairings	Totals
Service class	47	4	8	59
Percentage	79.7	6.8	13.6	100.1
Intermediate class	20	2	8	30
Percentage	66.7	6.7	26.7	100.1
Working class	14	5	12	31
Percentage	45.2	16.1	38.7	100.0
Totals	81	11	28	120
Percentage	67.5	9.2	23.3	100.0

Table 6.9   Mean mark obtained on the tennis item in the interview context by social class and response strategy (counts as in Table 6.8) (1 mark available)

	'Esoteric' pairings	Other (typically mixed)	'Realistic' pairings	Totals
Service class	1.00	0.75	0.00	0.85
Intermediate class	1.00	1.00	0.25	0.80
Working class	1.00	0.80	0.25	0.68
Totals	1.00	0.82	0.18	0.79

three pairs using all six names as 'realistic' – it becomes particularly important to look in more detail at what happened when, in the interview, the children were given a 'second chance' to try to find all of the possible pairs. Given the apparent tendency for working-class children to 'choose' more frequently an 'inappropriate' self-defeating strategy in their initial response it becomes a critical question whether those children who initially produced three pairs might have produced the nine pairs had they not 'chosen' to begin with this apparently 'realistic' response style. In other words, is there some sense in which such children might be able, in some cases, to carry out the mathematics 'pure and simple', given a minor cue that they have 'misrecognized' the context. Now, in fact, the cue was merely the request, once they had clearly finished writing some number of pairs fewer than nine, to consider whether they had obtained all the pairs. One example of what happened in a number of cases follows. The child here is a girl from the intermediate-class grouping.[3]

Intermediate-class girl
She writes the three pairs thus:

Rob and Katy
Rashid and Gita
David and Ann

MD: Done that one?
E: Yeah.
MD: OK, so tell me how you worked that one out.
E: I put those two names and – so I did those two there can and I did those.
MD: David and Ann, Rashid and Gita, OK.
E: Mm.
MD: OK, see where it says there find all the possible ways that girls and boys can be paired, do you think you've found all the possible ways?
F·   No.
MD: You could find some more?
E: Yeah.
MD: OK, let me just do that, so I'll know where you stopped for the beginning. [The interviewer adds a mark at this point to indicate the first response (for later coding).] OK, go on then. [She works at the problem, silently. She then adds six pairs to give:]

Rob and Katy
Rashid and Gita   Katy and David
David and Ann   Ann and Rob
                     Ann and Rashid

Gita and David
Gita and Rob
Katy and Rashid

MD: OK, so have you finished that one now?
E: Mm.
MD: And you think you've got all of them?
E: Yeah.
MD: OK, do you know? – when you first did it you stopped, after three, why did you stop after three?
E: I don't know.
MD: You don't know, but why didn't you continue?
E: I didn't think that you were supposed to.
MD: OK, that's a good reason, but why didn't you think you were supposed to? [The interview continues with the child being apparently unable or unwilling to give a reason.]

It can be seen that this girl initially produced three pairs but then obtained nine pairs, with six of these beginning with girls rather than boys, when encouraged to reflect on whether this was enough. Her account of why she stopped at three pairs points to the sort of subconscious behaviour which Bourdieu (1990b) describes via his concept of *habitus*. She did not think she was 'supposed to' do nine – a rather rule-like formulation. How common was this pattern of initial and subsequent response? Table 6.10 sets out the details of the 12 cases where an initial response of three pairs was followed, after the 'cue', by a subsequent response resulting in nine pairs. We have coded each second response by the child in terms of whether we 'compromised' their response via leading questions, etc. None of these 12 cases were 'compromised' on this coding. Of the other seven children who had produced three pairs initially, two stuck at three on their second attempt, two produced seven pairs, one produced eight, one a very idiosyncratic set of ten pairs, and one we seem to have failed to offer a second chance to (the last two cases appear under 'other' in Tables 6.11 and 6.12). It can be seen that some ten per cent of the sample under discussion here fell into the trap of initially producing a 'realistic' three pairs and yet recovered fully from this 'inappropriate' response when offered a chance to reconsider.[4] Furthermore, children from intermediate and working social class backgrounds were over-represented amongst this group and children from service-class backgrounds under-represented, as Table 6.11 shows. Notwithstanding the small numbers involved, this result seems to suggest that differentiated responses to items of this particular type might have some important consequences in producing social class-related patterns of success and failure in national testing. There is also a slight tendency for girls to be over-represented amongst this group (Table 6.12) and for the children to have lower than average 'ability' scores. Their mean quantitative CAT score, for example, is 96.08 (n = 12), while for the sample as a whole it is 104.17 (n = 122 here).

We can see that in the case of this test item a child's apparent response style can lead to his or her 'mathematical' competence being underestimated because of the way in which he or she 'chooses' to read the question. These 12 cases, some ten per cent of the total, are arguably all 'false negatives' on first response – given that the children could do what was required when cued to reconsider what they had written.[5] In the terms of the model described in Chapter 4, their *performance* has not reflected their *mathematical competence* – at least in the sense of the capacity to produce nine pairs from two groups of three items – and this seems to be related to the children's capacity to recognize correctly or not the 'legitimate' demands of the context as defined by the test designers. This 'capacity to recognize' might, of course, be described as a *cultural competence* at another level of analysis. Bourdieu's (1986) use of the phrase 'cultural

Table 6.10 Details of the 12 cases where, in the interview, the production of three pairs was followed by the subsequent construction of nine

Initial pairs	Initial response strategy	Pairs after 'second chance'	Overall response strategy	Social class	Sex	Verbal 'ability'	Quantitative 'ability'	Non-verbal 'ability'
3	'realistic'	9	'realistic'	service	male	75	70	79
3	'realistic'	9	'realistic'	intermediate	male	88	92	100
3	'realistic'	9	'realistic'	working	female	101	94	108
3	'realistic'	9	'realistic'	intermediate	female	89	83	87
3	'realistic'	9	'realistic'	intermediate	male	92	94	106
3	'realistic'	9	'realistic'	working	male	89	89	91
3	'realistic'	9	mixed	intermediate	female	95	88	100
3	'realistic'	9	'realistic'	intermediate	female	84	94	89
3	'realistic'	9	'realistic'	working	female	91	96	94
3	'realistic'	9	'realistic'	service	female	99	108	104
3	'realistic'	9	mixed	working	male	110	116	114
3	'realistic'	9	'realistic'	service	female	125	129	123

Table 6.11 Social class distribution of first and second responses on the tennis item in the interview

Response pattern		Service class	Intermediate class	Working class	Total
other	count	6	1	5	12
	column %	10.0	3.3	15.2	9.8
3 then 3	count	1	0	1	2
	column %	1.7	0	3	1.6
3 then 4, 5, 6, 7, or 8	count	0	0	2	2
	column %	0	0	6.1	1.6
3 then 9	count	3	5	4	12
	column %	5.0	16.7	12.1	9.8
9 pairs first time	count	50	24	21	95
	column %	83.3	80.0	63.6	77.2
	Total count	60	30	33	123

Table 6.12 Sex distribution of first and second responses on the tennis item in the interview

Response pattern		Girls	Boys	Total
other	count	5	7	12
	column %	9.3	9.9	9.6
3 then 3	count	0	2	2
	column %	0	2.8	1.6
3 then 4, 5, 6, 7, or 8	count	1	2	3
	column %	1.9	2.8	2.4
3 then 9	count	7	5	12
	column %	13.0	7.0	9.6
9 pairs first time	count	41	55	96
	column %	75.9	77.5	76.8
	Total count	54	71	125

competence' would seem to be at this level. In these terms, the first response of the 12 children, resulting perhaps from their particular mix of cultural competences, has the effect of rendering their 'mathematical' competence less visible – initially at least. In the light of Holland's (1981) work with Bernstein on children's preferred classifying strategies it seems that the over-representation of intermediate- and working-class children amongst these false negatives is something we might have expected.

The traffic and tennis items compared

What can we learn from a comparison of the children's responses to these two 'realistic' items, one multiple-choice and one open-ended? The threats to valid and 'fair' assessment of 'competence' inherent in both types of question can be noted. In the case of the traffic item, the children, because of the question's multiple-choice nature, could obtain marks by 'inappropriately' employing their 'everyday' knowledge. The nature of the response mode hides this from the assessor. This validity problem could have been avoided by making the given survey data less typical of everyday settings known to the children, i.e. by introducing 'realistic'/'esoteric' dissonance. Lorries might have been shown as passing the school more frequently than cars, for example (see Figure 4.4). However, had this been done, we perhaps would have found the second problem coming to the fore – the equity problem that we found in the case of the tennis item. On such a revised traffic item, working-class children might have tended to have lost marks not because they could not reason probabilistically but because they referred more to their 'everyday' knowledge and experience than their service-class companions. We saw, in the case of the tennis item, that children who had the 'mathematical competence' did not always demonstrate it, without the elaboration of their response induced by the interviewer, and that this behaviour was apparently related to the social class distribution of recognition rules. Some children just did not see the 'obviousness' of what the test designers required; other children did.

Before we leave these items, there is one other important question to address. If, as we have suggested in Chapter 4, there are predispositions, grounded in cultural differences, at work in responses to 'realistic' items, then it should be possible to discern some relationship between responses to the traffic item on the one hand and the tennis item on the other. Table 6.13 shows that there is a tendency for children who employ their everyday experience on the traffic item, either alone or in addition to the given data, to be more likely to produce either mixed or 'realistic' responses to the tennis item. This becomes much clearer if we collapse the two columns involving 'realistic' responses to the traffic item (see Table 6.14). The 53 children operating 'esoterically' on the tennis item and using the given data only on the traffic item have a mean quantitative 'ability' score of 109, while the seven children (in Table 6.13) operating 'realistically' on the tennis item and employing only their everyday experience on the traffic item have a mean of 86 points. But, alongside this difference, the groups are also quite different in respect of social class background. Of the 53, 60.4 per cent come from service-class families, 28.3 per cent from the intermediate class, and 11.3 per cent from the working class. Amongst the seven, one child comes from a service-class

Table 6.13 Relation between responses on traffic and tennis items in the interview

Initial tennis response		Traffic response			Total
		Given data used	Mixed use of given data and everyday experience	Everyday experience used	
Esoteric	count	53	12	16	81
	column %	77.9	46.2	66.7	68.6
Mixed	count	6	4	1	11
	column %	8.8	15.4	4.2	9.3
Realistic	count	9	10	7	26
	column %	13.2	38.5	29.2	22.0
	Total count	68	26	24	118

Table 6.14 Relation between responses on traffic and tennis items in the interview

Initial tennis response		Traffic response		Total
		Given data only used	Partial or total use of everyday experience	
Esoteric	count	53	28	81
	column %	77.9	56.0	68.6
Mixed	count	6	5	11
	column %	8.8	10.0	9.3
Realistic	count	9	17	26
	column %	13.2	34.0	22.0
	Total count	68	50	118

background, with three coming from the intermediate- and three from the working-class group. The overall distribution of social class amongst these 118 children is service class: 49.2 per cent; intermediate class: 25.4 per cent; and working class: 25.4 per cent. It is clear that both social class and 'ability' are associated with these responses patterns. Considering sex, the 118 children comprise 49 girls (41.5 per cent) and 69 boys (58.5 per cent). Amongst the 53 'esoteric' responders, there are 20 girls (37.7 per cent) and 33 boys (62.3 per cent). Amongst the seven, there are three girls (42.9 per cent) and four boys (57.1 per cent). There is, therefore, a weak association between sex and mode of response here, with girls being slightly under-represented in the 'esoteric' group of 53 relative to boys.

Lastly, we might note that five of the seven children initially produced three pairs, with the other two producing sets of nine pairs that were not set out 'esoterically' as previously defined. Of the latter two, one was of intermediate-class and one was of working-class background. Of the five former children, three, on their second attempt, produced a full nine pairs. One of these children was of service-class origin; two were of intermediate-class origin. The two working-class children in this group of five did not succeed in producing nine. One stuck at three; one produced more pairs, but not the full set of nine.

Summary

This chapter has concentrated on just two test items. In the previous chapter, we reported a statistical analysis, by social class and gender, of children's degrees of success on two broad classes of test items, termed by us 'realistic' and 'esoteric'. The 'realistic' items embed mathematical operations within contexts containing people and/or non-mathematical everyday objects while the 'esoteric' do not. Both of the items discussed in this chapter have been coded as 'realistic'. For two examples of 'esoteric' items see Figures 5.3 and 5.4. We found in Chapter 5 a greater difference between service- and working-class mean performances for the category of 'realistic' than for the category of 'esoteric' items. The current chapter shows that *part* of an explanation of this general finding might be found in social class differences in the interpretation of the demands of 'realistic' questions, with working-class and intermediate-class children being more likely than service-class children to draw 'inappropriately' on their everyday knowledge when responding to items. This relative failure (and it is relative, not absolute) to recognize the strongly classified nature of school mathematics in the face of surface appearances which suggest the relevance of everyday knowledge may be an aspect of the overall sociocultural predispositions discussed by Bourdieu and Bernstein. The realized meaning of both items discussed here seems to vary with social class, with the resulting negative effects on performance leading, in the case of the tennis item, to the underestimation of the actual competence of more intermediate- and working-class than service-class children. Had the traffic item been designed so that its given data conflicted with, rather than mirrored, data available from typical 'everyday' experience, we might well have seen a similar social class effect on performance in the case of this item.

We have argued in earlier chapters that there is sociological work which would lend plausibility to the claim that children are differently predisposed to draw on 'everyday' or 'esoteric' knowledge in their initial responses to 'realistic' problems in educational contexts. We have shown here that there is a correlation between the nature of children's responses to the two examined items. Not only are service-class children less likely to respond in 'everyday' terms than others, but it is also the case that children's responses on one item tend to predict their response on the other. This lends some support to the view that a predisposition is at work, though we would not claim that the findings here are enough to demonstrate this beyond any doubt. We certainly do believe, however, that these findings suggest that this is an area worthy of further research. We would claim that test designers should pay careful attention to the lessons that can be learned from some of these children's initial constructions of 'inappropriate' goals from the clues available to them – and to the apparent consequences for validity and fairness in testing.

We now turn, in Chapter 7, to the analysis of the data from our sample of older children, aged 13–14 years at the time of the research. Here our initial focus is on the ways in which secondary schools have distributed their pupils over the hierarchical tiers of the KS3 tests and the apparent consequences of this distribution for measured achievement by school.

Notes

1 The ratio of service-class to working-class scores on the traffic item is 1.08/ 1.00, i.e. 1.08, whereas for 'realistic' items as a whole it was 59.21/49.60, i.e. 1.19 (see Table 5.19). In the interview context, the service-class/working-class ratio for the traffic item falls to 1.02.
2 We noted in note 1 that the traffic item was less social class differentiating in the test context than the 'realistic' items as a whole. The tennis item is, by contrast, more differentiating than the 'realistic' items in general. The ratio of service-class to working-class means is 0.58 / 0.39, i.e. 1.49, while the comparable ratio for 'realistic' items as a whole is 1.19. The comparable ratio for the tennis item in the interview context falls to 1.30. The greater difference between test and interview scores for the tennis item in comparison with the traffic item may result partially from the tennis item's later position in the test paper.
3 For a working-class case, see Mike's discussion of his tennis response in Chapter 4.
4 In Holland's (1981) work with Bernstein on children's classifying strategies, the working-class children tended to reproduce their initial non-esoteric classifications a second time. This was also the case with the tennis item. Ten of these 12 children ended up with a set of nine pairs, which we coded as 'realistic', and two with a 'mixed' set. To some extent, of course, this result was constrained by their typically adding further pairs to their first 'realistic' set of three, rather than starting completely anew.
5 From an assessment point of view, this is when the context was manipulated to allow a better chance to produce the 'best' response.

7

Social class, sex, selection for tiers
and performance: a quantitative
analysis at Key Stage 3

Introduction

Our focus in this chapter shifts away from the analysis of the comparative performance of children on 'realistic' and 'esoteric' items. Instead, we explore the distribution of overall performance on the National Curriculum (NC) Key Stage 3 tests of children in three secondary schools. For the KS3 tests, taken by 13–14-year-olds, children can be entered by the school for one of four overlapping tiers designed to be of increasing difficulty and, optionally, for an extension paper. The statistical analysis of our secondary school data is complicated by the existence of this tiered testing coupled, as it is, with schools' different practices in respect of entering children for more or less demanding tests. It will be recalled that, in Chapter 5, we presented an argument for the use of percentages based on raw scores in our analyses of children's performances rather than NC 'levels'. Our being able to carry through this form of analysis was dependent on all the younger children having taken the same tests. Here, at KS3, because of the distribution of children over different samples of items as a result of the selective processes involved in the practice of tiered testing, we will be constrained to employ NC levels. Since children's eventual measured NC level of achievement is constrained by the tier of test for which they are entered, we incorporate within our analysis an examination of the ways in which the three secondary schools distributed children of varying 'abilities' over the tiers of the tests taken in May 1996. This is an important topic of research in itself. We should also remind the reader that we lack social class data for a large proportion of the children in one of the three schools (see Chapter 2). This, alongside the problem of our having to use NC levels, will prevent us from analysing the performance of the whole sample by social class, sex and measured 'ability' in quite the same way as the primary school data were analysed in Chapter 5.

Furthermore, as a consequence of the very limited number of 'esoteric' items taken in common by the majority of the KS3 children, we will not attempt to reproduce the comparison of performance on 'esoteric' and 'realistic' items undertaken in Chapter 5. In fact, the May 1996 KS3 tests were largely comprised of 'realistic' items on our definition (see p. 84). Moving through the four tiered levels from 3–5 to 6–8 the percentage of esoteric items and sub-items, as we have defined them, in these tests are, respectively, zero, 6.5, 12.7 and 16.0 per cent. It can be seen that there is a relationship between expected level of attainment and type of item. In particular, those children expected to perform least well receive a test comprising just 'realistic' items. We return to the possible consequences of this relationship between tier and item type when we discuss social class and performance at KS3.

Schools, selection for tiers, 'ability' and performance

In May 1996 children had to be entered for one of four tiered pairs of tests, respectively covering 'levels of attainment' 3–5, 4–6, 5–7 and 6–8. For each tier there was a Paper 1 and 2. There was also an extension paper available for children who had been entered for 6–8, but this option was not taken up by any of our schools. The test papers for the tiers overlapped considerably, with, for example, level 4 and 5 items from the 3–5 papers being carried over into the papers for 4–6, and so on. In each of the four tiers it was possible for a child to be awarded a level below the lowest level picked out by the tier's label. For example, in the case of tier 3–5, a child could be awarded levels 2–5. The details of this procedure for the May 1996 tests are set out in Table 7.1.

Table 7.1 Mark ranges for the Key Stage 3 tests in May 1996 (from SCAA, no date b)

Level	Tier 3–5	Tier 4–6	Tier 5–7	Tier 6–8	Extension paper
2	20–29				
3	30–60	24–31			
4	61–87	32–54	22–29		
5	88+	55–78	30–47	22–29	
6		79+	48–80	30–53	
7			81+	54–85	
8				86+	
Exceptional performance					28+

Table 7.2   The distribution of achieved NC levels within each school (May 1996)

NC test level awarded	School D	School F	School E
2		2.1%	4.7%
3	6.5%	16.8%	27.9%
4	24.8%	33.7%	40.7%
5	26.6%	25.3%	14.0%
6	33.2%	20.0%	10.5%
7	7.9%	2.1%	1.2%
8	0.9%		1.2%
n	214	95	86

Table 7.3   Mean measured 'ability' by school (KS3)

	School D	School F	School E
Verbal 'ability'	99	92	87
Quantitative 'ability'	98	89	87
Non-verbal 'ability'	105	98	96
Number of children	214	95	86

We will begin by describing children's achieved *levels*. Initially we will employ that part of the KS3 sample for which we have both May 1996 test scores and quantitative CAT scores. This will provide an overview of the three schools' performances as well as the manner in which they enter children of various 'abilities' to tiers. However, we wish eventually to use social class in our analyses and, at that point, we were constrained to work with a reduced sample, especially in the case of School D. Table 7.2 shows the levels achieved across the three schools by the 395 children for whom we have quantitative CAT scores. In Table 7.2 we have shaded the two largest 'level' groups in each school. It is clear that, as far as achieved levels are concerned, School D achieves better than both School E and School F. Comparing the latter two schools, School F children outperform those from School E. In Table 7.3 we set out the measured 'ability' of the children in the three schools. It can be seen that, in the case of each of the CAT scores, the schools are distributed in the same fashion as they are on the levels awarded by the mathematics tests, with mean scores dropping as we move from School D through School F to School E.

This raises the question of whether the differences in achieved levels can be 'explained' by the differences in the children's 'ability'. At first glance the pattern of results in Table 7.2 and 7.3 suggests that the school differences can be so 'explained' – in the sense of a correlation existing

Table 7.4   Tier of entry to test by school and quantitative 'ability' for May 1996 tests

	Tier 3–5 taken		Tier 4–6 taken		Tier 5–7 taken		Tier 6–8 taken	
	Row %	Count	Row %	Count	Row %	Count	Row %	Count
Lowest 'ability'								
School D	95.8%	23	4.2%	1				
School F	80.0%	24	20.0%	6				
School E	77.8%	28	22.2%	8				
Second lowest 'ability'								
School D	72.9%	35	27.1%	13				
School F	44.8%	13	41.4%	12	13.8%	4		
School E	21.7%	5	78.3%	18				
Second highest 'ability'								
School D	16.4%	9	69.1%	38	12.7%	7	1.8%	1
School F	17.4%	4	34.8%	8	47.8%	11		
School E			87.5%	14	12.5%	2		
Highest 'ability'								
School D	3.4%	3	43.7%	38	42.5%	37	10.3%	9
School F			23.1%	3	76.9%	10		
School E			27.3%	3	54.5%	6	18.2%	2

– by 'ability'. However, apart from the issue of whether the CAT score is a valid measure of children's 'ability' in relation to mathematics, there is a further difficulty arising from the practice of tiering to be addressed before we can accept this conclusion. Within each school, teachers have to decide on an appropriate tier for each child. Whatever it is about children that the CAT score captures, it is possible that teachers in each of the schools treat this differently in their decisions on appropriate tiers. In Table 7.4 we have set out, within each of four approximately equally sized categories of CAT score, the tiers for which children were entered.[1] Table 7.4 seems to show that the schools differ considerably in the ways they distribute their children by CAT score across the tiers. In particular School E enters children for higher tiers than School D for any given CAT score. This is brought out more clearly in Table 7.5 where the mean tier of test for which children have been entered is shown by school and CAT score (the dependent variable here is constructed by coding tier 3–5 as 4, tier 4–6 as 5, and so on). An analysis of variance of tier entered by school and CAT finds both significant.[2]

Since School D enters children, when considered against CAT scores, for lower tiers it is tending to cap its children's performance at lower levels. However, we know that this school produces the best overall performance. There are two reasons for this. First, as Table 7.3 showed,

Table 7.5 Mean tier of entry by school and quantitative 'ability' for May 1996 tests

	Mean NC test tier of entry	Count
Lowest 'ability'		
School D	4.04	24
School F	4.20	30
School E	4.22	36
Second lowest 'ability'		
School D	4.27	48
School F	4.69	29
School E	4.78	23
Second highest 'ability'		
School D	5.00	55
School F	5.30	23
School E	5.13	16
Highest 'ability'		
School D	5.60	87
School F	5.77	13
School E	5.91	11

School D has a higher mean CAT score than the two other schools and this clearly, following our argument in Chapter 2, 'predicts' a higher performance. This higher mean 'ability', as we will see later, is associated with a different social composition of the intake to this school. Second, it is the case that children in School D, for any given tier of test, do better in the May 1996 tests than children in the other two schools (with the exception of tier 6–8 where the numbers are very small). This is shown in Table 7.6. It seems likely that this pattern reflects the higher mean CAT scores found in those taking any given tier of the test in School D (with the exception of tier 6–8) as compared with the other schools – a pattern shown in Table 7.7. It is possible to push this analysis further. We have explored the considerable overlap of scores on baskets of common items across neighbouring tiers (e.g. 3–5, 4–6) of the May 1996 tests. As an illustration, the distribution of marks on the 61 common items and sub-items, drawn only from the May 1996 tests, are shown for the two groups entered for tiers 3–5 and 4–6 in Figures 7.1 and 7.2. Eight children, who were entered for the 3–5 test but who score better than the mean mark of 52.3 achieved by children entered for the 4–6 test, appear at the right of Figure 7.1. Thirteen, including these eight, score 50 or above.

Now, in order to allow some comparisons across the younger and older children, we had introduced a few Key Stage 2 items of appropriate 'levels' of difficulty into our February 1996 KS3 test. In particular, the

Table 7.6 Mean NC level achieved by school and tier of entry for May 1996 tests

	Mean level achieved	Count
Tier 3–5 entered		
School D	3.91	70
School F	3.59	41
School E	3.18	33
Tier 4–6 entered		
School D	5.34	90
School F	4.69	29
School E	4.26	43
Tier 5–7 entered		
School D	6.20	44
School F	5.80	25
School E	5.75	8
Tier 6–8 entered		
School D	7.20	10
School F	n/a	0
School E	7.50	2

n/a, not applicable

Table 7.7 Mean quantitative 'ability' by school and tier of entry for May 1996 tests

	Tier 3–5 taken		Tier 4–6 taken		Tier 5–7 taken		Tier 6–8 taken	
	Mean	*Count*	*Mean*	*Count*	*Mean*	*Count*	*Mean*	*Count*
School D	86	70	99	90	109	44	116	10
School F	82	41	91	29	101	25	n/a	0
School E	76	33	91	43	104	8	123	2

KS2 level 6 tennis item, previously discussed in Chapters 4 and 6, was taken by all children in the KS3 February 1996 test. Table 7.8 shows the mean scores on the tennis item for children entered for either tier 3–5 or 4–6 in May 1996 (the rows) and achieving either above or below the mean score achieved on the 3–5/4–6 basket of common items by 4–6 entrants (the columns). The eight children who were entered for 3–5, but who score above the 4–6 mean, all achieve perfect marks on the tennis item. Given the earlier results on CAT scores and tier entry by school (Table 7.5) it is notable that eight of the ten 'under-entered' children come from School D, two from School F, and none from School E. Their

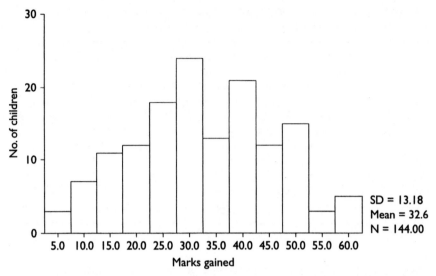

Figure 7.1 Distribution of children's scores on items common to the May 1996 3–5 and 4–6 tests for children who took the level 3–5 tests in May 1996

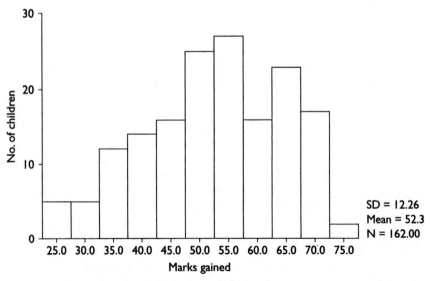

Figure 7.2 Distribution of children's scores on items common to the May 1996 3–5 and 4–6 tests for children who took the level 4–6 tests in May 1996

Table 7.8   Mean scores on the level 6 tennis item (1 mark available) by tier taken and performance on items common to tiers 3–5/4–6

Tier taken	Children scoring below 4–6 entrants' mean on items common to 3–5 and 4–6		Children scoring above 4–6 entrants' mean on items common to 3–5 and 4–6		Totals	
	Mean on tennis item	Count	Mean on tennis item	Count	Mean on tennis item	Count
3–5	0.42	136	1.00	8	0.45	144
4–6	0.61	77	0.82	85	0.72	162
Totals	0.49	213	0.84	93	0.59	306

better score overall on the 3–5/4–6 common items than the 4–6 entrants' mean, coupled with this perfect performance on a confusing level 6 item, suggests that they might have been entered safely for tier 4–6. Of course, we have not presented, with the exception of the tennis item, any direct evidence of the performance of the 3–5 entrants on level 6 items. Therefore this suggestion should be treated with caution. Neither is it a surprising finding, since schools can hardly be expected to get selection for tiers 'just right'. However, it does remind us that one threat to valid assessment inherent in the testing arrangements for KS3 resides in this difficult area of tier placement. Table 7.9 shows the comparable results if we split the columns at the less conservative mark of 50, rather than the mean of 52.3. Here the 13 children who scored 50 or more on the common items but took the 3–5 test slightly outperform on the tennis item the 95 children who score 50 or more but took the 4–6 test, gaining a mean of 0.85 against one of 0.82. Ten of the 13 are from School D, and three from School F.

A comparable analysis to that of Table 7.8 is set out in Table 7.10 for those items taken in common by children entered for tiers 4–6 and 5–7. Here there are 13 children who were entered for 4–6 yet scored higher than the mean on the common items of those children who were entered for 5–7. Twelve of these 13 answered the tennis item correctly, giving them a mean score of 0.92 compared with the 0.94 gained by the children who took the 5–7 test. Twelve of these 13 children came from School D and one from School F – a finding in line with the suggestion developed from the earlier analyses that School D tends to under-enter its children for tiers relative to the other schools, and to School E in particular.

This initial analysis suggests that internal practices are important mediating factors in the production of levels of achievement in these schools (for classic studies of such processes see Cicourel and Kitsuse 1963, and

Table 7.9 Mean scores on the level 6 tennis item (1 mark available) by tier taken and performance on items common to tiers 3–5/4–6

Tier taken	Children scoring below 50 on items common to 3–5 and 4–6		Children scoring 50 and above on items common to 3–5 and 4–6		Totals	
	Mean on tennis item	Count	Mean on tennis item	Count	Mean on tennis item	Count
3–5	0.41	131	0.85	13	0.45	144
4–6	0.58	67	0.82	95	0.72	162
Totals	0.47	198	0.82	108	0.59	306

Table 7.10 Mean scores on the level 6 tennis item (1 mark available) by tier taken and performance on items common to tiers 4–6/5–7

Tier taken	Children scoring below 5–7 entrants' mean on items common to 4–6 and 5–7		Children scoring above 5–7 entrants' mean on items common to 4–6 and 5–7		Totals	
	Mean on tennis item	Count	Mean on tennis item	Count	Mean on tennis item	Count
4–6	0.70	149	0.92	13	0.72	162
5–7	0.92	39	0.95	38	0.94	77
Totals	0.75	188	0.94	51	0.79	239

Lacey 1970). In the case of School D it seems clear that a relatively cautious approach is employed, consciously or otherwise, when entering children for tiers of the tests. In School E, on the other hand, children are apparently entered for relatively high tiers of the test in relation to their CAT scores. Our analysis in terms of quantitative CAT scores, employed here as predictors of mathematical achievement, supports such an interpretation from one side, and the additional analysis of performance on the tennis item lends further support. The levels achieved by the children from the three schools, set out by tier of entry and by the categories of quantitative CAT score employed in this analysis, are shown in Table 7.11. The figures in the last column of Table 7.11 show that children from School D outperform children from School E at all levels of quantitative CAT scores. The case of School F is harder to summarize. However, if we collapse the quantitative CAT scores into just two groups, the performance of School F children falls clearly between that of the other two schools in both CAT groups (see Table 7.12).

Table 7.11 Mean NC levels achieved on May 1996 tests by school, quantitative 'ability' and tier of entry (with 3–5 coded 4, 4–6 as 5, etc.)

Tier of test:	3–5		4–6		5–7		6–8		Total	
	Mean	Count	Mean	Count	Mean	Count	Mean	Count	Mean	Count
Lowest 'ability'										
School D	3.57	23	5.00	1	–		–		3.63	24
School F	3.21	24	4.17	6	–		–		3.40	30
School E	3.14	28	3.75	8	–		–		3.28	36
Group total	3.29	75	4.00	15	–		–		3.41	90
Second lowest 'ability'										
School D	4.06	35	5.00	13	–		–		4.31	48
School F	4.00	13	4.75	12	5.25	4	–		4.48	29
School E	3.40	5	4.22	18	–		–		4.04	23
Group total	3.98	53	4.60	43	5.25	4	–		4.30	100
Second highest 'ability'										
School D	4.11	9	5.24	38	6.14	7	7.00	1	5.20	55
School F	4.50	4	5.00	8	5.73	11	–		5.26	23
School E	–		4.43	14	6.00	2	–		4.63	16
Group total	4.23	13	5.02	60	5.90	20	7.00	1	5.12	94
Highest 'ability'										
School D	4.33	3	5.58	38	6.22	37	7.22	9	5.98	87
School F	–		4.67	3	6.10	10	–		5.77	13
School E	–		5.00	3	5.67	6	7.50	2	5.82	11
Group total	4.33	3	5.48	44	6.13	53	7.27	11	5.94	111
Table total	3.65	144	4.94	162	6.03	77	7.25	12	4.75	395

Table 7.12 Mean NC levels achieved on May 1996 tests by school and lower and higher quantitative 'ability'

| | Test level achieved | |
	Mean	Count
Lower 'ability'		
School D	4.08	72
School F	3.93	59
School E	3.58	59
Group total	3.88	190
Higher 'ability'		
School D	5.68	142
School F	5.44	36
School E	5.11	27
Group total	5.56	205
Table total	4.75	395

It is possible to explore some other relevant data in this context. Table 7.13 shows the mean percentages of items or sub-items apparently not reached by children in the May 1996 tests. These figures are based on the counts of items following each child's last written marks on his or her paper. Since children in School D have been entered, relatively speaking, for lower tiers in relation to their 'ability' as measured by CAT scores, we might expect them, all other things being equal, to find the test items less threatening. If this were to be so, then we might also expect them, within any particular 'ability' group, to complete a higher proportion of items in their May 1996 tests than the children from the other schools, and from those in School E in particular. The pair-wise comparisons between School D and School E children in the final column of means in Table 7.13 lend some support to this interpretation. For example, in the lowest (approximate) quartile of CAT scores, the mean of apparently non-reached items for School D children is 3.63 per cent, while for School E children it is 8.94 per cent. This pattern is similar in the other three quartiles of 'ability'. Children from School F fall in between these two schools in three of the four comparisons. It should be noted, though, that the school's entry policy is at best a partial explanation of the children's coverage of items. In the lowest quartile of CAT scores, for example, children from School F and School E have different percentages of apparently non-reached items (4.14 per cent against 8.94 per cent) even though they have been entered in very similar proportions for 3–5 and 4–6 tiers of test.

We have discussed the May 1996 performance across the three schools, with reference to measured 'ability', and with a special focus on the issue

Table 7.13 Percentages of items/sub-items not apparently reached by quantitative 'ability', school and tier of test taken

	3–5		4–6		5–7		6–8		Total	
	Mean	Count	Mean	Count	Mean	Count	Mean	Count	Mean	Count
Lowest 'ability'										
School D	3.65	23	3.26	1					3.63	24
School F	3.46	24	6.88	6					4.14	30
School E	8.43	28	10.73	8					8.94	36
Second lowest 'ability'										
School D	2.01	35	2.76	13					2.21	48
School F	1.23	13	4.80	12	2.22	4			2.84	29
School E	2.55	5	4.29	18					3.91	23
Second highest 'ability'										
School D	0.59	9	2.60	38	1.27	7	4.00	1	2.13	55
School F	1.60	4	4.08	8	4.26	11			3.73	23
School E			3.49	14	1.27	2			3.21	16
Highest 'ability'										
School D	0.35	3	2.26	38	2.57	37	2.67	9	2.37	87
School F			6.52	3	2.78	10			3.64	13
School E			7.25	3	6.75	6	0.00	2	5.66	11

of tier placement and its possible consequences for the valid measurement of children's knowledge of National Curriculum mathematics. We have shown that one school, School D, seems, relative to quantitative CAT scores, to have 'under-entered' its children when compared with the other two schools. This is associated with the children from this school attempting more items than the children from the other two schools and, in particular, from School E, the school where children were most clearly 'over-entered' in CAT-relative terms. Children in School D may have found their experience less demanding, if their lower rate of non-reached items is taken as an indicator. Furthermore, these children from School D did best in terms of overall levels achieved when judged against CAT scores (Table 7.12). However, the analysis of performance on items common to neighbouring tiers and on the tennis item, though clearly only suggestive, does bring out the difficulties of placing children 'appropriately'. Clearly, some children entered for one tier may have been capable of performing successfully on the next higher tier. The analysis here pointed to School D as the school that was most likely to have some children entered for too low a tier relative to others. Ironically, then, although School D did best in CAT adjusted terms, it is possible that its children's mean levels might have been higher still had the school adopted a slightly less cautious entry policy.

These findings, taken overall, raise important issues concerning any potential comparison of schools by tiered tests. Schools have to make difficult decisions about entry to tiers. When schools are compared via NC levels produced by tiered tests it is apparent that, alongside the children's mathematical skills and understanding, the teachers' skills in the area of placing children 'appropriately' are also being tested. Of course, this is not just a matter of teachers' 'skills'. Teachers will take into account a range of factors, including judgements about the effects of testing on children's motivation, as well as more diffuse judgements of children, when deciding on tiers (Cicourel and Kitsuse 1963; Lacey 1970; Dunne 1994, 1998). What is clear is that any comparison of secondary schools via NC tests ought not to be seen as anything but a very complex process. In fact, we have simplified the analysis of this process considerably to this point. No reference has been made yet to differences in performance by social class and sex. We will turn to these factors now, but, in the case of social class, we will be constrained to work with a reduced sample.

Sex and test performance

Tables 7.14 and 7.15 show that boys outperformed girls across the three schools. The first of these tables shows the distribution of levels achieved and the second shows the mean levels achieved for each school/sex

Table 7.14   NC levels achieved by sex and school (May 1996)

NC test level	School E		School F		School D	
	Girls %	Boys %	Girls %	Boys %	Girls %	Boys %
2	10.0		2.1	2.1		
3	27.5	28.3	18.8	14.9	8.6	4.6
4	37.5	43.5	37.5	29.8	25.7	23.9
5	15.0	13.0	22.9	27.7	25.7	27.5
6	10.0	10.9	14.6	25.5	32.4	33.9
7		2.2	4.2		7.6	8.3
8		2.2				1.8

Table 7.15   Mean NC levels achieved by sex and school (May 1996)

NC test level	School E		School F		School D	
	Mean	Count	Mean	Count	Mean	Count
Girls	3.88	40	4.42	48	5.05	105
Boys	4.22	46	4.60	47	5.23	109

combination. However, Table 7.16 shows that in two schools, School E and School D, boys have higher mean CAT scores than the girls. The situation in School F is less clear, with the boys here being higher than the girls on the quantitative measure of 'ability' but lower on the other two measures. This begs the questions – can the sex differences in performance be 'explained' statistically in terms of the CAT score differences? Or is it necessary to take other factors such as tier placement into account?

Table 7.17 shows how the tier of test taken varies by sex and school (unadjusted for CAT scores). In each school, boys are entered for a higher mean tier. If we adjust for quantitative CAT, using the simple method of dividing, for each child, his or her tier of entry (with 3–5 coded as 4, etc.) by quantitative CAT score and then multiplying by 100, we obtain the results shown in Table 7.18. Here we see the sex difference in tier placement reversed once CAT scores are taken into account, with girls being entered for higher mean levels than boys. These results can be further illuminated by an analysis of variance employing unadjusted tier placement as the dependent variable, with school, sex and quantitative CAT as the independent variables. Almost 60 per cent of the variance is accounted for, with quantitative CAT and the school attended as the significant factors. Sex, once 'ability' is controlled, does not reach statistical significance as a predictor of tier placement.

Table 7.16 Mean 'ability' scores by sex and school

'Ability' scores	Verbal mean	Quantitative mean	Non-verbal mean
School E Girls	86	85	94
School E Boys	88	89	98
School F Girls	93	88	99
School F Boys	90	90	97
School D Girls	98	97	104
School D Boys	101	99	106

Table 7.17 Mean tier of test taken by sex and school (May 1996)

| | School E | | School F | | School D | |
	Mean	Count	Mean	Count	Mean	Count
Girls	4.70	40	4.79	48	4.95	105
Boys	4.80	46	4.87	47	4.99	109

Table 7.18 Mean tier of test taken, adjusted for quantitative 'ability', by sex and school (May 1996)

| | School E | | School F | | School D | |
	Mean	Count	Mean	Count	Mean	Count
Girls	5.55	40	5.43	48	5.12	105
Boys	5.43	46	5.39	47	5.05	109

Table 7.19 NC level, adjusted by quantitative 'ability', by sex and school (May 1996)

| | School E | | School F | | School D | |
	Mean	Count	Mean	Count	Mean	Count
Girls	4.49	40	4.95	48	5.18	105
Boys	4.72	46	5.03	47	5.26	109

Now we can return to the initial question. Once 'ability' is controlled, via quantitative CAT score, do the differences between the sexes in levels achieved (Table 7.15) also 'disappear'? Table 7.19 shows how a simple CAT-adjusted measure of achievement – NC level achieved divided by quantitative CAT then multiplied by 100 – is distributed over the sexes and schools. There is a slight and consistent tendency for boys to have a higher adjusted score than girls, but it seems that these differences are small compared with the school effects (which, of course, will include effects of social class here). For both boys and girls, we have the same ordering of schools in this table, running upwards from School E through School F to School D. An analysis of variance of unadjusted NC level achieved by school, sex and quantitative CAT brings this pattern out. Sixty-eight per cent of the variance in unadjusted levels achieved is explained by CAT, school and sex taken together. Sex, however, is not a significant variable in this model. In fact, if sex is removed, we still find almost exactly the same proportion of variance accounted for. It appears that, considered against the background of CAT scores, sex is not an important factor in accounting for levels achieved. School differences seem more important and they seem to operate similarly, in our sample, for boys and girls. However, two points need to be made. First, it may be that quantitative CAT scores do not reflect adequately sex differences in mathematical 'ability' and hence are not an adequate control here. Second, we have not yet brought social class into the analysis, and it may be that the school effect is actually an effect of social class composition. We turn now to consider social class.

Social class and performance

We now unfortunately have to work with a reduced sample, particularly in the case of School D. While, in all schools, there was a problem of non-response, we experienced particular difficulties in the latter school in collecting data on parental occupations, as we noted in Chapter 2. Given these difficulties we will begin with a description of the differences between the children who remain in this analysis and those who were dropped. Amongst the 395 children discussed so far in this chapter, there are 159 for whom we have no social class information. Table 7.20 shows that these children are concentrated in School D, where we lack social class data on just over half of the sample discussed so far. Table 7.21, however, shows that, using CAT scores as an indicator, the children with and without social class data seem to be similar, at the level of means. Table 7.22 shows that the sexes are distributed similarly over the two groups. Taken together, these two tables suggest that our reduced sample is not likely to provide too misleading a picture of the ways social class, sex and 'ability' are related to achieved levels within these schools. It should be noted, though, that some cell sizes will become small in some analyses.

We will begin by examining performance by social class and school. Table 7.23 shows that, within each school, service-class children achieve

Table 7.20   Availability and non-availability of social class data for children by school

Social class	School E		School F		School D	
	Count	Col %	Count	Col %	Count	Col %
No data	24	27.9	16	16.8	119	55.6
Service class	7	8.1	18	18.9	34	15.9
Intermediate class	12	14.0	19	20.0	34	15.9
Working class	43	50.0	42	44.2	27	12.6

Table 7.21   Mean 'ability' scores by availability and non-availability of social class data

'Ability' scores	Children without class data		Children with class data	
	Mean	Count	Mean	Count
Verbal	94	159	95	236
Quantitative	94	159	93	236
Non-verbal	101	159	102	236

Table 7.22   Availability and non-availability of social class data by sex

'Ability' scores	Girls		Boys	
	Count	Row %	Count	Row %
Without social class data	79	49.7	80	50.3
With social class data	114	48.3	122	51.7

Table 7.23   Unadjusted mean NC levels achieved by social class and school

	School E		School F		School D	
	Mean	Count	Mean	Count	Mean	Count
Service class	5.14	7	5.06	18	5.68	34
Intermediate class	4.75	12	4.84	19	5.09	34
Working class	4.09	43	4.19	42	4.85	27

Table 7.24 Mean NC levels achieved, adjusted for quantitative 'ability', by social class and school

	School E		School F		School D	
	Mean	*Count*	*Mean*	*Count*	*Mean*	*Count*
Service class	5.13	7	5.41	18	5.51	34
Intermediate class	5.03	12	5.17	19	5.22	34
Working class	4.68	43	4.77	42	5.05	27

higher mean levels than intermediate-class children, who in turn outperform working-class children. Broadly speaking, within social class groupings, the school effects remain as we have seen before, with School D ahead of the others. Table 7.24 shows the results when quantitative CAT-adjusted measures of achievement are employed. Again the variable is constructed by dividing NC level by quantitative CAT and then multiplying by 100. The social class effects remain, and here the school effects remain clearly visible. School D outperforms the other two schools in all three social class groups, and School F similarly outperforms School E. However, an analysis of variance of unadjusted NC level achieved by school, social class and quantitative CAT finds 69 per cent of variance accounted for, with CAT and social class significant and school *not* significant. In this model, it is 'ability' that is accounting for almost all of the variance explained. Adding sex to this model achieves no increase in variance accounted for. As we argued in earlier chapters, how one understands these findings hinges on what view is taken of the capacity of CAT tests to reflect 'ability' in ways that are independent of any relevant cultural differences linked to social class. It is worth noting, in this respect, that a model without quantitative CAT, but with sex, still explains 16 per cent of the variance in level achieved, with social class and school being significant variables, but not sex.

Given the results of the earlier analysis of tier entry, we should, before concluding this chapter, explore how the distribution of children across the tiers varies by social class, sex, school and 'ability' taken together. Tables 7.25 and 7.26 show how tier of entry, unadjusted and CAT-adjusted respectively, varies by social class, sex and school. The pattern in the CAT-adjusted data in Table 7.26 does suggest that, within each of the six combinations of sex and social class, School D under-enters its children relative to School E. Also, within each school, service-class children are entered for higher tiers than working-class children. Working-class boys in School D have the lowest 'ability'-adjusted tier of entry. An analysis of variance of unadjusted tier of entry by social class, sex, school and quantitative CAT explains 61 per cent of the variance, with CAT,

Table 7.25 NC tier taken (3–5 coded as 4, 4–6 as 5, etc.) by social class, sex and school

| | School E | | School F | | School D | |
	Mean	Count	Mean	Count	Mean	Count
Service-class girls	6.00	1	5.14	7	5.44	16
Service-class boys	5.50	6	5.18	11	5.28	18
Intermediate-class girls	5.00	5	5.25	8	5.06	18
Intermediate-class boys	5.00	7	5.09	11	4.94	16
Working-class girls	4.77	22	4.50	22	4.73	15
Working-class boys	4.81	21	4.60	20	4.50	12

Table 7.26 NC tier taken (3–5 coded as 4, 4–6 as 5, etc.), adjusted for quantitative 'ability', by social class, sex and school

| | School E | | School F | | School D | |
	Mean	Count	Mean	Count	Mean	Count
Service-class girls	5.71	1	5.47	7	5.21	16
Service-class boys	5.73	6	5.62	11	5.22	18
Intermediate-class girls	5.36	5	5.61	8	5.27	18
Intermediate-class boys	5.33	7	5.54	11	5.02	16
Working-class girls	5.60	22	5.33	22	5.10	15
Working-class boys	5.45	21	5.14	20	4.56	12

school and social class, but not sex, appearing as significant variables in accounting for tier of entry.

There is just one last point to raise here. We noted, towards the end of the introduction to this chapter, that the four tiers of the tests have different proportions of 'realistic' and 'esoteric' items. Tier 3–5 has only 'realistic' items and the proportion then falls monotonically as we move through to tier 6–8, where it is 84 per cent. The result of this, given the observed distribution of children across tiers by social class, is that working-class children, since they are entered, on average, for lower tiers, are tested relatively more than others by 'realistic' items. We showed, in Chapter 5, that at the ages of 10–11 years working-class children performed relatively least well on this 'realistic' type of item in comparison with 'esoteric' items. This raises the intriguing possibility that some part of the social class difference in achievement shown in Tables 7.23 and 7.24 might be accounted for by the effects of the association of social class with item type, with this association being produced by the way children are distributed across the differentially 'realistic' tiers of the test. However, given that non-neighbouring tiers have only a minority of their items in common, we are not in a position to explore this further.

Conclusion

Schools, teachers and pupils are increasingly compared with one another through the medium of league tables based on National Curriculum assessment data, of which paper and pencil test results form a key component.[3] In earlier chapters, we explored the ways in which, in the primary school context, the nature of test items might interact with social class, sex and 'ability' to produce gaps between children's actual levels of mathematical understanding and skills and their test performance. Here, because of the existence of tiered testing in secondary schools, we have chosen to highlight a different potential problem – that of the effects on schools' potential league table positions of their decisions on the distribution of their pupils over the available tiers of the tests. We have shown that our schools seemed to have differed considerably in their approach to this problem, with the result that the tiers of the tests were taken by children of different measured 'ability' across the three schools. In addition, we have, in an exploratory way, used data on common items from neighbouring and overlapping tiers of the May 1996 test plus data from one item taken in February 1996 by all the children in our research – the tennis item – to show that one school does seem to have underestimated what some of its pupils might have achieved. The implication of this finding seems straightforward. A school's position in any potential league tables will reflect not only its relative strengths as a provider of teaching in mathematics but, employing an economic analogy, also its skills in judging accurately for which tiers to enter its 'raw material' in order to obtain the greatest level of 'output'.

Employing the reduced sample for which we have social class data, we have also analysed the ways in which performance on these largely 'realistic' tests varies by social class, sex, school and measured 'ability'. In this analysis we have found that tier of entry is associated with 'ability', social class and school but not the sex of the child. As far as actual performance is concerned, we have found 'ability' and social class to be the most important factors, with sex not significant and the school effects becoming non-significant in an analysis including social class and 'ability'. We also discussed briefly, and speculatively, the possibility that the differing proportions of 'realistic' items in the four tiers of the KS3 test might be implicated in the production of a part of the observed relation between social class and NC achievement.

We now return to the exploration of the ways in which children interact with some individual 'realistic' items. Our focus in Chapters 8 and 9 will be on KS3 children and items, though we will explore initially the ways in which both KS2 and KS3 children coped with the demands of a level 5 item, which originally appeared in a KS2 test.

Notes

1 Category 4 is 102 and over; category 3 is 93–101; category 2 is 84–92; and category 1 is 83 and below.
2 We will use analyses of variance throughout this chapter to provide some degree of statistical control for our interpretations. It should be noted, how-ever, that the dependent variable – a discrete and limited range of levels – is not ideally suited for entry into such analyses.
3 In the case of 14-year-olds, there was an initial move away from planned league tables by the Conservative government as a result of teacher resistance in 1993 and 1994. Later, both major political parties argued for such league tables in the run up to the national election of 1997. It now seems likely that, at some point in the future, the Key Stage 3 results will be used for the purpose of comparing schools, either directly or as part of a value-added measure assessing progress between 14 and 16 years of age.

8

Children's answers to items and explicitness: examples from Key Stage 2 and Key Stage 3

Introduction

In this and the following chapter, we return to the analysis of individual items, concentrating – though not exclusively – on KS3. As part of our research we have carried out analyses of children's responses to the KS3 items comparable to those reported earlier for KS2, drawing on both test and interview data. Comparing data from these two sources, we have been struck frequently by one particular feature of children's responses to items. There are several items in both KS2 and KS3 tests where some children lose marks because they fail to meet criteria for the degree of explicitness of their response rather than because they lack the required mathematical understanding. In Bernstein's (1996) terms, they lack knowledge of, or fail to employ their knowledge of, the realization rule for the testing context. Children frequently fail to provide a sufficiently explicit and/or full account of an answer to gain marks on a particular item, even though the interview data show that they could have done so. Since one major aspect of Bernstein's early work on social class, culture and language concerned variations between social classes in the typical degree of explicitness of communication in certain contexts, it seemed to us important to explore not only the extent to which children fell into this trap but also whether there was any apparent relation between the tendency to do so and a child's social class origins. We begin our discussion with an item concerning an imagined survey of sex differences in the types of socks children wear at school.

Boys, girls and socks – not saying enough

We have already met in Chapter 4 the Key Stage 2, level 5, item concerning sex differences in the types of socks worn (see Figure 4.1). In that chapter we compared the responses to its demands of just two children. We saw that it is an item that can cause a child to invoke his or her everyday experience rather than respond to the given data. It shares this feature with the traffic survey item discussed in Chapters 4 and 6. Of the 107 children we believe reached this item in the KS2 test context, six referred only to their 'real world' experience in answering part a, and a further three referred partly to their 'real world' experience. If we consider just the 106 of these children (52 service; 28 intermediate, 26 working) for whom we have social class data, the number of solely 'real world' referrers remains at six and partial 'real world' referrers at three. Of the former, four are service-class children, one is intermediate class, and one is working class. Of the latter, one is service class and two are working-class children. The socks item was one of the few from KS2 that we included, for purposes of comparison by age, in our KS3 test in February 1996. Amongst the 252 13–14-year-olds we believe reached the item and whose responses we have coded, 16 referred only to the 'real world' in answering part a, and a further nine referred partly to the 'real world'. If we consider just the 235 of these children (60 service; 63 intermediate; 112 working) for whom we have social class data, the number of solely 'real world' referrers reduces to 13. Of these, ten are working-class children, and three from the intermediate class. There are now six children who refer partly to the 'real world'. All are working class. While amongst the younger children, the 'real world' responders are spread across the social class groups, we can see that amongst the older children, it is primarily those from working-class backgrounds who respond in this way to this particular item. This suggests that, by the age of 13–14, service-class children are typically well-aware of the 'irrelevance' of their everyday experience to items of this type, but that some working-class children are not.

However, in this chapter we address a different aspect of this item and children's associated responses. If we look carefully at the item, we can see that the child is required to make sense of some potentially ambiguous messages. First of all, we might ask whether it is 'obvious' that the statements 'there are 35 girls' and 'there are 30 boys' refer to the respective total populations of girls and boys involved rather than just to the girls and boys wearing patterned socks. Clearly, for those who understand the conventions of this type of question, which sets the proportional nature of the percentages against the absolute numbers in the samples, this may be 'obvious'. However, for those lacking such familiarity, it is possible to link these statements with Anne's saying that 'more girls than boys wore patterned socks', to give a reading of the information which results in the belief that the two 20 per cents represent respectively 35 girls and 30 boys, rather than the intended seven girls and six boys. In fact, we can see that a child believing this, who writes down as the reason 'there are more girls', nevertheless will receive a mark from the marking scheme. It is also possible that some children will not see these two statements as part of the 'graphs', thus adding to their problems of interpreting the item's demands.

The major problem, however, concerns the reference to giving 'as many reasons as you can why she is right'. We can ask ourselves whether this was intended to distract the child from the 'real' reasons, but, since the marking scheme (see p. 45) does not penalize the child for giving 'wrong' reasons, we are led to search for another account of this instruction. It seems plausible that the test designers intended this instruction to encourage children to move beyond such responses as 'because there are more girls', worth one mark, to more linguistically elaborated responses that refer simultaneously to the relation between the different population sizes of boys and girls, the same percentages and the resulting different absolute numbers of boys and girls wearing patterned socks. The marking scheme lends support to this interpretation, since the only apparent 'reasons' given as examples are all *part* of the single 'correct' coherent explanation. But, there is a paradox here. If a child who understands percentages is predisposed to provide an elaborated response, then this instruction is not required. If, on the other hand, such a child is predisposed to give a less elaborate response, such as 'there are more girls', and he or she 'believes' that this is an adequate rendering of the 'correct' reasoning, then he or she may be left wondering what other reasons there are to provide. This might be expected to result in the production of 'inappropriate' reasons, including those that refer outside of the given data. Similarly, the child who has given a fully elaborated response, but who regards it as comprising just one reason rather than several, and is therefore puzzled by the request to give 'as many reasons as you can', may also produce other 'inappropriate' additional responses.

We have coded children's test responses to the item, at both Key Stages, concentrating on the component 'reasons' set out in the marking scheme. The results, by social class and sex, are set out in Tables 8.1 and 8.2 for KS2 and KS3, respectively, for children we believe reached the item, and for whom we have both social class and quantitative CAT data. We are particularly interested, given the considerations discussed above, in the cases where children wrote just 'there are more girls than boys' or its equivalent. Looking first at the Key Stage 2 responses in Table 8.1, we find that just over half the sample (51.9 per cent) produced such a truncated response, with the proportions rising as we move from the service-class through the intermediate-class to the working-class children, where 73.1 per cent produce this unelaborated response. With the exception of just one working-class child, it is the service-class children who offered more elaborated versions of the 'correct' reason. In the KS3 sample in Table 8.2, 34.9 per cent produce the truncated response. Here the

Table 8.1 Key Stage 2 children's written responses to the socks item, part a, in the test

		Service-class girls	Service-class boys	Intermediate-class girls	Intermediate-class boys	Working-class girls	Working-class boys	Total
Ann isn't right / is wrong (20% = 20%)	number	4	0	1	0	1	0	6
	col %	18.2	0	7.7	0	11.1	0	5.8
Ann isn't right / is wrong (other reason)	number	0	1	0	0	0	0	1
	col %	0	3.6	0	0	0	0	1.0
There are more girls than boys	number	7	11	7	10	7	12	54
	col %	31.8	39.3	53.8	66.7	77.8	70.6	51.9
There are more girls than boys, + the percentages are the same	number	2	5	0	0	0	0	7
	col %	9.1	17.9	0	0	0	0	6.7
There are more girls than boys, + the percentages are the same, + reference to this giving two different numbers	number	4	1	0	0	1	0	6
	col %	18.2	3.6	0	0	11.1	0	5.8
Other	number	4	7	3	2	0	3	19
	col %	18.2	25	23.1	13.3	0	17.6	18.3
Blank	number	0	3	1	3	0	2	9
	col %	0	10.7	7.7	20.0	0	11.8	8.7
Reference to the same percentages only	number	1	0	1	0	0	0	2
	col %	4.5	0	7.7	0	0	0	1.9
Total	number	22	28	13	15	9	17	104

Table 8.2 Key Stage 3 children's written responses to the socks item, part a, in the test

		Service-class girls	Service-class boys	Intermediate-class girls	Intermediate-class boys	Working-class girls	Working-class boys	Total
Ann isn't right / is wrong (20% = 20%)	number	1	2	0	3	2	2	10
	col %	4.8	5.3	0	10.3	3.3	3.8	4.3
Ann isn't right / is wrong (other reason)	number	0	0	0	0	1	2	3
	col %	0	0	0	0	1.7	3.8	1.3
There are more girls than boys	number	8	13	12	6	25	17	81
	col %	38.1	34.2	37.5	20.7	41.7	32.7	34.9
There are more girls than boys, + the percentages are the same	number	1	0	1	2	1	2	7
	col %	4.8	0	3.1	6.9	1.7	3.8	3.0
There are more girls than boys, + the percentages are the same, + reference to this giving two different numbers	number	6	14	8	10	8	8	54
	col %	28.6	36.8	25.0	34.5	13.3	15.4	23.3
Other	number	0	2	1	0	2	4	9
	col %	0	5.3	3.1	0	3.3	7.7	3.9
Blank	number	3	4	7	4	4	4	26
	col %	14.3	10.5	21.9	13.8	6.7	7.7	11.2
Reference to the same percentages only	number	1	0	0	1	0	0	2
	col %	4.8	0	0	3.4	0	0	0.9
Ann is right, incorrect reason given	number	1	3	3	3	17	13	40
	col %	4.8	7.9	9.4	10.3	28.3	25	17.2
Total	number	21	38	32	29	60	52	232

working-class children produce the highest percentage of such responses (37.5 per cent), but there is no clear pattern by social class (with the service class producing 35.6 per cent and the intermediate class 29.5 per cent). Girls, however, produce a higher percentage of such responses than boys in each social class grouping.

It is possible, of course, to analyse these responses further. In particular, we can consider whether measured 'ability' is of any apparent relevance. In order to achieve this, we have further subdivided the responses by quantitative CAT score, breaking the data into two approximately equal sized groups, divided at a score of 104.5 for the KS2 children and 92.5 for the KS3 children. The results show that, at KS2, it is mainly amongst the children with higher CAT scores that the relation between type of response and social class discussed above is generated. For working-class children with higher CAT scores, this response or its equivalent is produced by ten of the 11 such children (90.9 per cent). For the comparable service-class children the percentage is 31.4 per cent, and for the intermediate group it is 86.7 per cent. The percentages for the KS2 children with lower CAT scores are 46.7 per cent for the service class; 30.8 per cent for the intermediate class; and 60 per cent for the working class. It is also the case that, amongst the older children, it is the working class higher CAT scorers who produce the largest percentage of these responses (47.6 per cent against, for example, 39.5 per cent for service-class higher CAT scorers, and 22.9 per cent for intermediate-class higher CAT scorers).

The question which begs to be further examined is whether the children producing the non-elaborated 'there are more girls than boys' responses actually had a full understanding of the 'reasons' for Ann being right but failed to demonstrate this in their written response, possibly because of a predisposition to produce less linguistically elaborated responses in contexts where the audience might be expected to understand such a less than fully elaborated response. We can address this question but, to do so, we need to turn to our interview data.

Table 8.3 shows the coded responses from the interviews of KS2 children for whom we have both social class and quantitative 'ability' data. Here, because we prioritized this item in our interviews, we have a larger sample of children than we did in the case of the test, where we omitted those we believe did not reach the item (which was positioned towards the end of the test paper). What we see here, in this larger sample, but different context, is a major difference in the rate of production of the truncated response between the service-class children and the rest. Amongst service-class children as a whole 29.8 per cent produce the truncated response, with figures for the intermediate class and working class of 51.7 per cent and 46.9 per cent, respectively. Again, as in the case of the test data, if we divide the sample by CAT score (at 104.5 with 54 below and 64 above), we find that it is amongst the higher scorers that

Table 8.3 Key Stage 2 children's initial responses to the socks item, part a, in the interview

		Service-class girls	Service-class boys	Intermediate-class girls	Intermediate-class boys	Working-class girls	Working-class boys	Total
Ann isn't right / is wrong (20% = 20%)	number	5	5	3	5	2	5	25
	col %	20.8	15.2	23.1	31.3	16.7	25.0	21.2
Ann isn't right / is wrong (other reason)	number	0	2	0	0	0	0	2
	col %	0	6.1	0	0	0	0	1.7
There are more girls than boys	number	7	10	7	8	5	10	47
	col %	29.2	30.3	53.8	50.0	41.7	50	39.8
There are more girls than boys, + the percentages are the same	number	6	4	1	1	0	0	12
	col %	25	12.1	7.7	6.3	0	0	10.2
There are more girls than boys, + reference to this giving two different numbers	number	2	6	1	0	1	0	10
	col %	8.3	18.2	7.7	0	8.3	0	8.5
Other	number	2	4	1	1	2	3	13
	col %	8.3	12.1	7.7	6.3	16.7	15.0	11.0
Blank	number	0	1	0	1	0	2	4
	col %	0	3.0	0	6.3	0	10.0	3.4
Reference to the same percentages only	number	0	0	0	0	1	0	1
	col %	0	0	0	0	8.3	0	0.8
Ann is right, incorrect reason given	number	2	1	0	0	1	0	4
	col %	8.3	3.0	0	0	8.3	0	3.4
Total	number	24	33	13	16	12	20	118

the social class effect is generated. Amongst these 64 children, 26.3 per cent of the service class, 66.7 per cent of the intermediate class, and 72.7 per cent of the working class, produce the truncated response. For the 54 lower CAT scorers, the corresponding figures are 36.8 per cent, 35.7 per cent and 33.3 per cent.

While in the case of the younger children, the test sample is contained within the interview sample, the situation with the older children is different (see Table 8.4). Again there were some children who were interviewed who did not reach, as far as we can tell, the socks item in their test. These children, of whom there are seven, appear therefore in our interview sample but did not previously appear in the test sample. With these exceptions, the interview sample is a subset of the test sample (see Chapter 2). Here, unlike the case of the younger children, there is little sign of any relation between social class and the production of truncated responses. What is noteworthy is the increase between the test and the interview contexts in the proportion of children stating that 'Ann isn't right'. If we just consider data for the 106 children amongst the 113 interviewees who also appear to have reached this item in the test, the percentage claiming 'Ann isn't right' jumps from 3.8 per cent in the test to 25.5 per cent in the interview. The percentage of blank responses drops from 8.5 per cent to 1.9 per cent, suggesting that part of the change results from the interviewer encouraging the child to make some response. In the test, some children puzzled by the item, but believing Ann to be wrong, may have left the item blank and moved on. The same pattern holds for the younger children. If we consider just the 104 children we believe reached the item in the test, then 6.7 per cent in the test, and 21.2 per cent in the interview, stated that 'Ann isn't right', while blank responses reduced from 8.7 per cent to 3.8 per cent. The other great change was the reduction in responses coded as 'other' from 18.3 per cent to 9.6 per cent. We will return to those children who claimed that Ann was wrong later. The question we now explore is whether, amongst the children who produced truncated responses, there are some – and if so, who they are – who, when encouraged to elaborate their initial response, show that they could have produced initially, from the perspective of their existing 'mathematical' understanding as opposed to that of their apparent understanding of the rules of the assessment game, a fuller answer. This requires us to turn to our interview transcripts.

Of the 118 KS2 children (Table 8.3) considered above, 36 appear, from our tape-recordings, not to have been offered a chance to elaborate their answers during the interview. Amongst the remaining 82 the relation between social class and the production of the truncated response becomes much less clear. Twenty-nine of these 82 children produce the response 'there are more girls than boys' or its equivalent. Amongst the service-class children 12 of 37 (32.4 per cent) do so; amongst the intermediate-class

Table 8.4 Key Stage 3 children's initial responses to the socks item, part a, in the interview

		Service-class girls	Service-class boys	Intermediate-class girls	Intermediate-class boys	Working-class girls	Working-class boys	Total
Ann isn't right / is wrong (20% = 20%)	number	0	4	6	4	7	8	29
	col %	0	21.1	42.9	28.6	25.0	33.3	25.7
Ann isn't right / is wrong (other reason)	number	0	0	0	0	2	1	3
	col %	0	0	0	0	7.1	4.2	2.7
There are more girls than boys	number	5	4	3	0	9	6	27
	col %	35.7	21.1	21.4	0	32.1	25.0	23.9
There are more girls than boys, + the percentages are the same	number	1	1	1	0	2	1	6
	col %	7.1	5.3	7.1	0	7.1	4.2	5.3
There are more girls than boys, + the percentages are the same, + reference to this giving two different numbers	number	7	7	2	8	5	6	35
	col %	50.0	36.8	14.3	57.1	17.9	25.0	31.0
Other	number	0	1	1	2	0	0	4
	col %	0	5.3	7.1	14.3	0	0	3.5
Blank	number	0	1	0	0	2	0	3
	col %	0	5.3	0	0	7.1	0	2.7
Ann is right, incorrect reason given	number	1	1	1	0	1	2	6
	col %	7.1	5.3	7.1	0	3.6	8.3	5.3
Total	number	14	19	14	14	28	24	113

children 9 of 21 (42.9 per cent); and amongst the working-class children 8 of 24 (33.3 per cent) do so. Of these 29 children taken together, 20 (69.0 per cent) improved their mark when their verbal elaboration was taken into account. The 'improvers' figures for the three social class groups were 8 of 12 for the service class (66.7 per cent), 7 of 9 for the intermediate class (77.8 per cent), and 4 of the 8 for the working class (50.0 per cent). It is clear that, amongst all three social class groups, children were able to improve their marks when allowed to elaborate their initial written response. The working-class children were least likely to elaborate their truncated responses successfully during interview. Since the mean quantitative CAT scores for the three social class groups comprising these 29 children are, from service through intermediate to working respectively, 111, 106 and 102, it appears plausible that the initial truncated responses of children from the working class are less likely to be standing in for full understanding than those of the service class. We illustrate below both improvers and non-improvers, beginning with a working class boy (with a quantitative CAT score of 115) who wrote initially, 'There are more girls than boys', but who, when encouraged by the interviewer to expand this, apparently shows a correct understanding of the relation between the percentages and the absolute numbers involved.

MD: What did you say?
Alan: She's right because there's more girls than boys.
MD: OK, there are more girls than boys.
Alan: Yeah.
MD: OK. What about this 20 per cent, you see it says 20 per cent there?
Alan: Um.
MD: And 20 per cent there, does that make a difference?
Alan: Yeah, because there'll be 20 per cent of girls and 20, 20 per cent of boys but more girls will wear them because there's 35 girls and 30 boys.
MD: OK, so if you worked out 20 per cent of 35 . . . ?
Alan: It'll work out more than the 30.

While Alan seems to have been able to demonstrate an understanding of percentages in what he said, the elaboration by the following working-class girl does not. She also wrote the truncated response initially, 'Because they are more girls than boys', but her elaboration of this in the interview shows that the awarding of one mark both for her response and the 'same' response of Alan's – as the marking scheme does – is somewhat questionable with respect to validity.

MD: Explain the first bit to me then.
Elle: Using both graphs give as many reasons as you can why she is right. She says more girls than boys wore patterned socks. I said because there are more girls than boys.

MD: How do you know there's more girls than boys?

Elle: Because it says here, there are 35 girls, so there's really only about 5 per cent more of the girls wore white socks than the boys

MD: OK, she's talking about patterned socks though right?

Elle: Yeh.

MD: Alright, so it says there are 35 girls and 30 boys, yeh?

Elle: Yeh.

MD: But see where it says patterned and it's got 20 per cent and it's got patterned 20 per cent, so they're both 20 per cent, so is she still right then?

Elle: Yeh.

MD: Because . . .

Elle: There's more girls than boys.

MD: So if you worked out 20 per cent, what . . .

Elle: Twenty per cent would add up more to the boys 'coz if she just take away the five and put it on to the patterned that would make 25 per cent and the boys would just be left to 20 per cent

MD: OK.

Elle: But it would still be the same amount of boys and girls there, but the per cent, the per . . . , hundred would be more than a hundred on the boys.

MD: OK, so there would still be more girls?

Elle: Yeh.

Here we have a child, whose quantitative CAT is 94, who does not apparently understand the relation between percentages and absolute numbers, at least in the context of this item. Nevertheless, she gains one mark, as did Alan, who does seem to understand the relation. On the other hand, the following child, a service-class girl with a similar CAT score (98) does seem, like Alan, to understand the relation. She had written 'There are more girls anyway more boys wore grey socks than girls' with no punctuation to enable the reader to ascertain whether the 'anyway' belongs to its preceding or following clause – though the interviewer assumes the former in his questioning, apparently correctly.

BC: I wanted to ask you a bit about the first part as well. You have written that there are more girls anyway and you've written that more boys wore grey socks than girls, why are they good reasons then?

Frances: Because there's five more girls anyway, so there would be more girls wearing patterned socks because there's more of them.

BC: Did you look at the percentages when you were thinking about that?

Frances: Yeah.

BC: What did you did you find when you look at the percentages?
Frances: They are the same but there's more girls.
BC: And why did you write that more boys wore grey socks, what has that got to do with it?
Frances: Er, because that's filling up more of the chart, no girls wore grey socks.
BC: OK, but why does that help you sort out patterned socks?
Frances: Er.
BC: What I'm wondering is whether you did it because it says give as many reasons and you thought you had better write more than one?
Frances: Yeah.

As is the case with many of these transcripts, it is possible to argue that Frances did not elaborate her response enough to show without any doubt that she understood the relations involved here. The interviewer should have allowed her more space. However, it seems likely that she did have this understanding, and what is certainly clear is that her elaboration involves the addition of the point concerning 'the same percentages' to her answer. This would have gained her another mark, had it been written initially. The interviewer may have been too structuring of the child's response in the last part of the exchange, but Frances does agree that she was led by the request for 'as many reasons as you can' to provide the reference to grey socks. It is very difficult to decide, retrospectively, whether references like those of Frances to 'grey socks' indicate faulty understanding of the relations between percentages and absolutes or, perhaps, merely the temporary bracketing out of knowledge and understanding while attempting to respond to an authoritative request for *more* reasons.

However, the example of the next child (intermediate class, CAT of 117) shows much more clearly that the request for 'as many reasons as you can' could cause an interpretative problem. He wrote 'Because there are more girls than boys.' He asks the interviewer whether just one reason would be enough. She replies 'yes', but then, after he has written his initial response, asks him whether he can think of 'anything else'.

Andy: Is it alright if I can only think of one reason?
NR: Yep, do you think you can think of anything else?
Andy: No.
NR: No, how did you get that part then?
Andy: 'Cause well they, they've both got 20 per cent but there's 30 boys and 35 girls so, 20 per cent of 35 is more than 20 per cent of 30.
NR: OK so, is that more than one reason then do you think? Because there are more boys than girls.

Table 8.5 Socks item: nature of 'second attempts', after production of the truncated response, by social class and sex (KS2)

		Service-class girls	Service-class boys	Intermediate-class girls	Intermediate-class boys	Working-class girls	Working-class boys	Total
No second attempt made even though prompted	number	0	0	1	0	0	0	1
	col %	0	0	20.0	0	0	0	3.4
Second attempt leads to fewer marks	number	0	0	0	0	0	2	2
	col %	0	0	0	0	0	33.3	6.9
Second attempt leaves marks unchanged	number	2	2	1	0	1	1	7
	col %	33.3	33.3	20.0	0	50.0	16.7	24.1
Second attempt improves marks	number	4	4	3	4	1	3	19
	col %	66.7	66.7	60.0	100	50.0	50.0	65.5
Total	number	6	6	5	4	2	6	29

Andy: More girls.

NR: More girls than boys sorry, but what you just said there, 'cause they're both 20 per cent, 20 per cent of 35 is more than 20 per cent of 30, yeah. OK so why did you write that [interviewer points to his written response] down instead of what you told me?

Andy: 'Cause that was the first thing that came into my head.

NR: That was the first thing, but once you thought about it did you come up with the other things?

Andy: Yeah.

NR: Yeah, OK, do you want to write anything else or are you happy with that?

Andy: I'm happy with that.

Here we have a clear understanding, orally expressed, of the relations between percentages and absolute numbers. However, in spite of his elaborating his response in the required direction, Andy feels no need to expand his written response. He clearly sees it as adequately representing his (correct) thinking. Neither has the exchange with the interviewer led him to see that a reference to the same percentages might, from one perspective at least, constitute another reason.

We can see from these examples that children writing 'there are more girls than boys', and hence receiving one mark, may or may not have an adequate understanding of percentages and their relation to absolute numbers. Some children, like Andy, clearly will lose marks not because they lack the necessary mathematical understanding but rather because they fail to produce an adequately explicit account of what they do know. They appear not to know well enough the rules of the game being played here. However, it appears that, in this case, at KS2, it is service- and intermediate-class children, rather than working-class children, whose truncated responses are more likely to be elaborated successfully in interview, as Table 8.5 shows – though it should be remembered that this table is based on just the 29 children previously discussed. In fact, two of the eight working-class children worsen their mark as a result of the elaboration of their response in the interview. It should be remembered that the working-class children here have the lowest mean CAT scores amongst these 29. The numbers involved do not justify any statistical exploration of the relations by measured 'ability', though it is interesting to note (Table 8.6) that there is an apparent relation between CAT score and improvement in the service- and intermediate-class groups, but not in the working-class group. Table 8.5 also shows that it is two boys from the working-class who worsen their mark during their interview, but again the numbers do not allow much more to be said about sex in this case.

Table 8.6 Quantitative 'ability' by social class and the nature of the second attempt for children making the truncated response to the socks item (KS2)

	Service class		Intermediate class		Working class	
	Mean	Count	Mean	Count	Mean	Count
No second attempt even though prompted	–	–	83.00	1	–	–
Second attempt leads to fewer marks	–	–	–	–	107.50	2
Second attempt leaves mark unchanged	106.00	4	94.00	1	101.00	2
Second attempt improves marks	113.25	8	111.29	7	98.75	4

Of the 113 older children considered earlier (Table 8.4), 33 appear, from our tape-recordings, not to have been offered a chance to elaborate their answers during the interview. Amongst the remaining 80, 19 (23.8 per cent) produce the truncated response. Fifteen of these children (78.9 per cent) expand their response with some success in the interview. Table 8.7, comparable to Table 8.5, shows that it is again the service- and intermediate-class children amongst these whose truncated responses are more likely to be expanded successfully in the interview (100 per cent of each group). Table 8.8 shows how CAT scores are distributed over these response categories by social class.

Returning to the wording 'as many reasons as you can', the interview with the last child in particular, Andy, demonstrates how the way in which this item is worded might cause children to search for more 'reasons' than they might have done had the wording been something like 'explain as carefully as you can why Ann is right'. The previously quoted child, Frances, seems to have added an incorrect reason because of the wording. Given that irrelevant and/or incorrect reasons are not penalized, this seems not to have been deliberately intended by the test designers.

Boys, girls and socks – turning the text on its head

Although our main focus in this chapter is on the production and meaning of 'truncated responses', which fail to meet the specified criteria for explicitness, we also consider one other aspect of the socks item before turning to discuss a second example of an item that elicits inadequately explicit responses. In particular, we consider those children who wrote or said initially that 'Ann isn't right'. Returning to Tables 8.3 and 8.4 we

Table 8.7 Socks item: nature of 'second attempts', after production of the truncated response, by social class and sex (KS3)

		Service-class girls	Service-class boys	Intermediate-class girls	Intermediate-class boys	Working-class girls	Working-class boys	Total
No second attempt made even though prompted	number	0	0	0	0	1	0	1
	col %	0	0	0	0	20.0	0	5.3
Second attempt leads to fewer marks	number	0	0	0	0	0	1	1
	col %	0	0	0	0	0	33.3	5.3
Second attempt leaves marks unchanged	number	0	0	0	0	2	0	2
	col %	0	0	0	0	40.0	0	10.5
Second attempt improves marks	number	5	3	3	0	2	2	15
	col %	100	100	100	n/a	40.0	66.7	78.9
Total	number	5	3	3	0	5	3	19

Table 8.8 Quantitative 'ability' by social class and the nature of the second attempt for children making the truncated response to the socks item (KS3)

	Service class		Intermediate class		Working class	
	Mean	Count	Mean	Count	Mean	Count
No second attempt even though prompted	–	–	–	–	95.00	1
Second attempt leads to fewer marks	–	–	–	–	91.00	1
Second attempt leaves mark unchanged	–	–	–	–	95.50	2
Second attempt improves marks	94.38	8	90.67	3	90.00	4

can see that 25 of the 118 younger children and 29 of the 113 older children gave as their initial response some version of 'Ann isn't right, because the percentages were the same'. What view might we take of these responses? First, consider the following extract from a school mathematics text (*School Mathematics Project: Book 3T* 1970: 218–19), which follows some introductory material on percentages, including the use of the standard denominator 100:

Example 7
A town of 55000 men of working age has 1750 unemployed. Is there much cause for alarm?
Expressing the data in fraction form we get:

$$\text{the fraction of men unemployed is } \frac{1750}{55000} = \frac{7}{220}$$

Another way is to express the original fraction with the standard denominator 100:

$$\frac{1750}{55000} = \frac{7}{220} = \frac{3.14}{100}$$

that is, 3.14 per cent of the men of working age are unemployed. This makes it easy to compare it with, for instance, the national figure. Is 3.14 a low figure?

This example clearly predates later concerns over gender and mathematics texts. No doubt much else could be said about its implicit politics, and its arithmetic accuracy (shouldn't it be 3.18 rather than 3.14, whether π is everywhere or not?). However, it has at its core the message that percentages have, as one function, the purpose of allowing meaningful comparisons between groups of different absolute size: here, the town population of 55000 and the national population, presumably much greater. Now, if we consider the socks item in the light of this typical introductory material on percentages, we can see further interpretative complexities arising for the child considering the socks item. He or she is asked to consider whether Ann is right. If the message of mathematics textbooks about meaningful comparisons is taken seriously, then it would seem reasonable to argue that she is not. After all, once we have used the standard denominator of 100, and found that 20 per cent of both boys and girls wear patterned socks, it would appear that the sampled propensities to wear patterned socks by sex are the same, and that girls do not wear patterned socks *more* than boys. The careful reader will note that the word 'more' in the preceding sentence is differently placed to the word 'more' in the item itself, but this displacement would hardly seem to justify the marking scheme's assumption that Ann must be seen as being right. Perhaps the child is supposed to assume that if a test item, supplied by responsible adults, implies Ann is right, then any knowledge or understanding that might suggest she is not should be bracketed out. This might be very puzzling for a child who has recently undertaken a classroom survey of favourite television programmes, which involved the calculation of percentages in order to compare boys' preferences against those of girls, for example.

We will now examine some of the interview responses of the 29 children amongst the older 113 who argued Ann is right (and who might be assumed to have seen such textbook accounts of comparisons as that quoted above). The interesting question is: were these responses based on the understanding, whether derived from mathematics lessons or elsewhere, that meaningful comparisons between groups of different sizes require initial adjustment of denominators? We can begin by looking at how many, among these 29 older children, succeeded in improving their mark when given a chance to reconsider their initial answer. In fact, breaking this down by social class, all four service-class children, seven of the ten intermediate-class children, and twelve of the fifteen working-class children improved their mark. However, as we have said earlier, marks can be gained by writing 'there are more girls than boys', but this statement does not necessarily imply an understanding on the part of a child of the relations between percentages and absolute numbers. The same point applies to children's second attempts. We have decided therefore to present here a few cases in some detail rather than attempt any statistical analysis. Our purpose in doing so is to further illustrate the difficulties raised by an item of this type for the valid measurement of children's mathematical understanding. Indeed, it will be seen from these examples, that determining a child's degree of understanding remains a difficult task even on the basis of interview data.

First we can look at a case where marks were not improved via a second attempt, and where no clear evidence of the required understanding emerges in the interview discussion. Charlie, an intermediate-class boy with a quantitative CAT score of 110, wrote, 'She is not right because there are the same amount of patterned socks in each graph'. The interviewer draws his attention to the 35/30 statements. It seems that he had not noticed them initially, possibly because he had not seen them as part of the 'graphs'. Now, it is possible that his reference to 'more per cent' does hide an adequate understanding but, if so, the interviewer did not succeed in bringing this out before Charlie develops his reasoning in inappropriate ways by referring to the irrelevant percentages of white socks:

BC: Let's look at the first one [i.e. part a]. When you read the first one, did you read all the words down to here do you think? [Interviewer points at the sentences mentioning 35 and 30.]

Charlie: Yes.

BC: Ok, let's look at it again, because you've said she's wrong, haven't you?

Charlie: Um.

BC: These charts show the colour of socks worn on one school day – girls' socks, boys' socks. There's the two pie charts. You've said the patterned and the patterned are the same. Did you read this bit – there are 35 girls and 30 boys?

Charlie: [inaudible]

BC: Sorry?

Charlie: I didn't see that part.

BC: You didn't see that part – does that make any difference?

Charlie: Yeah.

BC: What difference does it make?

Charlie: There's more per cent of girls that wear patterned socks and boys, there's more boys, more girls than there is boys.

BC: There's more per cent?

Charlie: Um.

BC: The per cent's the same isn't it?

Charlie: Yeah.

BC: Twenty and 20 – so what do you mean – there's more?

Charlie: Well in the pie charts, none of the boys, no, none per cent of the boys wear white socks, whereas in this one 40 per cent wear white socks, so, and the others is 20 per cent, and 20 per cent is the same, but more girls wear white socks than there are boys.

BC: What about the 35 and the 30 – what difference does that make in particular?

Charlie: There's five more girls than there is boys.
BC:　　Right. OK, number six next please.

Here is another case, that of Shelly, an intermediate-class girl with a CAT score of 95, who improves her marks, because of the addition of the 'there are more girls than boys' statement during her second attempt, but where it is still not entirely clear whether her initial claim that 'Ann is wrong' was based on the approach to comparison via percentages set out in textbooks. However, the use of the word 'chance' here may well indicate an understanding that 20 per cent of 35 is a larger number than 20 per cent of 30, though the form of expression is not that recommended in mathematics texts! The previous reference to there being more girls 'that would be able to wear them' is compatible with this interpretation:

Shelly: [pause] Mm.
BC:　　What are you thinking?
Shelly: This is a bit confusing 'cos like they both wear, there's both the same amount of patterned.
BC:　　Right.
Shelly: And you have to write down the reasons why she's right, but you can't.
BC:　　You think she's wrong?
Shelly: Yeah.
BC:　　Have you read all the words down to here do you think?
Shelly: Yeah, I think so.
BC:　　Do you want to read them through again, see if it makes any difference?
Shelly: [pause] Um.
BC:　　Still think that's wrong?
Shelly: Yeah.
BC:　　OK, do you remember what you wrote in the test, or did you miss it out?
Shelly: Don't know, I'm not sure what I done.
BC:　　Oh right.
Shelly: I think I might have missed it out.
BC:　　OK, well just look, this bit here where it says that these charts show the colour of socks worn on one school day.
Shelly: Mm.
BC:　　And you've noticed that it's patterned 20 per cent and patterned 20 per cent?
Shelly: Yeah.
BC:　　And it says that there are 35 girls, there are 30 boys, Ann says more girls than boys wore patterned socks. Now can you think of any reason why she might be right even though it's 20 per cent and 20 per cent?

Shelly: 'Cos there are more girls.
BC: How does that make her right?
Shelly: 'Cos there are more girls to, that would be able to wear them than there are boys.
BC: Do you think you can explain that.
Shelly: Er, [pause] I'm trying to think.
BC: You're not sure?
Shelly: No.
BC: How about just in words to me rather than writing it down.
Shelly: 'Cos there's five more girls there's er, more chance of girls wearing them than there are boys.
BC: Even though it's 20 per cent and 20 per cent?
Shelly: Yeah.

The next child, Zoe, an intermediate-class girl with a CAT score of 103, is apparently convinced, at least initially, that there is no reason available why Ann is right:

NR: OK do you want to go to number four.
[Zoe considers the item.]
Zoe: There ain't a reason, I can't think of one. They're both 20 per cent ain't they. They're more varied, there's more an equal amount of them than there is, and there's more, like mostly grey so they've got a dominating colour. They're both the same amount of patterned so you can't say more girls wore patterned socks.
NR: Just have another look in the box, is there anything you haven't seen before?
Zoe: Oh yeah I see it. Took me a while last time as well.

After this prompt from the interviewer to 'have another look in the box', she wrote: 'Because there are 35 girls being questioned, while only 30 boys were questioned'. This response apparently assumes a context of a survey of some sort – exactly the type of context in which a comparison employing percentages would be more appropriate than one using absolute numbers. Ironically, her cued response is of the truncated variety and, because the interviewer chooses not to probe further, we cannot be sure whether she fully understands the relations between proportions and absolutes here. Her test response had been fuller, suggesting that she read the requirements of the two contexts differently, and, in spite of some carelessness, Zoe's test response does suggest that she understands the relations involved. She wrote: 'There are 35 girls and 30 boys. Each of the groups wear 20% patterned by ['but' intended?] there are more girls than boys so 30% ['20%' intended?] means more than boys'. Taking her two responses together, especially given the implied reference to a survey, we can suggest that she may well have been genuinely puzzled by Ann's claim, possibly initially seeing her as employing a flawed method of comparison rather than as making a statement concerning raw numbers. As she says, it took her some time to see through the item's ambiguities 'last time', in the test, and we have seen in her transcript that it was only after a cue that she rejected the alternative interpretation of the item in the interview context.

We cannot be sure what the intentions of the designers of this item were. It is possible the ambiguity over 'more' was intended, but it seems at least strange to make the marks dependent on children's being able to bracket out what we presume they have been taught to regard as good practice when making comparisons between differently sized samples. The socks item is one of a number in these tests that have been described by their designers as being likely to have the effect of improving the mathematical understanding of children via their effects on teachers' ped-agogical practices. Whatever one thinks about such claims, we can see that, until children understand much more about their peculiarities, such items are not likely to lead to valid assessment of what children know. Not only do children frequently fail to respond explicitly enough to in-dicate their actual understanding, as we saw earlier, but also, in this particular case, they are arguably required to turn the usual advice of mathematics texts on its head in order to make sense of what is required. We return now to the issue of the degree of explicitness required of children in their response and, in particular, to the demands of a KS3 item assessing understanding of probability, which appeared in tiers 5–7 and 6–8 of the test. Since this item was taken mainly by more 'able' children (see Table 7.7) we will be able to focus on their degree of under-standing of the realization rules for items demanding extended explana-tion. Does being 'able', according to the measures generated by CAT tests, ensure knowledge of the 'rules of the game'?

Throwing dice

For our second illustration of the 'not explicit enough' response problem, we will consider children's responses to the item from tiers 5–7 and 6–8 shown in Figure 8.1 (SCAA 1995b). The instructions for marking the initial part of the item are shown in Table 8.9. We begin our discussion by considering our test data.

Shana's dice: test data

This item appeared in the tests that the KS3 children took in February 1996 at the two tiered levels of 5–7 and 6–8. The written responses were marked by us following the marking scheme shown in Table 8.9. Our

This dice with 4 faces has one blue, one green, one red and one yellow face.

Five pupils did an experiment to investigate whether the dice was biased or not.

The data they collected are shown in this table.

Pupil's name	Number of throws	Face landed on			
		Red	Blue	Green	Yellow
Peter	20	9	7	2	2
Caryl	60	23	20	8	9
Shana	250	85	90	36	39
Keith	40	15	15	6	4
Paul	150	47	54	23	26

(a) Which pupil's data is **most likely** to give the best estimate of the probability of getting each colour on the dice?

_____

Explain your answer.

Figure 8.1   Dice item, part a (SCAA 1995b)

interpretation of these instructions is that marks should not be given, in part a, if children do not state the correct reason explicitly in their own words. There were 120 children in our sample who took these tiers of our test and for whom we have quantitative CAT data. However, since the item appeared at different points in the 5–7 and 6–8 tiers of the test, it is important to take out children we believe may have not reached this item (which appeared quite late, as item 20, in the 5–7 test). This leaves 91 children we believe read and/or attempted the item.

Of these 91 children 32 (35.2 per cent) gained the mark for part a. Girls (34.8 per cent) were very slightly less successful than boys (35.6 per cent), but this difference was not statistically significant. There were large, and statistically significant, differences between the schools. Of these 91 children, 46.2 per cent of School D children; 25.9 per cent of School F children; and only 8.3 per cent of School E children succeed in gaining

Table 8.9 Marking scheme for the 4-sided dice item (SCAA 1995b)

SoA	Mark	Correct response (part a)	Additional guidance
5/7b Understand and use relative frequency as an estimate of probability	1m	Indicates Shana and explains that more throws are likely to lead to more accurate estimates e.g. • 'Shana's. She threw the dice more times than the others so her findings will be more consistent.' • 'Shana. Because the more throws will give more accurate probabilities.' • 'Shana, because the more throws the more reliable your estimates can be.' • 'Shana's. Because there are more throws to see that it wasn't just a fluke.' • 'Shana. Because she has thrown the dice more times and this gives a clearer picture.'	Do not accept an explanation that says that Shana has thrown the dice the most and/or paraphrases the question with no reference to increased accuracy or similar e.g. • 'Shana. Because she did the most throws.' • 'Shana. She threw it more times so she will get the best estimate.'

the mark for part a. We saw in the previous chapter that these schools varied considerably in their practices concerning tier of entry for the tests, with School D effectively setting a higher CAT threshold for entry to any given tier. As a result the sample of children taking the Shana item in the different schools varies by quantitative CAT score, with the mean scores being 110 in School D, 100 in School F and 99 in School E. However, the difference between School F and School E is very much larger than the difference in CAT scores, suggesting some other factor is at work here. Candidate factors might include differential curriculum coverage or some external factor such as social class, which might, for example, affect the degree of explicitness of children's answers (see Bernstein 1973).

These 91 children include those for whom we do not have social class data. If we look at the test data just for the 59 children amongst the 91 for whom we have social class data as well as quantitative CAT scores, we again find boys and girls performing almost equally well (34.5 per cent and 33.3 per cent respectively gaining the mark). We also find the school differences as before (Table 8.10). Again the difference between School F and School E seems larger than can be accounted for by CAT scores. In fact, the children from School E have a slightly higher mean quantitative

Table 8.10 Performance in test on dice item, part a, of 59 children

		Zero marks	One mark	Total
School D	number	11	13	24
	row %	45.8	54.2	100.0
School E	number	10	1	11
	row %	90.9	9.1	100.0
School F	number	18	6	24
	row %	75.0	25.0	100.0
Total	number	39	20	59
	row %	66.1	33.9	100.0

Table 8.11 Quantitative 'ability' scores of the 59 children in Table 8.10

	Tier 5–7 taken		Tier 6–8 taken		Total	
	Mean	Count	Mean	Count	Mean	Count
School D	109.71	21	118.33	3	110.79	24
School E	91.50	6	112.60	5	101.09	11
School F	100.67	24	–	–	100.67	24
Total	103.31	51	114.75	8	104.86	59

Table 8.12 Performance in test on dice item, part a, of 59 children by social class and school (1 mark available)

	Service class		Intermediate class		Working class		Total	
	Mean	Count	Mean	Count	Mean	Count	Mean	Count
School D	0.73	11	0.40	10	0.33	3	0.54	24
School E	0	3	0.33	3	0	5	0.09	11
School F	0.44	9	0.25	8	0	7	0.25	24
Total	0.52	23	0.33	21	0.07	15	0.34	59

'ability' score than those from School F in this case (Table 8.11). Only one of the 11 children from School E gains a mark (Table 8.10), perhaps pointing to curriculum coverage, or lack of it, as a likely relevant factor here.

In fact, Table 8.12 seems to show both school and social class 'effects' operating here, though the small sample from School E behaves differently by social class than those from the other two schools. Service-class children have a mean score of 0.52; intermediate-class children one of 0.33; and working-class children one of only 0.07.

We now turn to the interview data to explore one possible basis of this social class difference in achievement on this item – a difference in the 'chosen' degree of explicitness of a child's answer by social class. Since we are now operating with smaller numbers of children, the analysis in the next section should be seen as exploratory. Since, however, there are frequently items in the English testing programme, which, like this one and the socks item discussed earlier, call upon the child to provide an elaborated explanation of an answer, any evidence that some children might lose marks, not because of a lack of mathematical understanding, but because of their 'choice' of less explicit modes of response needs to be taken seriously by both test designers and the children's teachers.

Shana's dice: interview data

We interviewed 46 children undertaking this item. Of these children, 12 initially wrote Shana, while also giving what we judged to be an acceptable written reason, while 17 wrote Shana but failed, in our judgement, to provide acceptably explicit enough reasons according to the marking scheme in their initial written response explaining their answer. We should stress here that these responses (and the written test responses) were not always easy to code. Examples of written responses in the interviews that seem clearly not to meet the 'explicitness' requirements of the marking scheme are:

> Shana. 'Because she had thrown it the most times.'
> Shana. 'Because she did it the most times.'

Responses that seem to meet the requirements include:

> Shana. 'She threw the dice more times so it would be more accurate.'
> Shana. 'She threw the dice most times. Her results are more likely to "average out".'

Cases where we are less sure about our coding include:

> Shana. 'She threw the dice more times so will have more results than the others.'
> Shana. 'Shana trew (sic) the dice more times so there were more chances to get a different reading.'

Both of the last two responses were coded as not explicit enough to gain marks, but the second coding of the pair in particular is perhaps contestable. Our problems here, and elsewhere, in employing the marking scheme as part of our coding remind us how difficult it is to produce sets of 'rules' to cover a range of not entirely predictable responses. Notwithstanding these coding difficulties, there existed a group of children who selected Shana, but failed to convince us, in their initial written response, that they had met the explicitness requirements of the marking scheme.

However, our interviews show that some children writing non-explicit answers, or paraphrasing the question, do understand the mathematical point involved but have failed to express it with the required degree of explicitness. Of the 17 children we coded as producing not explicit enough responses, our records show that we offered to 14 children a chance to elaborate their explanation of their choice of Shana. Of these 14 children, ten gave acceptably explicit reasons when the interviewer asked them to explain why they had chosen Shana. This suggests that an important minority of children are not yet currently aware of the 'rules of the game' for this type of item and that, as a result, their mathematical capacities may have been underestimated. Ten may seem a small number, but we interviewed, it will be recalled, just 46 children for this item. An illustrative transcript follows where it can be seen that, when questioned about her response, this child, an intermediate-class girl with a quantitative CAT of 106, was able to produce exactly one of the phrases ('a clearer picture') given in the marking scheme as evidence of understanding. Her initial written response had been 'Shana. She rolled the most times':

> BC: Can I ask you about these? You say Shana because she threw the dice more. Why's that better?
>
> Child: 'Cos the more throws you do, the more clear your results could be.
>
> BC: Why's that? It's the right answer – I'm just trying to get your full explanation.
>
> Child: 'Cos the more clearer picture you have. If you threw it 20 times you haven't got much information to go on, you need, you need more numbers.

We can compare these replies with one of the marking scheme's examples of a 'correct response': 'Shana. Because she has thrown the dice more times and this gives a clearer picture.' This child clearly knew more, or had a deeper understanding, than her written response would have indicated.

We want now to explore which children make which responses. We can look at which children it is amongst the 29 children writing Shana plus some reason who initially make more or less explicit responses, and who it is amongst the initially not-explicit enough responders who subsequently make the move to more explicit responses when offered the opportunity. Among the 29 children, there is a slight tendency for girls to be more likely than boys to provide not explicit enough responses (61.5 per cent against 56.25 per cent), though the difference is not statistically significant (see counts by sex in Table 8.13). If we look at the social class distribution of responses in Table 8.13, we find that the working-class children are much more likely to produce not explicit enough responses than the other two groups. Numbers in the cells are too small to allow a chi-squared test. Four of the five working-class children initially write a

Table 8.13 Quantitative 'ability' score of the 29 children writing 'Shana' plus a reason by social class, sex and nature of response

Social class and sex	Explicit responses		Implicit responses	
	Mean	Count	Mean	Count
Service-class girls	113.25	4	110.50	2
Service-class boys	88.00	1	109.00	5
Intermediate-class girls	95.00	1	103.00	2
Intermediate-class boys	109.60	5	116.75	4
Working-class girls	–	–	93.75	4
Working-class boys	106.00	1	–	–

not explicit enough response. These four are all girls and are spread across all three schools, with two from School E. This tendency of girls to respond not explicitly enough is also found in the intermediate class, but is reversed in the service-class sample. Since the numbers here are very small, however, it is possibly safer to regard this more as a finding worthy of further exploration rather than as anything firmer. It is also the case that these four children have the lowest mean CAT score of any group in Table 8.13. However, the overall pattern of scores across the cells of Table 8.13 does not suggest that CAT score determines response mode here.

If we now consider just the 14 children of the 17 in the final column of Table 8.13 who were coded as giving a not explicit enough reason for their choice of Shana and who were offered a chance to elaborate their response, we found, as we noted above, that ten of these successfully expanded their reason orally when encouraged to further explain it to the interviewer (Table 8.14). These included three of the four working-class girls. Here is how one of them responded in the interview, and one other in both the test and interview. Lucy, the first of these girls, wrote nothing for this item in her test, probably only having reached the item just preceding it. In her interview, she wrote, 'Shana. Because that was the one with the most number of throws.' Clearly she received no marks for this written statement (see Table 8.9). The following exchange then occurred, which seems to justify the award of a mark, given her explicit linking of the greater number of throws with improved 'accuracy' (see, again, Table 8.9):

NR: OK, let's go back here then. So you think it's Shana?
Lucy: Yeh.
NR: For that and so . . .
Lucy: Because there's the most numbers of throws. The more you do the more accurate it's gonna be.

Table 8.14 Results of second attempts by fourteen children for the dice item, part a

		No second attempt even though prompted	Second attempt leaves marks unchanged	Second attempt improves marks	Total
Service-class girls	count	–	–	2	2
	row %	–	–	100	100
Service-class boys	count	1	–	3	4
	row %	25.0	–	75.0	100
Intermediate-class girls	count	–	1	1	2
	row %	–	50.0	50.0	100
Intermediate-class boys	count	–	1	1	2
	row %	–	50.0	50.0	100
Working-class girls	count	–	1	3	4
	row %	–	25.0	75.0	100
	Total	1	3	10	14
	row %	7.1	21.4	71.4	99.9

The second child, Sue, wrote in her test, thus gaining no mark: 'Shana. Because she threw the 4 faced dice more times than the rest'. In her interview she wrote, again gaining no mark: 'Shana. She threw the 4 faced dice more than the rest.' The following exchange then occurred, in which she refers explicitly to the notion of a 'fair test':

NR: OK, so over here when you say Shana, so she threw the four faced dice more than the rest so, what would that mean?
Sue: She gets a better answer.
NR: How is it a better answer?
Sue: 'Cause if you just throw it like 40 times then you don't get that much of a fair test, but throw it like how many Shana did, 250, it's a fair test.

Neither of these two children would have gained any mark on the basis of their written response, but they can, we would argue, be seen to have the required degree of mathematical understanding on the basis of their oral elaborations in the interview context.

Of course, it is not only working-class children in our sample who fall into this group. Consider John, a child who has been categorized as of intermediate social class origin (though, interestingly, this is one of the cases where we wondered whether working class might not have been more accurate, since the child owes his categorization to his father's self-employed status rather than his occupational role of chauffeur). In his test he wrote, 'Shana. Because she threw it the most times.' In his interview he wrote, 'Shana. Because she had thrown the dice the most times.' Clearly, following the marking scheme, no marks could be given for either of these responses. In his interview, this exchange occurred:

> *NR:* OK what do you think about that question?
>
> *John:* Er, that was quite easy.
>
> *NR:* Quite easy. So this first part here where you said Shana because she's thrown the dice more times. Why would that be better then?
>
> *John:* Because if you throw the dice more times you're more likely to get a fair result because of all the times you've thrown it, it lands – I can't explain it.

This appears, in its reference to the relation between more throws and a 'fair result', to meet the criteria for receiving a mark. We have here several children who know more than their initial marks would have indicated. This disparity between their knowledge and their initial mark seems to have arisen as a result of their 'choice' of a response mode that leaves too much to be filled out by the reader. Of course, it can be argued that the reader knows enough to fill in what is missing. Not only is the child aware that the marker 'knows the answer' but, in everyday language settings, much of the meaning of utterances is left to be filled in by the listener. However, in the special context of a mathematics test, different and specialized linguistic 'rules of the game' operate, and these children appear to be unaware of what these 'rules' or conventions are. As we have stressed the numbers here are small. But we would nevertheless want to argue that the relation of the 'choice' of a non-explicit response mode to social class is worthy of further research by those concerned with equity issues in assessment. A variety of arguments can be advanced for the use of items like this dice problem in mathematics tests. However, it is important that the possible unintended consequences of using such items as part of the process, which labels children as more or less 'mathematical', receive more attention. It is also of interest that the four working-class children in our small group making non-explicit responses are girls. On the other hand, in the service class, it is boys who predominate in this non-explicit group. There is no sign of any simple association of explicitness of response with sex here, though one might, of course, appear in a larger sample.

Conclusion

In this chapter we have examined, in an exploratory fashion, some ways in which two items, which demand relatively extended responses from children, might not give us an accurate insight into their mathematical understanding. It is easier to sum up our findings concerning the second item, from the KS3 tests and concerning probability, than those for the first item, concerning a survey of clothing habits whose results are presented in terms of percentages. In the case of the probability item, which asked higher-attaining children of 13–14 years of age to provide a reason for their choice of a previously selected answer from a range of five, we found, in interviewing children, that they frequently wrote down only a part of what they actually knew and understood about the textually represented dice-throwing situation. Though it should be remembered that the numbers involved are small, there was a clear tendency for working-class children to be likely to produce initially not-explicit enough responses, with four of the five amongst our group of 29 relevant interviewees doing so. Furthermore, these were all girls – though it should be noted that, amongst the service class, it was boys who were much more likely to produce such 'inappropriate' responses initially. Three of these four working-class girls improved their mark when given a chance to elaborate their initial response. Overall, amongst our total of 46 interviewees for this item, ten of the 14 children who had written initially a not explicit enough response gained the mark for the item when they were cued to elaborate their initial reason for choosing the correct name of Shana. It seems clear that, at the time of our research, and even amongst higher attaining children, there were many who were apparently unaware of the 'rules of the game' in which they were being required to participate. It may, of course, be the case that these children would readily respond to instruction from teachers, were it to be given, aimed at teaching these rules for the 'appropriate' degree of explicitness of communication in the context of mathematics tests. On the other hand, if Bernstein (1973) is correct in his claim that the social classes differ in their predisposition to use such explicit language in certain contexts, then such instruction might be more readily taken on board by some children than others. This must be a matter for further research.

Turning to the case of the KS2 item concerning a survey of the types of socks worn by boys and girls, we again found that many children, both at KS2 and KS3, offered up answers not explicit enough to gain themselves full marks. Amongst the KS2 children there was a clear tendency, especially amongst children with higher rather than lower measured 'ability', for social class to be associated with the production of a 'truncated' response to this item. The results for KS3, on the other hand, showed no clear relation to social class. However, analysis of children's interview transcripts showed that these 'truncated' responses, worth one of the three available marks, in some cases 'hid' a complete understanding, worth three marks had it been written out fully and explicitly, but in other cases 'hid' a lack of understanding. At both KS2 and KS3, when children who had provided the 'truncated' response were given a chance to elaborate it, there was, as with the dice-throwing item, improvement in marks across all three social class groups. However, in this case, because of (1) the apparently confusing request to the child 'to give as many reasons as you can' and (2) the fact that the item is set up in a way which conflicts with what children are likely to have been taught about the use of percentages in making comparisons, it is very difficult to determine, in some cases, just what a child's understanding and knowledge actually are. We think it is justified, on the basis of our evidence, to conclude that the item is not well-suited for the context of a paper and pencil test, though it might well be a useful focus of discussion in a mathematics lesson on interpreting data. We must conclude that both of these items, in interaction with some children's apparent tendency to provide only partially explicit elaborations of what they know and understand, are problematic from the perspective of validity. We cannot, on the other hand, on the basis of the findings in this chapter, offer a definite answer to the question of whether this type of item is fair across children from different social backgrounds (especially as we are not in a position to eliminate any effects of differential curriculum coverage of the mathematical knowledge demanded by these items within and between our research schools). There is though, in our opinion, enough suggestive evidence to indicate that test designers should pay more attention to the ways in which items like these might cause particular difficulties to children who, for whatever reason, are less aware than others of the rules of the assessment game as currently defined by NC marking schemes.

9

Constructing the right goal:
a comparative analysis of
two Key Stage 3 items

Same but different?

In the previous chapter we discussed a KS3 item which was taken by only a minority of our sample, those taking the February 1996 test at levels 5–7 and 6–8. We want now to look at two items taken across the three tiers 3–5, 4–6 and 5–7 of the February test. This will enable us to employ a larger sample size, but, on the other hand, will also mean that we will have to take special care over the issue of whether, in the test, children did or did not reach items positioned at different points in the different tiers of test. We want to look at these two items in some detail. They are described as having the same SoA, 3/5b, *Express a simple function symbolically*. They are originally from the same test year 1995. Taking each item, its SoA *and its associated marking scheme* into account, one item (Figure 9.1 and Table 9.1) apparently concerns the constructing and simplifying of expressions, set in the context of a problem concerning perimeters, and the other (Figure 9.2 and Table 9.2) the same tasks in the context of an imagined orchard. Originally, the perimeters item appeared in the first of the two papers taken at the three levels, and the cherries item in the second. In our single test, taken in February 1996, this order was reversed, with cherries appearing first for the child. A key difference between the items, given that both marking schemes require simplification of the constructed expressions, is that the perimeters item demands this explicitly, while the cherries item does not until the final part. In the latter case, given what the marking scheme says, the SoA is apparently seen by the test designers as *implying* simplification in earlier parts.

What is immediately of interest is how different the items seem to be, superficially, in the cognitive demands they make on the child. Notwithstanding the shared SoA, and intended level of difficulty, they seem quite different. The perimeters item provides a visual demonstration of

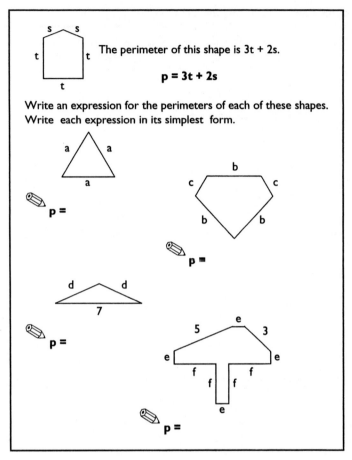

The perimeter of this shape is 3t + 2s.

p = 3t + 2s

Write an expression for the perimeters of each of these shapes. Write each expression in its simplest form.

Figure 9.1   The perimeters item (SCAA 1995b)

the derivation of the required expression in such a way that a child can succeed, at least in the first two parts of the item, by reflecting on the relation between the figure, with its labelled sides, and the given expression. In this respect, the item is rather like one from a test of intelligence. Children do not need to know the meaning of either 'perimeter' or 'expression' to proceed, though clearly knowledge of both should be of help. As far as the first two parts are concerned, they do not even need to have previous experience of simplifying expressions, as long as they follow the model provided. The child might be seen as being asked to construct expressions and then to simplify them further if necessary, but this construction – if the given example is taken as a template – seems reducible to following a provided model of a relation between terms in a labelled plane figure and terms in a given expression. There are two 's's,

Table 9.1   Marking scheme for the perimeters item (SCAA 1995b)

1m	3a	Accept alternative orders or use of multiplication sign e.g. 'a × 3'
1m	3b + 2c	'c × 2 + b3'
1m	2d + 7	'2 × d + 1 × 7'
		Accept use of capital letters e.g. '3A' '2c + B3'
		Accept use of extra zeros e.g. '3a + 00' '2d + 07'
		Do not accept use of repeated addition instead of multiplication e.g. 'a + a + a' 'b + 2b + c + c'
		Do not accept multiplication by 1 without use of a multiplication sign e.g. '2d + 17' '2d + 1.7'
		Do not accept missing addition signs e.g. '3b, 2c'
		Do not accept use of s to indicate plurality e.g. '3a's' '3bs + 2cs'
		Do not accept incorrect use of indices e.g. 'b^3 + 2c'
1m	4e + 4f + 8	Accept factorisation e.g. '4(e + f) + 8' '4(e + f + 2)'
		Accept '5 + 3' for 8

and so you write '2s', etc. Admittedly, there are still further decisions to make, e.g. about the order of '3b' and '2c' in the second part, but the item seems to ask something of the child that could be achieved partly by a process of imitation.

The cherries example seems quite different. Here the context is a verbal account rather than a labelled figure. This item, *when considered with its*

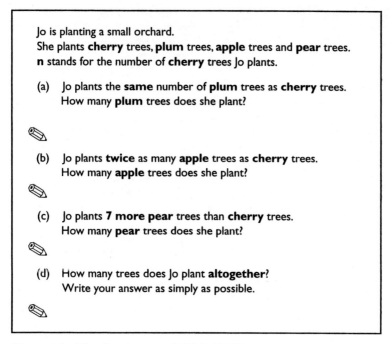

Jo is planting a small orchard.
She plants **cherry** trees, **plum** trees, **apple** trees and **pear** trees.
n stands for the number of **cherry** trees Jo plants.

(a) Jo plants the **same** number of **plum** trees as **cherry** trees.
How many **plum** trees does she plant?

(b) Jo plants **twice** as many **apple** trees as **cherry** trees.
How many **apple** trees does she plant?

(c) Jo plants **7 more pear** trees than **cherry** trees.
How many **pear** trees does she plant?

(d) How many trees does Jo plant **altogether**?
Write your answer as simply as possible.

Figure 9.2 The cherries item (SCAA 1995b)

marking scheme, seems to ask the child to construct an algebraic expression to represent a verbally described context and then to simplify it, though the task of simplification is only referred to in part d. This seems, on superficial examination, to be a more difficult task than the perimeters item. Here the 'n' has to be seen as standing for an unknown number, while in the perimeters item, it is not clear that this conceptual move is required. It might be worth noting here that the cherries item was the only one we included in our test at the request of a participating school. The head of mathematics in School E had been concerned at the problems this had caused his pupils in their statutory test in May 1995, and had asked us to include it in our research. The *implicit* nature of the cherries item's demand for the constructing and simplifying of expressions is particularly worthy of note. The text does not actually ask the child to 'write an expression' as the perimeters item does. Even if the intended task of algebraic construction is correctly recognized, it may not be obvious to the child that simplification is also required throughout. Furthermore, the item phrases its requests in the language of everyday number, asking repeatedly 'how many ... trees does she plant?'. In Newman *et al.*'s (1989) terms, this might be expected to result in many children constructing the 'wrong' goal for the problem. The problem may be recognized not as one involving general terms standing for unknown

Table 9.2 Marking scheme for the cherries item (SCAA 1995b)

1m a n	Accept equivalent expressions e.g. '1n' 'n × 1' Accept use of capital letter Accept consistent use of a single alternative term equivalent to n e.g. 'c cherry trees, c plum trees, 2c apple trees' etc.
1m b 2n	Accept equivalent expressions e.g. '2 × n' 'n2' Do not accept repeated addition instead of multiplication e.g. 'n + n' Do not accept the use of s to indicate plurality e.g. '2n's'
1m c n + 7	Accept equivalent expressions e.g. '7 + n'

2m d For 2m indicates
simplified total
e.g. '5n + 7'
    '7 + n × 5'
 	
For only 1m indicates an
equivalent expression in
which the 'n's have not
been collected
e.g. 'n + n + 2n + n + 7'
    '7 + n + n + n + n + n'
	Award only 1m for correctly simplified
	expression in which the number of cherry trees
	has been overlooked
	e.g. '4n + 7'
	    '7 + n × 4'
	
	Do not accept follow through from incorrect
	responses to earlier parts of the question.
	
	Do not accept incorrect use of indices
	e.g. 'n^5 + 7'
	
	Do not accept use of s to indicate plurality
	'5ns + 7'

numbers but as a variety of an arithmetic word problem. Indeed we shall see later that many children set themselves the radically underdetermined task of finding a concrete number of trees for part a of the cherries item.

We might add that both the marking schemes for these items employ rather contestable criteria for judging 'correctness'. In the case of cherries, for example, the answer to part b is given as '2n'. The marker is told to accept 'equivalent expressions' such as '2 × n' or 'n2', but is specifically told not to accept repeated addition as in 'n + n'. Presumably this is because the SoA is seen by the test designers as implying the simplifying of constructed expressions. However, unless it is assumed that the child should know this conventional 'rule of the game', perhaps reading it off from the original appearance of 3/5b at the right of each part of the item, it is difficult to see why 'n + n' should not be treated as a mathematically correct response. Its being ruled out seems arbitrary. At best, it is based on the assumption that the child reads the *unstated* goal of the item as intended. In the case of the cherries item, where there is no explicit reference in part b to simplest form, we have, in the marking scheme, what seems to be an excessive concern with correct form. On the other hand, in the case of perimeters, where there is an explicit reference to simplifying expressions, the child is allowed to replace lower case with upper case letters and still receive marks. Also, the marker is told, in the last part, to accept '5 + 3' for '8', hardly the simplest form. It is also ironic that the marking scheme for the cherries item rules out the use of an 's' to indicate 'plurality', but actually uses such an approach in the marking scheme instructions concerning part d. This presumably demonstrates a belief that this plural usage does unambiguously convey meaning from test designer to marker, but that it cannot be accepted as doing so from child to marker. All this serves to remind us of the considerable degree of discretion involved in determining correct responses, even in a supposedly precise discipline like mathematics, and even in the case of two items assessing identical SoAs in two comparable tests. The main concern of the head of mathematics in School E, however, seems to have been his children's difficulties in leaping the hurdle presented in the cherries item by the embedding of the task in the 'story' about an or-chard. (Note, by the way, the apparent assumption that an 'orchard' is a meaningful term for children. Again, though, the child might *surmise* it has something to do with trees. Or perhaps it is a variety of plant? One child read it out aloud as 'orchid' during his interview.)

What we want to do here is explore how children coped with mainly the initial parts of these items, in both tests and interviews. We have a sample of 421 children who took one of the three levels of the February 1996 test containing these items, and for whom we have quantitative CAT scores. However, some of these children did not reach the item. In the case of the cherries item, which appeared first, 17 of the 160 children who took tier 3–5 seem not to have attempted it. In the case of the perimeters item, which appeared a little later, 36 of these 3–5 entrants seem not to have attempted it, reflecting its position nearer the end of their paper. Also one 4–6 entrant seems not to have reached it. The 37 children who do not seem to have attempted the perimeters item include

Table 9.3 Marks gained for cherries item, part a, in the test by school and sex (maximum = 1)

School	Girls		Boys		Total	
	Mean	Count	Mean	Count	Mean	Count
School D	0.41	101	0.46	111	0.43	212
School E	0.18	40	0.16	37	0.17	77
School F	0.23	48	0.38	47	0.31	95
Total	0.31	189	0.38	195	0.35	384

the 17 who do not seem to have attempted the cherries item. We will omit them from this analysis, which will therefore only include children who seem to have reached both items in the test. This leaves us with data from 384 children. This sample includes those for whom we do not have social class data.

The marks obtained for part a of each item by these children are very different. While only 34.9 per cent of these children obtained the mark for the first part of cherries, 72.9 per cent obtained the mark for the first part of perimeters. Clearly this is a large difference, especially considering that the items are supposedly assessing the same goal (SoA) at the same level. The problem in the case of the cherries item seems to have been one, as suggested by the head of mathematics in School E, of not knowing where to begin. Of all the children we believe reached the cherries item in their test, we have analysed and coded test responses on these items of 254 and, of those we believe reached perimeters, of 241.[1] In the case of cherries, 29.9 per cent of these children left part a blank in spite of having written something in response to subsequent questions (our indicator of the item having been reached). The comparable figure for part a of perimeters is 8.3 per cent. Clearly, something about the cherries item prevented children from 'having a go' much more frequently than in the perimeters case. This is perhaps ironic given its more obviously everyday context.

Before moving on to discuss the subsample of the 384 children for whom we have social class data, we can examine, within the larger sample, the relation between performance on part a of cherries, sex and school. Table 9.3 shows that School D outperforms School F which in turn outperforms School E, and that boys do better than girls in both School D and School F, but not School E. Table 9.4, for perimeters part a, seems to show a lower degree of difference between the schools than for cherries part a. In fact, looking at a cross-tabulation of school by mark (0,1) and employing the contingency coefficient to measure the degree of association in the two cases, we obtain a higher value for cherries than for perimeters (0.215 against 0.143; both statistically significant). For sex

Table 9.4 Marks gained for perimeters item, part a, in the test by school and sex (maximum = 1)

School	Girls		Boys		Total	
	Mean	Count	Mean	Count	Mean	Count
School D	0.71	101	0.77	111	0.74	212
School E	0.68	40	0.54	37	0.61	77
School F	0.77	48	0.83	47	0.80	95
Total	0.72	189	0.74	195	0.73	384

Table 9.5 Responses to cherries item, part a, in the test by school

Response		School D	School E	School F	Total
Blank	count	31	19	26	76
	col %	31.0	26.8	31.3	29.9
Correct response	count	44	13	22	79
	col %	44.0	18.3	26.5	31.1
Incorrect answers	count	1	0	3	4
(using 'algebraic' terms)	col %	1.0	0.0	3.6	1.6
Incorrect answers (mainly	count	24	39	32	95
referring to concrete numbers)	col %	24.0	54.9	38.6	37.4
Total number of children		100	71	83	254

by mark (0,1), the two corresponding values are 0.076 for cherries and 0.021 for perimeters; neither reaching significance. We explore below what might be happening here in more detail using the sample of children for whom we have social class data. First, however, we want to explore whether there is any sex or school difference in the tendency to 'give up' on part a of cherries. For this, we return to the 254 children whose test responses we have coded for cherries. The results can be seen in Tables 9.5 and 9.6. Children in School E in fact produced fewer blank responses than those in School D or School F. What particularly characterized the responses from School E was a greater tendency to provide inappropriate answers, such as a number like 'ten' rather than a term like 'n'. This difference may reflect differences between the schools in curriculum coverage and test preparation, coupled with the different school intakes and policies over tier entry.[2] If we look at the sex differences in Table 9.6 we find that girls were more likely than boys to produce blank responses, but more or less equally likely to produce responses oriented to a concrete number.

Table 9.6   Responses to cherries item, part a, in the test by sex

Response		Girls	Boys	Total
Blank	count	42	34	76
	col %	33.9	26.2	29.9
Correct response	count	32	47	79
	col %	25.8	36.2	31.1
Incorrect answers (using 'algebraic' terms)	count	3	1	4
	col %	2.4	0.8	1.6
Incorrect answers (mainly referring to	count	47	48	95
concrete numbers)	col %	37.9	36.9	37.4
Total number of children		124	130	254

Table 9.7   Marks gained for cherries item, part a, in the test by social class and sex (maximum = 1)

Social class	Girls		Boys		Total	
	Mean	Count	Mean	Count	Mean	Count
Service	0.30	20	0.44	36	0.39	56
Intermediate	0.34	32	0.48	27	0.41	59
Working	0.20	59	0.29	49	0.24	108
Total	0.26	111	0.38	112	0.32	223

We now consider the test performance on part a of these two items for the subsample of the 384 for whom we have social class data. There are 223 children in this sample. What is the relation between social class, sex and performance? We can see from Tables 9.7 and 9.8 that these 223 children found the cherries item much more difficult in the test than they found the perimeters item. Working-class children had a very low rate of success on the cherries item in relation to their success on the perimeters item. Also, the cherries item seems to have been found relatively more difficult by girls in relation to boys than the perimeters item. Whatever it is about this item that makes it difficult, it seems to be associated with social class and sex (though we should note that working-class girls have the lowest mean scores on both items). However, there are clearly other possible factors to examine here, including school and measured 'ability'.

In fact, looking at a cross-tabulation of social class by mark (0,1) and employing the contingency coefficient to measure the degree of association in the two cases, we obtain a higher value for cherries than for perimeters (0.168 against 0.09; the first alone statistically significant). For sex

Table 9.8 Marks gained for perimeters item, part a, in the test by social class and sex (maximum = 1)

| Social class | Girls | | Boys | | Total | |
	Mean	Count	Mean	Count	Mean	Count
Service	0.75	20	0.81	36	0.79	56
Intermediate	0.81	32	0.74	27	0.78	59
Working	0.66	59	0.76	49	0.70	108
Total	0.72	111	0.77	112	0.75	223

by mark (0,1), the two corresponding values are 0.13 for cherries and 0.054 for perimeters; neither reaching significance (though the first is just on the boundary at p = 0.0501). For school by mark (0,1), the two corresponding values are 0.187 for cherries and 0.161 for perimeters; the first reaches significance and the second is very near the boundary at p = 0.052. There is also a higher association between quantitative CAT and cherries than between quantitative CAT and perimeters. Employing *ETA* as our statistic, we obtain values of 0.385 and 0.358 respectively, both significant. If we use a three-way categorical breakdown of quantitative CAT, we obtain values for the contingency coefficient for CAT by mark (0,1) of 0.361 for cherries and 0.338 for perimeters, both significant. This set of relations is clearly difficult to interpret, as a result of the strong associations between social class and 'ability', and school and social class, in particular. However, it is interesting to note that it is in the case of social class that one item falls each side of statistical significance, lending some support to the idea that these items do behave differently with respect to social class.

It is possible to obtain some further idea of whether social class is important independently of measured 'ability' (which, it will be recalled, we argued in Chapter 2 is not likely to be measurable completely independently of social class) by examining the associations between marks on the two items and social class within two 'ability' groupings, selected to divide the 223 children into approximate halves. None of the four values reach statistical significance (Table 9.9). However, even with only a twofold division, the procedures for calculating significance become unreliable as a result of small expected values in some cells of the tables of social class by mark by CAT score, and we therefore discuss the pattern of the contingency coefficients themselves in an exploratory manner here. The results (Table 9.9) show that, for both items, the largest social class by mark associations are for the higher 'ability' children. In fact, in the case of cherries, it is the relative failure of higher 'ability' working-class children on this item relative to others in this 'ability' group that

Table 9.9 Mark by social class contingency coefficients for part a of cherries and perimeters items

Social class by mark (0,1)	Cherries part a	Perimeters part a	n
Quantitative 'ability': lower half	0.098 ns	0.133 ns	111
Quantitative 'ability': higher half	0.142 ns	0.143 ns	112
Total	0.168 s	0.090 ns	223

ns, not significant
s, significant

Table 9.10 Mark by sex contingency coefficients for part a of cherries and perimeters items

Sex by mark (0,1)	Cherries part a	Perimeters part a	n
Quantitative 'ability': lower half	0.281 s	0.042 ns	111
Quantitative 'ability': higher half	0.014 ns	0.027 ns	112
Total	0.130 (p = 0.0501)	0.054 ns	223

ns, not significant
s, significant

produces the pattern we have been discussing. While 53 per cent of both service- and intermediate-class higher 'ability' children gain the mark for cherries part a, only 38 per cent of the corresponding working-class children do so. It is also interesting to note how in Table 9.9 the associations found within the 'ability' levels for the perimeters item are reduced when the whole sample is considered together. This results from the service-class children being the best performers on perimeters part a in the lower 'ability' group, but the worst performers in the higher 'ability' group. If we turn to sex (Table 9.10), whose association with the cherries mark (0,1) for the 223 children taken as a whole is on the conventional boundary of significance (p = 0.0501), we find that it is for the lower 'ability' children that sex is most strongly, and significantly, related to achievement on cherries part a.

It is possible to approach this pattern of results from the other direction. What is the relation between CAT score and mark, for the two items, across the six sex by social class groups? We will use the coefficient of correlation ETA here. The majority of the component associations in Table 9.11 are significant. There are some notable exceptions, however. The lowest associations between measured 'ability' and mark for the cherries item are those for intermediate- and working-class boys, both non-significant. The figure for working-class girls is also markedly lower

Table 9.11 *ETA* for quantitative 'ability' and mark (0,1) by social class and sex for cherries and perimeters items

'Ability' by mark (0,1)	ETA cherries part a	ETA perimeters part a	Mean CAT	n
Service-class girls	0.407 ns (p = 0.075)	0.262 ns	99.15	20
Service-class boys	0.580 s	0.282 ns (p = 0.096)	96.03	36
Intermediate-class girls	0.646 s	0.358 s	93.94	32
Intermediate-class boys	0.001 ns	0.451 s	97.63	27
Working-class girls	0.366 s	0.365 s	87.76	59
Working-class boys	0.191 ns	0.352 s	93.24	49
Total	0.385 s	0.358 s	93.40	223

ns, not significant
s, significant

Table 9.12 *ETA* for quantitative 'ability' and mark (0,1) by social class for cherries and perimeters items

'Ability' by mark (0,1)	ETA cherries part a	ETA perimeters part a	Mean 'ability'	n
Service class	0.500 s	0.260 ns (p = 0.053)	97.14	56
Intermediate class	0.317 s	0.387 s	95.63	59
Working class	0.302 s	0.371 s	90.25	108
Total	0.385 s	0.358 s	93.40	223

ns, not significant
s, significant

than those for service-class girls and boys and intermediate-class girls. If we look at the comparable figures for social class alone,[3] we find it is the working-class children who have the lowest value for cherries (Table 9.12). This might be open to the interpretation that it is the difficulty of the item, coupled with working-class pupils' lower mean 'ability', which produces the lower association (via restriction of variance in the distribution of marks). The same argument, in reverse, could be suggested as an explanation for the lower service-class association, in relation to other children, for the perimeters item (Table 9.12). This is, however, merely a technical 'explanation'. It still begs the issue of what it is that makes the items differentially difficult, and whether this difference might be related to social class. It is this issue to which we turn now.

Table 9.13 *ETA for quantitative 'ability' and mark (0,1) by sex for cherries and perimeters items*

'Ability' by mark (0,1)	ETA cherries part a	ETA perimeters part a	Mean 'ability'	n
Girls	0.453 s	0.360 s	91.59	111
Boys	0.299 s	0.347 s	95.20	112
Total	0.385 s	0.358 s	93.40	223

s, significant

First of all, for the 107 children who we believe reached both items in their test and who were subsequently interviewed, what was the relation between their performance on the test and the interview for the two items?[4] In the case of cherries, of the 35 who succeeded in the test on part a, 30 succeeded in the interview. A further 19 children, who had not succeeded in the test, succeeded in the interview. In the case of perimeters, of the 82 who succeeded in part a on the test, 78 succeeded in the interview. A further 17 children, who had not succeeded in the test, succeeded in the interview. The additional successes perhaps reflect the fact that, in the interview, children were encouraged to undertake the item rather than give up when it first puzzled them. What we do now is look at the children's initial responses to these two items, mainly in the interviews. This should provide some clues as to why cherries is more difficult than perimeters and, possibly, why the former item is more social class/sex differentiating than the latter item. We will begin by considering some examples of how those children who constructed the cherries item initially as one concerning the finding of a concrete number coped with the problem of finding the 'missing' number. There are a variety of approaches available to such children, ranging from guessing through to some fairly complex, if idiosyncratic, strategies. Robert, an intermediate-class boy with a CAT score of 102, guesses that 'n' equals 25:

NR: OK, so what about this question?
Robert: It was a bit hard up here 'cos – hard to understand sort of.
NR: So you've said that n equals 25.
Robert: Yeh.
NR: OK, so where did you get that from then?
Robert: I made it up.
NR: You just made . . .
Robert: 'Cos I can't see anything else . . .
NR: OK.
Robert: . . . to say what number it stands for.

On the other hand, Robert had no problem producing four correct answers for the perimeters item. In that case, the researcher asked him, when he had finished, to explain his '2d + 7' for part c. He seems to have used the template provided by the example to solve the problem.

NR: . . . OK, what do you think about that question then?
Robert: Quite easy.
NR: Quite an easy one.
Robert: Mm.
NR: How did you do that one there then?
Robert: Well there's two 'd's and I put two 'd's plus the 7 'coz it's on its own.
NR: OK, and did you look at this one up here to help you?
Robert: Yeh.
NR: Would you have known how to do it without looking at this, was it something you've done before?
Robert: I haven't done it before, I don't think.
NR: No, so you used the way that they did this to help you?
Robert: Yeh.
NR: But you thought that was quite easy?
Robert: Yeh.

Gill, a working-class girl with a CAT score of 96, tried yet another way to make sense of the cherries dilemma. In the test she had written 'nine' for part a, '18' for part b, '9+7   16' for part c, and '9+18+16   53 trees' for part d. In the interview, she wrote, initially, '9 plum' for part a, and continued in this fashion for the other parts. It becomes clear in her interview, that 'nine' was not a meaningless choice, at least from her perspective:

NR: OK so, right how have you done this one then?
Gill: In the test before we had done it, we hadn't done the 'n' bit, so in the test I just guessed that it was nine.
NR: OK so, where did you guess nine from then?
Gill: From the 'n', I thought that the 'n' standed for nine because it was the beginning of the number.
NR: Sorry what? 'n' was nine because?
Gill: It was the beginning letter of the number.
NR: Beginning? Oh right I see, 'n' stands for the number nine written out. OK, right, and so what did you just, you guessed at that or?
Gill: Yeah.

This may seem a strange approach to take. Certainly the interviewer seemed surprised. However, as we argued above, if the problem is interpreted as requiring a concrete solution, some way out of its radically underdetermined nature is required. Children have to use their imagination. They have to find a way of making sense of the apparently ill-structured problem, which results from their belief that a concrete number is required. Gill's 'solution' allows her to proceed, which is, of course, a typical background goal in the situation of a test or interview comprising serially presented items. Here is another example, perhaps showing some influence of work the child may well have done in the past on counting letters in texts as part of producing a frequency count, or perhaps similar work on code breaking:

NR: What do you think about this question?
Emma: Didn't really understand it at first.
NR: Didn't understand it at first, and then, what made you understand it?
Emma: When I've, I read that through a few times . . . [tape ends and is turned over] . . . and it says the 'n' stands for the number of cherry trees that Jo planted, and then I thought, count how many 'n's' there are in that sentence, and I counted four, and then it says there's twice as many apples as the cherry trees, so I just doubled the four and made it 8, and then Jo plants 7 pear trees, more than cherry trees, so 4 and 7 equals 11, and then I added all of that together to make 23.
NR: So, 'n' stands for the number of cherry trees, so you looked for 'n's' in this sentence . . .
Emma: Yeah.
NR: 'Cause, what, you just didn't know what it was asking for, so you thought – what did you think?
Emma: I thought well it might mean that, I don't think it does but I thought it might mean that.
NR: Was that a hard question or an easy one?
Emma: Quite easy, but I didn't understand it until I read that through a few times.
NR: So once you understood it, it was quite easy then really?
Emma: Yeah.

Given that Emma, an intermediate-class girl with a CAT score of 98, seems far from convinced about the correctness of her approach, her willingness to employ it suggests she does not expect to find much meaning in mathematics test items, but that an overriding goal is to complete the item and move on. She gained marks for the first two parts of the perimeters item in the test, and the first three parts in the interview, though only after the question had been read through and a cue given by the interviewer to follow the example. Another idiosyncratic approach was taken by Joe, a service-class boy with a CAT of 86, after he had initially announced he did not 'get' the problem but was encouraged by the interviewer to think further about it. He began by remembering this had been a problem in the test (where he had left the item blank):

Joe: I remember that.

NR: You remember that one?

Joe: Yeah. I don't even get this one.

NR: You don't get it?

Joe: My friend Sam didn't get it as well.

NR: Let's have a look at it. It says, Jo's planting a small orchard, she plants cherry trees, plum trees, apple trees and pear trees.

Joe: Yeah.

NR: Alright – n stands for the number of cherry trees Jo plants. So Jo plants the same number of plum trees as cherry trees.

Joe: Ah.

NR: Have you got any ideas?

Joe: No.

NR: No? What is it that's confusing you then?

Joe: Well I just don't understand how I'm supposed to find out how many trees she planted, plum trees.

NR: It says n stands for the number of cherry trees, right, so n stands for the number of cherry trees, and so Jo plants the same number of plum trees as cherry trees.

Joe: Where 'n' stands for the number, ah yeah, 'n' stands for, what does it say?

NR: There's no number is there? Are you looking for a number?

Joe: Yeah. Well, 15? . . . Thirteen, it could be.

NR: So how have you got 13?

Joe: Well, the alphabet, and the thirteenth letter in the alphabet, may be it's the 13 like that, or.

NR: So you want a number then do you?

Joe: What?

NR: You're looking for a number?

Joe: Yeah, I wouldn't mind a number!

Joe clearly is searching for a concrete number. Given the absence of 'appropriate' conditions or constraints in the text that would generate such a number, and under pressure from the interviewer to produce a response, he follows Emma in generating a method which enables the resolution of this difficulty. In the test, apparently similarly confused, but without the pressure from the interviewer, he had left the item blank. He apparently had experienced no similar problem in getting started on the perimeters item where, in both the test and interview, he gained marks for parts a and b.

Jenny, a working-class girl with a CAT of 91, chose to use a numeric approach, even though she seems to have been aware of the nature of 'n'.

She argues that she chose 'one' for a possible value of 'n' to make the arithmetic easier. She justifies this on the seemingly rational grounds that 'n' can stand for anything! Then, challenged by the researcher to consider another approach, she offers, seemingly with no great enthusiasm, 'n' as a possible answer. Whether, unconsciously, she had been dragged away from this initially by 'how many . . . ?' is impossible to decide from the transcript, but it seems more likely that she had, in the absence of any instructions to leave the answer in terms of 'n', employed her belief that 'n' 'could stand for anything' to allow a move to use a simple number:

MD: OK, alright, so explain to me part (a) of question 10, how did you get to that answer?

Jenny: Well, 'n' is supposed to stand for any number you like.

MD: OK.

Jenny: So I just put one there.

MD: So does anybody know that 'n' stands for one?

Jenny: [no reply]

MD: Does everybody know that?

Jenny: Well, it doesn't actually have to stand for one it could stand for anything.

MD: OK, so why have you chosen one?

Jenny: It would be easier to add up at the end.

MD: OK, and you wanted to put it into numbers.

Jenny: Mm.

MD: OK, go on then, so you did part one and you decided that 'n' stands for one.

Jenny: Mm.

MD: Do you think you should have written it?

Jenny: [inaudible]

MD: Do you, do you think you should have written, like, 'n' – if 'n' equals one, could you have done it without using the numbers?

Jenny: Don't really know.

MD: No, OK, if you had to do it without using the numbers, could you explain what happens in the first one, Jo plants the same number of plum as cherry trees, how many plum trees does she plant?

Jenny: Do I do it without any numbers?

MD: Mm.

Jenny: What, just using the 'n'.

MD: Mm.

Jenny: Well, I suppose you could actually.

MD: What could you write there? What would you write for the first one then if you could – Jo plants the same number of

> plum trees as cherry trees, how many plum trees does she plant?
>
> *Jenny:* I suppose you'd just put 'n' down or something.

These examples make it clear what made the cherries item difficult for many children. To reiterate, it was possible to construct a goal for this problem, because of the phrase 'how many . . . trees did she plant?', which concerned finding a concrete number. Such a goal is, after all, common enough in school mathematics to make this readily believable. Once such a goal has been constructed, there follows a search for a way of choosing a number that makes some sense to the child and allows him or her to move to the next item.

There was, however, another way of apparently resolving the dilemma, and one which perhaps can be seen as closer to what the test designers seem to have intended. In his test response, one child wrote, for cherries part a, 'however many cherry trees are planted' rather than guess a number. This was an approach used by a few children. Rachel, for example, an intermediate-class girl with a CAT of 87 wrote as her initial interview response 'the same amount as cherry trees'. For part b, she wrote, 'twice as many'. It is instructive to consider whether this apparently 'circular' response is worthy of a mark. The mark scheme instructs the marker to award a mark for part a for 'n', but to accept 'equivalent expressions' such as '1n' or 'n × 1'. The child is also allowed to substitute a term such as 'c' for 'n', if he or she uses the 'c' consistently throughout the four parts. We have interpreted the marking scheme as not allowing responses like 'the same amount as cherry trees' since all the examples given use some term like 'n' or 'c' and, in the context of the SoA, *Express a simple function symbolically*, we are fairly confident that this is what was intended. Reflecting on our decision, the 'obviousness' of ruling Rachel's response to be incorrect begins to disappear. The child is asked to find the number of plum trees. Unless he or she interprets this request within the framework of a discipline that concerns 'propositions about any things or about some things, without specification of definite particular things' (Whitehead 1911/48: 7), i.e. as a problem in 'pure mathematics' in spite of the setting, then he or she is quite likely to want to find an answer that goes beyond the given information rather than merely re-codes it from everyday English to a language comprising numbers, arithmetic operators and, crucially, 'n'. From this 'realistic' perspective, 'n' conveys no more – and perhaps less – information than 'the same amount as cherry trees'. Similarly, we can ask whether '2n' conveys more information than 'twice as many' as cherry trees. Given that the problem makes no explicit reference to using 'n' in the answer, it is not clear why these responses should be ruled to be incorrect, other than in terms of conventional rules of the mathematical game. Children like Rachel seem to either lack

Table 9.14 Nature of response to cherries item, part a, by social class and sex in the test context

Response		Service-class girls	Service-class boys	Intermediate-class girls	Intermediate-class boys	Working-class girls	Working-class boys	Total
Uncoded	count	0	0	0	0	2	2	4
	col %	0	0	0	0	3.4	4.1	1.8
Blank	count	7	9	10	5	20	12	63
	col %	35.0	25.0	31.3	18.5	33.9	24.5	28.3
Correct response	count	6	16	11	12	12	14	71
	col %	30.0	44.4	34.4	44.4	20.3	28.6	31.8
Incorrect answers (using 'algebraic' terms)	count	1	1	0	0	1	0	3
	col %	5.0	2.8	0	0	1.7	0	1.3
Incorrect answers (mainly concrete numbers)	count	6	10	11	10	24	21	82
	col %	30.0	27.8	34.4	37.0	40.7	42.9	36.8
Total number of children		20	36	32	27	59	49	223

knowledge of these rules or fail to see this as a place to apply what knowledge of them they do have. They are failing to recognize the embedded piece of algebra in the noise of the tree-planting setting. And, who, after all, would plant 'n' trees?

We previously noted that social class and sex differences in marks obtained in the test context were greater in the case of cherries part a than in perimeters part a. How might these differences in marks be related to the pattern of responses by social class and sex? If, for a moment, we return to the 223 children for whom we have social class information, we find that there is a tendency for working-class children, both boys and girls, to produce 'non-algebraic' answers (like '7', '25') to part a of cherries in the test setting more frequently than children from both of the other two social class groupings, and for intermediate-class children, both boys and girls, to be more likely to do so than service-class children (Table 9.14). It seems clear that the reading of this item as a request for a concrete number was a contributory factor in the production of failure. It also seems that such readings were differentially distributed by social class and that these readings were therefore one contributory factor in the production of social class differences on this item. Turning to sex, across each of the three social class groupings, girls were considerably more likely than boys to leave the item blank (remember, these are children who we believe reached the item in the test). Of course, whether these blanks in the test result from failures to determine a concrete number believed to be needed or from other ways of reading the item we can not be sure. Considering just the 102 of the 223 children who were later interviewed, we find that, in the test, girls in this subsample were more likely to produce blank responses (28.3 per cent against 24.5 per cent for boys). However, in the interview, this is reversed, with boys producing a greater percentage of blanks (40.8 per cent against 28.3 per cent for girls). This increase in blank responses from the boys between the test and interview contexts holds, by the way, for all three interviewers, two female and one male, taken separately. It seems that boys were less willing to take a chance on being wrong on this item in the interview context than in the test situation. Girls, on the other hand, produce the same percentage of blanks in both contexts, though it should be noted that these are not precisely the same girls in both contexts (ten of the 15 produce blanks in both).

Conclusion

Our results for the cherries item, against the background of the perimeters item, allow several points to be made. First of all, as with other items we have discussed, the importance of item design at the level of phrasing is clearly a critical issue. Unless the intention is to deliberately distract the test-taker from constructing the goal the test designer has in mind, then phrasing that points away from the intended goal needs to be more carefully avoided. Here the phrase 'how many . . . trees does she plant?', coupled with the embedding of the questions about 'n' in a story about tree-planting, seems to have pulled many children away from being able to show whether they could or could not construct and simplify expressions.

What we seem to have, in the case of the cherries item, is an item causing children to fail to recognize the goals that they were required to address, those of constructing and simplifying expressions. Our data suggest that, in the context of the non-explicitness of the relation between the item's surface features and the SoA *express a simple function symbolically* with its apparent additional but largely implicit requirement of simplification, working-class children in particular read the item as requiring a concrete number as the answer. Once they had made this 'mistake', children were more or less condemned to gain no marks for this item. What, in summary, the item seems to have been testing, as well as the skill of constructing and simplifying expressions, is the capacity to recognize a test designer's intentions when these are well-hidden within the noise of an everyday context. The problem is compounded by the fact that answers not employing 'n' – such as 'the same amount as cherries' – seem, on the face of it, 'rational' responses. Again, we see that what is apparently 'obvious' to test designers is far from obvious to 13–14-year-old children. Furthermore, on the side of the children, this sense of the 'obvious' is differentially distributed by social class. The result in the case of cherries is an item that clearly cannot be said to validly assess its associated SoA. The SoA refers to 'a simple function'. However, the amount of construct-irrelevant noise in the item seems to override the simplicity of the underlying function. Much more is being demanded of the child than the SoA states. Furthermore, compared with the perimeters item, the cherries item in the test context can be seen to produce greater social class and sex differentiation. This seems possibly to have resulted from working-class children's greater tendency to read the item as requiring a number as its solution, and from girls' greater tendency to leave the item blank. It seems likely, given children's apparent difficulties in constructing the same goal as that intended by the test designers, that these social class and sex differences overestimate the underlying differences in the capacity of children from these groups to reason about simple functions and expressions.

The item we have used for comparison also included a context, that of perimeters, but it seems that this did not provide the same distractions for the children from finding the intended goal. However, it is worth stressing that an alternative goal to that *apparently* intended at the start of the item – the alternative of following the template provided rather than using a definitional knowledge of perimeters – could gain the child some marks in the perimeters case, as the following example suggests (see also the earlier case of Robert):

> Sarah: Done it.
>
> MD: OK, explain to me how you got that one?
>
> Sarah: Um 'cos in the example it's got '3t's and two 's's so I done the same, two 'd' plus 7.
>
> MD: OK, what about here?
>
> Sarah: I done the same as well, added them the 'f's up make four and the 'e's make four and the three plus 5.

There is no apparent reference to perimeters, whether as a word or a concept. The goal of the perimeters item, for this child, has been constructed as something akin to a traditional analogies item from an intelligence test.

Of course, the designers of these items might well respond to our analysis of the cherries item in particular by claiming that they were interested precisely in children's ability to model an 'everyday' situation algebraically. However, this is certainly not the goal set out in the SoA associated with the cherries item – *express a simple function symbolically*. This SoA would seem to involve no necessary reference to an 'everyday' context. Furthermore, children, especially from working-class backgrounds, frequently failed to infer the intended goal of the cherries item. This finding suggests that short items of this nature in timed paper and pencil tests are not likely, unless children are given much more help in learning the rules of this game, to prove satisfactory routes to the valid and fair assessment of such goals.

Notes

1 These children were selected on the basis of the existence of social class information and/or being interviewees. For some of these, we do not have CAT data.
2 Entry policies for tiers of the tests in February 1996 were very similar across the schools to those for the May 1996 test. Relative to quantitative CAT score, School D entered children for lower tiers than School E, with School F falling between the two.
3 The comparable breakdown for sex is shown in Table 9.13.
4 This 107 includes two children for whom we have no quantitative CAT score.

10   Conclusions and reflections

English school mathematics and its assessment

We noted in Chapter 1 that 'school mathematics' is not some fixed and unchanging entity against which children's 'mathematical' knowledge and understanding can be straightforwardly measured and compared over periods of time. Neither is it the case that changes in school mathematics – or in school subjects in general – simply reflect changes in mathematical knowledge in élite disciplinary settings outside of the schools (Bernstein 1996). In the case of mathematics in England, debates within and about the subject in the late 1970s and early 1980s had resulted in a preference – at least at the level of rhetoric – for an approach in schools that favoured 'relevance', 'applications' and a relatively active learner (Cockcroft 1982; Cooper 1985a, 1994a). As a result of the subsequent introduction of the National Curriculum in the late 1980s, and the shift within NC assessment procedures to a primary emphasis on group testing via paper and pencil tests, a situation had arisen by the early 1990s in which children's knowledge and understanding were being assessed primarily by 'realistically' contextualized items in two timed test papers given at several points in their school career. Furthermore, as a result of an ever increasing degree of publication of children's and schools' performances in 'league tables', these assessments were 'high stakes' indeed.

The programme of research reported in this book has focused on a variety of ways in which this form of measurement of children's knowledge and understanding of mathematics might be less than valid. However, we have attempted to use the opportunity provided by this primary research focus also to address a set of more general, but related issues. These include differences between children in their predisposition to import their everyday knowledge and experience into the context of problem-solving in school mathematics, differences between children in their predisposition to use 'appropriately' explicit linguistic forms in the same contexts, and also several problems concerning selection within schools – but especially those arising from the requirement for secondary schools to enter children, at 13–14 years of age, for a particular level of a hierarchically ordered set of paper and pencil tests.

Our general approach

Throughout the research and the book itself we have analysed our data on children's interpretations of, and performance in, the National Curriculum mathematics tests in terms of their social class backgrounds, sex and, much of the time, their measured 'ability'. We have had two main reasons for taking this approach. First of all, much – though not all – of the argument for the use of a 'realistic' approach within school mathematics education seems to us to have been based as much on a general sense of what might plausibly 'work' with children as a whole, or particular groups of children, as on any reference to evidence concerning what actually 'works'. This becomes a particularly worrying problem when the assessment of children's knowledge and understanding depends on their understanding of the peculiar 'rules of the game' surrounding the interpretation and use of such 'realistic' items in school (see Chapter 3). Given that there is research suggesting that working-class children (Holland 1981) and girls (Boaler 1994) might be expected to experience greater problems than other children in responding 'appropriately' to 'realistic' problems, as well as a more general sociological tradition of great potential relevance (Bourdieu 1986; Bernstein 1996), we considered it important to analyse children's responses in terms of these social categories. Part of our rationale for this approach to our research, then, concerns equity and fairness issues (Darling-Hammond 1994). What might be the unintended consequences – the perverse effects – of assessing children largely via the use of 'realistic' items?

There is, however, a second reason for our analysing the data in this way. Much of the recent debate in mathematics education on problem-solving has stressed situational factors rather than what children bring to situations as a consequence of their previous experience in and out of school (for one recent view of the debates in this area, see Kirshner and Whitson 1998). At times, when reading the mathematics education research literature, one might be forgiven for wondering whether cultural experience leaves any traces at all! There are, of course, notable exceptions. Various attempts have been made to bring together individual agency and social structure in the analysis of individuals' 'mathematical' activity (e.g. Lave 1988 who makes some use of Bourdieu's work; and, from an alternative perspective, Walkerdine 1988). However, perhaps partly because of concerns about the dangers of 'essentialist' thinking (Sayer

1997), there has been a dearth of research in mathematics education using such categories as social class (Apple 1995a, 1995b). We wished in this research to make some contribution to addressing both the general problem of how previous socio-cultural experience might interact with mathematical problem solving as well as the more specific problem of whether cultural differences associated with social class and/or sex interact to inform children's sense-making when they are confronted by 'realistic' NC items.

Methods

In order to address these issues, we have collected data from two main settings for children of both 10–11 and 13–14 years of age from, respectively, three primary and three secondary schools. First of all, we have data on children's test performances across a range of 'realistic' and 'non-realistic' problems collected as children undertook three test papers comprising NC items. Two of these three papers were the statutory tests taken by children in May 1996. The other paper, designed by us but comprising NC items from previous years, was taken by the children at the beginning of 1996. Second, we have collected data for a subset of the test items in this latter test in the context of individual interviews in which children were asked to attempt their solutions in the presence of one or other of the researchers. In this context children were asked to offer accounts of their chosen approach and reasons for their choice of responses. They were also, in the case of some items, allowed and/or encouraged to reconsider their initial response. This collection of data on responses from the two settings has allowed us to compare and contrast, for a subset of 'realistic' items, the measure of children's mathematical knowledge and understanding derived from the group testing context – the context in which their performance is officially measured – with what we can learn about their understanding and knowledge from the interview. In order to enable us to analyse possible effects of social class, gender and school, we have also recorded, wherever possible, each parent's current or most recent occupation and status at work, as well as each child's sex and school. We have also collected data from the schools on children's measured 'ability'. Social class and 'ability' are difficult concepts to define and operationalize. The reader should carefully ponder the implications of this when considering each or any of our results (see Chapter 2).

We believe strongly that the results of educational research, including our own, should be read critically. We have already noted that the nature of some of our key organizing categories – especially social class and 'ability', is, and will remain, contestable. Before we summarize some of our findings and consider their implications, a variety of other issues readers should bear in mind should also be noted. First, it should be remembered that we have no data, other than what the children have said to us in interview, on children's cognitive activities outside of school. For example, when we refer to familial cultural and cognitive differences between children from different social class backgrounds as explanations of our findings, we are engaging in an inferential process that links the observed ways in which children respond to 'realistic' problems in the test and interview contexts with the accounts that writers such as Bernstein and Bourdieu have previously produced about the relations between the social division of labour and cultural orientations. We clearly consider the resulting explanations of children's differentiated ways of responding to be plausible or better, but the nature of our reasoning from our data on the one hand, and others' theoretical and empirical work on the other, should be noted. Second, our sample is from just one part of one region of England, and, given our orientating position concerning the potential importance of cultural differences in accounting for children's responses to 'realistic' items in particular, we should certainly point out that we cannot be sure that our findings would be reproduced were similar research to be carried out elsewhere. On the other hand, given the general importance of social class in constraining and enabling children's cultural development, we would expect to find similar social class effects elsewhere. We also, with hindsight, regret not having been able to include some children who attend private schools in our analyses. It is also the case that, in some of our analyses, cell sizes become fairly small and, in these particular cases, we would ask readers to regard our findings as worthy of further investigation rather than as definitive. These 'problems' arise from our decision to undertake a large number of in-depth interviews with children (we have carried out more than 250) rather than expand our test sample size by concentrating on the less labour intensive collection of group test data. Given our interest in the processes of interpretation children undertake when faced with test items, we have chosen to prioritize qualitative rather than quantitative data collection – though often we have analysed the resulting qualitative data in a quantitative fashion. Third, and linked to these points, it is also the case that we have not been able to undertake in-depth research into pedagogical differences between the schools in our sample. While we have attempted to control for such effects by considering school differences at various points in our analyses, this is again a point the careful reader should bear in mind. Lastly, it should be noted that, insofar as part of the children's understanding of these forms of assessment derives from their teachers' and perhaps their parents' own understanding of what is required by the current assessment regime in England, it is quite possible that findings of future research, even if undertaken in the same schools, would be different as a result of learning and changed pedagogic behaviour on the part of these adults (cf. Bhaskar 1979 and Lieberson 1985 on the status of laws, and their time-space dependence, in the social sciences). Having considered some of the aspects of this research, which might be relevant to assessments of its internal and external validity, we now summarize some of the findings.

Key findings and some implications

Before we turn to the empirical findings of our research, we should recall that the quality of several of the items we have described in this book, and their associated marking schemes, might be seen as less than satisfactory. In some cases, this is a matter of judgement about the relation of mathematics and the 'real', as in the case of the lift and basketball items described in Chapter 3 and the items concerning tree-measuring and tennis competitions in Chapter 4 (for other examples, see Cooper 1992, 1994b). In these cases, there is clearly a need for further debate about the ways in which, and the extent to which, 'realistic' considerations should be brought to bear in the process of solving such problems. In other cases, however, it can be argued that there are problems with the mathematical judgements *per se* implicit in the answers required by the marking schemes. In the case of the traffic item discussed in Chapters 4 and 6, for example, how it is possible, from the point of view of the mathematics of probability, to rule in and out particular responses (Cooper 1998a)? Similarly, given that no general request for simplification is expressed in the text of the cherries item discussed in Chapter 9, why does the marking scheme rule out 'n + n' as a way of expressing the 'correct answer' of '2n'? These peculiarities of NC marking rubrics have puzzled us at various times. Occasionally, in the case of more complex questions, they have caused us considerable difficulty. In fact, in the case of one KS2 item (that of a question concerning probability set in the context of estimating who might answer the telephone; SCAA 1995a), we abandoned our intention to use the item in our analysis because the three researchers involved could not agree a common interpretation of the marking rubric provided! We know that these items were often produced to tight deadlines, and in a context of a rapidly changing climate of opinion over the nature of NC assessment, but, having recognized these factors, we must nevertheless note these apparent weaknesses of design.

Key Stage 2

We began our analysis of children's responses to the KS2 items by presenting case studies of two children responding to a range of 'realistic'

NC test items, setting our account against the background of the work of Bernstein and Bourdieu on social class and cultural orientations (Chapter 4). Having established, at the level of a working hypothesis, that some children might experience a particular type of difficulty in negotiating the boundary between mathematical knowledge and extra-school everyday experience – and that these children might tend to be from working-class families – we turned in Chapter 5 to a statistical analysis of children's relative performances on 'realistic' and 'esoteric' items (see p. 84 for definitions). Having begun by rehearsing some of the difficulties associated with measuring and reporting children's and schools' performances through the use of a restricted range of NC levels of achievement, we then showed that there are, in our sample, social class differences in children's relative achievement on these two broad classes of test items. Our key finding is that, compared with service-class children, working- and intermediate-class children perform less well on 'realistic' items in comparison with 'esoteric' items. We have attempted to control for a variety of other possible explanations of this apparent effect of item type in interaction with social class, including children's 'ability', the wordiness of items, the difficulty level of items and, employing NC attainment targets, the mathematical topic being addressed. The effect of the interaction of social class with item type survives, though it is sometimes reduced. We have shown, in a simulation of a selection process employing different mixes of 'realistic' and 'esoteric' items, that the effect is large enough potentially to make a considerable difference to children's futures. We have found similar, though smaller, differences between the sexes, with boys performing better than girls on 'realistic' items in comparison with 'esoteric' items. In fact, within our six social class with sex combinations, it is the comparison of service-class boys with working-class girls that produces the largest difference in relative performance on the two broad item types (Table 5.21). However, the number of working-class girls is small, and this finding should be treated with caution. We have also stressed that these differences between the social classes and the smaller ones between the sexes are not differences of kind, but rather of degree. Figure 5.6, which shows the distribution of one of our key indicators within and between our social class groups, makes this clear.

The results of Chapters 4 and 5 taken together suggest that we do need to understand more about the ways children interpret and respond to 'realistic' items in particular. In Chapter 6 we began to address this issue by examining in some depth children's responses to two contrasting 'realistic' items, one concerning a traffic survey and one a tennis competition. Here we concentrated on whether children responded in an 'esoteric' or a 'realistic' manner to the items and the contrasting consequences of their 'choice' of response to each item. Children responding 'realistically' here are defined as those who draw on their extra-school everyday knowledge when addressing the test items. We found, in the case of both items, a clear relation between the child's social class background and mode of response. There was also a correlation between the nature of children's responses on the two items. Those who responded 'realistically' to one item were also likely to respond similarly to the other. In the case of the tennis item, we were able to use our interview data to show that children's initial responses often failed to indicate their actual capacity to carry out the 'mathematical' operation demanded by the item taken together with its marking scheme. Intermediate-class and working-class children were relatively more likely, compared with service-class children, to fall into the trap of responding initially in an 'inappropriately' 'realistic' manner – producing a response that the marking scheme rules 'incorrect'. However, asked to reconsider their initial response, many of these children were able to move to produce the 'correct' answer. The performance called forth by this item seemed, in some ten per cent of our sample, to underestimate the child's actual competence.

Taking Chapters 3–6 together, we believe this research has shown, in the case of 10–11-year-olds, that there are considerable grounds for concern over the use of 'realistic' items in the context of timed paper and pencil tests. Certainly, if such items are to be used, more attention needs to be paid to the ways in which children interpret their meaning in constructing an initial solution goal (cf. Newman *et al.* 1989). Much more thought also needs to be given to exactly what is being assessed. Is it primarily children's 'mathematical' knowledge and understanding *per se*, or is it primarily their capacity to negotiate the boundary between the 'mathematical' and the 'real' as part of the process of discovering the test designers' intentions for the item? Clearly, school mathematics can be so defined as to include the latter skill and, to some extent, has been in recent times. In the map of mathematics offered by the English National Curriculum at the time of our research, it was under Attainment Target 1, *Using and Applying Mathematics*, where such skills seemed most obviously to be located. However, and somewhat ironically given the stress on 'realistic' items in the tests, this AT was not to be assessed via the tests at all, but by teachers over a longer period of time. One aspect of what is now needed is some careful thinking about the relation between the 'mathematical' and the 'real'. Currently, as we argued in Chapter 3, mathematics educators tend to operate within a rather peculiar set of conventions about what is relevantly 'real' in the context of mathematics problems. In Dowling's (1998) terms, the myths surrounding this relation need to be carefully unpacked (see also Davis 1998). Furthermore, while, in some contexts, we might regard the peculiarities of 'realistic' mathematics items as a cause for amusement, we cannot apply such a charitable perspective as readily when such items appear in tests that, on the one hand, label children as 'mathematical' or otherwise and, on the other hand, label schools and their teachers as successes or failures.

Key Stage 3

In the case of KS3 we have concentrated on a different set of problems. In Chapter 7 we have addressed the problems that would arise for any process of school comparison as a result of the existence of tiered testing at Key Stage 3. Children of 13–14 years of age are distributed across the four bands of the papers (covering levels of achievement 3–5, 4–6, 5–7 and 6–8) by their teachers. In comparing our three secondary schools, we have found that one of these schools seems to have systematically entered its children, relative to both their measured 'ability' and subsequent attainment, for lower tiers of the test than the two other schools. On the basis of our evidence and analysis in Chapter 7 it seems plausible, though we would not claim to have demonstrated this beyond doubt, that this school could have gained a better set of overall results if it had taken a less cautious approach. The key point, however, is that any comparisons of secondary schools via NC levels of achievement derived from tiered testing would introduce another variable, that of teachers' skill in judging for which tier to enter children, into the process alongside both children's mathematical knowledge and understanding and their knowledge of the 'rules of the game' concerning 'realistic' items. Some teachers and departments are likely to be better than others at this aspect of the competition for public esteem or shame. We also provided some analysis of the relationship between the level of NC achievement gained by the children in May 1996 and their social class, sex, 'ability' and school. Here we had to use a more restricted sample as a result of one school's concerns over the collection of social class data (see Chapters 2 and 7). In these analyses we found that tier of entry is associated with 'ability', social class and school but not the sex of the child. Concerning the final level of achievement gained in the tests, we found 'ability' and social class to be the most important factors, with sex not significant and school effects becoming non-significant in an analysis including social class and 'ability'.

In Chapters 8 and 9 we returned to the in-depth analysis of children's responses to individual items, employing both our test and interview data. While, in Chapters 4 and 6, we were focusing on, in Bernstein's (1996) terms, children's access to the *recognition rules* for reading test items, in Chapter 8 we focused primarily on one aspect of his *realization rules*. In particular, our main concern here was the exploration of children's tendency to offer inadequately explicit answers to test items demanding, according to their associated marking schemes, elaborated responses. We began with an analysis of the ways in which both 10–11

and 13–14-year-olds attempted to make sense of a potentially very se-
mantically ambiguous KS2 item concerning a survey of children's sock-
wearing habits (Figure 4.1). This is a type of item that some test developers
have been heard at conferences to describe as likely to 'improve' pedagogy in schools – by encouraging the use of discussion in mathematics
lessons. We showed how the chosen wording of this item could cause
considerable confusion for children. Furthermore we showed that many
children who produced initially rather truncated, and somewhat implicit,
responses could successfully expand them in the interview, gaining more
marks in the process. Amongst the 10–11-year-olds, especially those with
higher 'ability' scores, there was a clear relation between social class and
the apparent degree of explicitness of response. Analysis of interview
transcripts showed that the truncated responses sometimes concealed a
full understanding of the 'mathematical' content of the item but, in other
cases, concealed a complete lack of understanding. Nevertheless, both
cases would gain the same mark in the test. However, as a result of the
design of the item and its marking scheme, it remained in several cases
very difficult to judge, even in an interview, whether children did or did
not understand the key mathematical point involved. Furthermore, we
showed that, given what mathematics textbooks say about the use of
percentages in the context of surveys, we might wonder whether many
of the definitely 'incorrect' answers offered by children in the test context
ought to be readily taken as indicators of misunderstanding or lack of
knowledge. They might rather be attempts to apply what has been learned
in lessons about surveys and percentages to a very confusing problem. We
then turned to an item concerning probability taken by higher-attaining
secondary pupils (Figure 8.1). Here, again, we found a large proportion
of these children initially responding not explicitly enough to gain the
mark for the item. However, many of them were able to expand their
initial response when encouraged to do with the result that they gained
the mark. Their lack of skill here appears to have been not 'mathematical'
per se but rather to have resided in the area of the 'rules' concerning the
nature of legitimate test responses. Though numbers became very small
in the final stages of this analysis, it was working-class pupils, and especially working-class girls, who tended to produce, initially, inadequately
explicit responses. Clearly, even amongst these higher attaining children
entered for tiers 5–7 and 6–8 of the tests, there were many who were
apparently unaware of the 'rules of the game' they were being invited
to play. As we noted in Chapter 8 itself, these children might readily
respond to instruction from teachers, were it to be given, aimed at teaching these rules for the 'appropriate' degree of explicitness of communication in the context of mathematics tests. On the other hand, if Bernstein
(1973) was correct in his claim that the social classes differ in their predisposition to use such explicit language in certain contexts, then such

instruction might be more effective for some children than others (cf. Morais *et al.* 1992).

In Chapter 9 we contrasted two KS3 algebra items and children's responses to them. One item set the tasks of constructing and simplifying expressions in the context of an imagined exercise in tree planting in an orchard; the other set this task in the context of working out the perimeters of labelled plane figures (one completed example having been provided). We pointed to problems in both the marking schemes, and in the relation of the orchard-based item to its supposed statement of attainment. However, our main focus was on children's difficulties in constructing the intended problem when confronted by the orchard-based item. Given the wording of the item, many had great difficulty in inferring the intended goal of the test designers (Newman *et al.* 1989). An alternative goal, the choice of which ensured that no marks would be obtained, could be easily constructed by children. As with many of the other 'realistic' items we have considered, we found that what is 'obvious' to test producers may not be at all 'obvious' to test takers. While this item (Figure 9.2) officially assesses the SoA *Express a simple function symbolically*, its successful solution actually requires much more than this. The child, as in so many other of these items, must also be adept at discovering, amidst all the noise generated by the 'realistic' setting, the underlying mathematical problem. Again, we are faced with an apparent lack of clarity about the nature of school mathematics and, in particular, about just what skills it should be seen as encompassing.

Final comments

This book has explored various unintended consequences, which seem to have arisen from the use of a particular type of test item in large-scale testing contexts. Clearly, the use of such test items – those which embed mathematics in 'realistic' contexts – reflected the assumptions of those then most influential in determining what counted as school mathematics and how it should be tested. Since the time of our research, there have been further changes in the assessment regime for mathematics, with the introduction of a greater element of oral testing of mental arithmetic and some re-emphasizing, at least rhetorically, of the importance of the assessment of children by their own teachers in the classroom (following the report by Dearing in 1993). The use of 'realistic' items in tests remains, however, a – perhaps the – central component of the assessment of children's work. Our discussion of our findings should be seen as part of a growing concern that more complex forms of assessment might be differentially valid, and associated with unfairness with respect to cultural background (e.g. Wood 1991; Darling-Hammond 1994; Gipps and Murphy 1994; Baker and O'Neil 1994; Gipps 1995; Murphy 1995; Secada *et al.* 1995; Murphy 1996). However, the related issue of consequential validity (Messick 1989) needs to be borne in mind. In particular, it needs to be noted that, if further research were to bear out the concerns raised in this book, there might be difficult decisions to be made about the use of forms of assessment item, which might, on the one hand, be expected to operate to 'improve' pedagogy as teachers refer their classroom work to them, but, on the other hand, might lead to less than fair assessment outcomes.

There are a number of reasons why further research in this area (and related areas such as the assessment of scientific understanding) is important. First of all, such research is clearly a contribution to our general understanding of the relations between socio-cultural background and cognitive processes and products. Second, the findings have important policy implications for those working in education, especially for those concerned with validity and equity issues in testing. Third, given these first two reasons, it is important that findings such as ours are subjected to further empirical tests. It is an unfortunate feature of much, though not all, educational research that its findings are not subjected to the test of replication. However, the overriding reason why research such as ours should continue to be undertaken is that mathematics remains one of the key areas of study within our formal educational institutions. Because of this, children's success or failure in mathematics is a major factor in the determination of their subsequent life chances. Formal measures and informal judgements of mathematical 'ability' and attainment are frequently used as part of both selection and allocation processes within and between schools (Dunne 1994). If children are denied subsequent opportunities as a consequence of the use of partly flawed and potentially unfair tests as part of these processes, this should be a matter of considerable concern to all of us working within education.

We would like to end by addressing a more general issue. While we have been undertaking the research reported here, the value of much educational research has been questioned from a variety of directions. At the very moment that we complete this book, we have just read yet another attack on the value of our enterprise – this time from Her Majesty's Chief Inspector of Schools, Chris Woodhead (*Guardian Education*, 15/12/98, p. 17). Apparently, most of the work we researchers undertake and publish is of little value to the educational enterprise as he understands it. The nature and the presentation of his arguments recall Ball's 'discourses of derision' (Ball 1990). In the Chief Inspector's piece, an unnamed, and inadequately referenced professor of education is represented by a three-word phrase. We are given no idea of the context from which it is taken, or even what topic the article from where it was taken addressed. We do not need to know, since the mere existence of the phrase, 'holistic problematised pedagogies' is clearly seen by Woodhead as self-condemning and as evidence enough for his claims. After all, as he goes on to tell us, he 'sometimes think(s)' that academics 'for obvious, if dubious, reasons' seek 'to render the straightforward complex'. No doubt this is sometimes true and, after all, he only 'sometimes' thinks it. We must leave it to our readers to judge whether we are guilty of this charge, or whether, insofar as there is complexity in this book, it reflects the complexity in the world. We have to say that we believe the world of educational problems and solutions to be more complex than the Chief Inspector appears to believe, but then we would, wouldn't we? Perhaps, anyway, we are taking his article too seriously, and it was only intended as a humorous provocation to debate? Whatever his intentions were, we hope that our readers will judge the value of our work in the light of their own goals, concerns and interests, and on the strengths and weaknesses of our research. No doubt there are some clumsy three-word phrases lurking in our text which could be put to good rhetorical use by those with agendas different to our own. There may even be some such phrases that, out of context, will appear conveniently ridiculous. Nevertheless, we would recommend other approaches to assessing the value of research as more valuable than undertaking a 'word search' (e.g. Hammersley 1998). We believe that what we have to report is of practical importance as well as of theoretical interest. More generally, those involved in educational research must defend the potential and actual relevance to practice of theoretically informed empirical research. The handing down to teachers from above of pedagogical and curricular goals, coupled with the absence of research into their effects, both intended and unintended, is no recipe for successful schools. The same applies to forms of assessment. We need to be able to learn from our mistakes. One way we can do this – and there are, of course, others – is by the application of broadly social scientific perspectives and methods in the study of educational practice. We offer this study as an intended contribution to this tradition of work. We welcome critical discussion of its theoretical assumptions, its methods, its results and their implications – but we would prefer not to be subjected to a 'discourse of derision'. The children in our schools deserve better than this.

References

Abbreviated Proceedings of the Oxford Mathematical Conference for Schoolteachers and Industrialists (1957). London: *The Times.*

Alexander, J.C. (1995) *Fin de Siècle Social Theory.* London: Verso.

Apple, M. (1989) How equality has been redefined in the conservative restoration, in W.G. Secada (ed.) *Equity and Education.* New York: Falmer Press.

Apple, M. (1992) Do the standards go far enough? Power, policy and practice in mathematics education? *Journal for Research in Mathematics Education,* 23(5): 412–31.

Apple, M. (1995a) Education, culture and class power: Basil Bernstein and the neo-Marxist sociology of education, in A. Sadovnik (ed.) *Knowledge and Pedagogy: the Sociology of Basil Bernstein.* Norwood, NJ: Ablex, pp. 59–82.

Apple, M. (1995b) Taking power seriously: new directions in equity in mathematics education and beyond, in W.G. Secada, E. Fennema and L.B. Adajian (eds) *New Directions For Equity In Mathematics Education.* Cambridge: Cambridge University Press, pp. 329–48.

Baker, E.L. and O'Neil, H.F. (1994) Performance assessment and equity: a view from the USA. *Assessment in Education,* 1(1): 11–26.

Ball, S.J. (1990) *Politics and Policy Making in Education.* London: Routledge.

Ball, S.J. (1994) *Education Reform.* Buckingham: Open University Press.

Baranes, R., Perry, M. and Stigler, J.W. (1989) Activation of real-world knowledge in the solution of word problems. *Cognition and Instruction,* 6(4): 287–318.

Belenky, M.F., Clinchy, B.M., Goldberger, N.R. and Tarule, J.M. (1986) *Women's Ways of Knowing: the Development of Self, Voice and Mind.* New York: Basic Books.

Bernstein, B. (1973) *Class, Codes and Control.* St Albans: Paladin.

Bernstein, B. (1990) *The Structuring of Pedagogic Discourse.* London: Routledge.

Bernstein, B. (1996) *Pedagogy, Symbolic Control and Identity: Theory, Research, Critique.* London: Taylor & Francis.

Bhaskar, R. (1978) *A Realist Theory of Science.* Sussex: Harvester.

Bhaskar, R. (1979) *The Possibility of Naturalism.* Sussex: Harvester.

Blackburn, R.M. and Mann, M. (1979) *The Working Class in the Labour Market.* London: Macmillan.

Boaler, J. (1993a) The role of contexts in the mathematics classroom: do they make mathematics more 'real'? *For the Learning of Mathematics*, 13(2): 12–17.

Boaler, J. (1993b) Encouraging the transfer of 'school' mathematics to the 'real world' through the integration of process and content, context and culture. *Educational Studies in Mathematics*, 25: 341–73.

Boaler, J. (1994) When do girls prefer football to fashion? An analysis of female underachievement in relation to 'realistic' mathematics contexts. *British Educational Research Journal*, 20(5): 551–64.

Boaler, J. (1997) *Experiencing School Mathematics: Teaching Styles, Sex and Setting*. Buckingham: Open University Press.

Bourdieu, P. (1986) *Distinction: A Social Critique of the Judgement of Taste*. London: RKP.

Bourdieu, P. (1987) What makes a social class? On the theoretical and practical existence of groups. *Berkeley Journal of Sociology*, 32: 1–17.

Bourdieu, P. (1990a) From rules to strategies, in P. Bourdieu (ed.) *In Other Words*. Cambridge: Polity.

Bourdieu, P. (1990b) *The Logic of Practice*. Oxford: Blackwell.

Bourdieu, P. (1994) *Raisons Pratiques. sur la théorie de l'action*. Paris: Seuil.

Bourdieu, P. and Passeron, J.-C. (1977) *Reproduction in Education, Society & Culture*. London: Sage.

Bourdieu, P. and Wacquant, L.J.D. (1992) *An Introduction to Reflexive Sociology*. Chicago: University of Chicago Press.

Brown, M. (1992) Elaborate nonsense? The muddled tale of Standard Assessment Tasks at Key Stage 3, in C. Gipps (ed.) *Developing Assessment for the National Curriculum*. London: Kogan Page & London University Institute of Education, pp. 6–19.

Brown, M. (1993) Clashing Epistemologies: the Battle for Control of the National Curriculum and its Assessment. Professorial Inaugural Lecture, King's College, London.

Cicourel, A.V. and Kitsuse, J.I. (1963) *The Educational Decision-Makers*. Indianapolis: Bobbs-Merrill.

Cobb, P. (1994) Where is the mind? Constructivist and sociocultural perspectives on mathematical development. *Educational Researcher*, 23(7): 13–23.

Cockcroft, W.H. (1982) *Mathematics Counts*. London: HMSO.

Cole, M. (1996) *Cultural Psychology*. Cambridge, MA: Belknap/Harvard University Press.

Cole, M., Gay, J., Glick, J.A. and Sharp, D.W. (1971) *The Cultural Context of Learning and Thinking*. London: Tavistock/Methuen.

Cooper, B. (1983) On explaining change in school subjects. *British Journal of Sociology of Education*, 4(3): 207–22.

Cooper, B. (1985a) *Renegotiating Secondary School Mathematics: a Study of Curriculum Change and Stability*. Basingstoke: Falmer Press.

Cooper, B. (1985b) Secondary school mathematics since 1950: reconstructing differentiation, in I.F. Goodson (ed.) *Social Histories of the Secondary Curriculum*. Basingstoke: Falmer Press: 89–119.

Cooper, B. (1992) Testing National Curriculum Mathematics: Some critical comments on the treatment of 'real' contexts for mathematics. *The Curriculum Journal*, 3(3): 231–43.

Cooper, B. (1994a) Secondary mathematics education in England: recent changes and their historical context, in M. Selinger (ed.) *Teaching Mathematics*. London: Routledge, pp. 5–26.

Cooper, B. (1994b) Authentic testing in mathematics? The boundary between everyday and mathematical knowledge in National Curriculum testing in English schools. *Assessment in Education: Principles, Policy and Practice*, 1(2): 143–66.

Cooper, B. (1995) Exploring children's interpretation of Key Stage 2 National Curriculum tests in mathematics. Paper presented to Standing Conference on Research into Social Perspectives of Mathematics Education, University of London Institute of Education, December 1995.

Cooper, B. (1996) Using data from clinical interviews to explore students' understanding of mathematics test items: Relating Bernstein and Bourdieu on culture to questions of fairness in testing. Paper presented to the Annual Meeting of the American Educational Research Association, New York, April 1996.

Cooper, B. (1998a) Assessing National Curriculum Mathematics in England: Exploring children's interpretation of Key Stage 2 tests in clinical interviews. *Educational Studies in Mathematics*, 35(1): 19–49.

Cooper, B. (1998b) Using Bernstein and Bourdieu to understand children's difficulties with 'realistic' mathematics testing: an exploratory study. *International Journal of Qualitative Studies in Education*, 11(4): 511–32.

Cooper, B. and Dunne, M. (1998) Anyone for tennis? Social class differences in children's responses to national curriculum mathematics testing. *The Sociological Review*, 46(1): 115–48.

Cooper, B., Dunne, M. and Rodgers, N. (1997) Social class, gender, item type and performance in national tests of primary school mathematics: some research evidence from England. Paper presented at the Annual Meeting of the American Educational Research Association, Chicago, March 1997.

Crompton, R. (1993) *Class and Stratification*. Cambridge: Polity Press.

Darling-Hammond, L. (1994) Performance-based assessment and educational equity. *Harvard Educational Review*, 64(1): 5–30.

Davis, A.J. (1998) *The Limits of Educational Assessment*. Oxford: Blackwell.

Davis, R.B. (1989) The culture of mathematics and the culture of schools. *Journal of Mathematical Behaviour*, 8: 143–60.

Davis, R.B. and Maher, C.A. (1993) (eds) *School, Mathematics and the World of Reality*. London: Allyn & Bacon.

De Abreu, G. (1995) Understanding how children experience the relationship between home and school mathematics. *Mind, Culture and Activity*, 2(2): 119–42.

De Corte, E., Verschaffel, L. and Lasure, S. (1995) Word problems: game or reality? Studies of children's beliefs about the role of real-world knowledge in mathematical modelling. Paper presented to Annual Meeting of the American Educational Research Association San Francisco, April 1995.

Dearing, R. (1993) The National Curriculum and its Assessment: Final Report. London: SCAA.

DES/WO (Department of Education and Science/Welsh Office) (1988) *National Curriculum: Task Group on Assessment and Testing: A Report*, DES/WO.

Devlin, K. (1997) *Mathematics: the Science of Patterns*. New York: Scientific American Library.

Douglas, J.W.B. (1964) *The Home and the School*. London: MacGibbon and Kee.

Dowling, P. (1991) A touch of class: ability, social class and intertext in SMP 11–16, in D. Pimm and E. Love (eds) *Teaching and Learning School Mathematics*. London, Hodder & Stoughton.

Dowling, P. (1998) *The Sociology of Mathematics Education: Mathematical Myths/ Pedagogic Texts*. London: Falmer Press.

Dunne, M. (1994) The construction of ability: a critical examination of teachers' accounts, DPhil. thesis, University of Birmingham, UK.

Dunne, M. (1998) Pupil entry for National Curriculum Mathematics tests: the public and private life of teacher assessment. Paper presented to Mathematics Education and Society: An International Conference, Nottingham, September 1998.

Eco, U. (1995) Does the audience have bad effects on television? in U. Eco *Apocalypse Postponed*. London: Flamingo.

Edwards, D. and Mercer, N. (1987) *Common Knowledge: The Development of Understanding in the Classroom*. Milton Keynes: Open University.

Erikson, R. and Goldthorpe, J.H. (1993) *The Constant Flux: A Study of Class Mobility in Industrial Societies*. Oxford: Clarendon.

Ernest, P. (1991) *The Philosophy of Mathematics Education*. Basingstoke: Falmer Press.

Featherman, D.L., Spenner, K.I. and Tsunematsu, N. (1988) Class and the socialisation of children: constancy, change or irrelevance? In E.M. Hetherington, R.M. Lerner and M. Perlmutter (eds) *Child Development in Life-Span Perspective*. Hillsdale, NJ: Lawrence Erlbaum.

Fennema, E., Carpenter, T.P., Jacobs, V.R., Franke, M.L. and Levi, L.W. (1998) A longitudinal study of gender differences in young children's mathematical thinking. *Educational Researcher*, 27(5): 6–11.

Gardner, H. (1983) *Frames of Mind*. New York: Basic Books.

Gilbert, N. (1993) *Analysing Tabular Data: Loglinear And Logistic Models For Social Researchers*. London: University College London Press.

Gilligan, C. (1982) *In a Different Voice: Psychological Theory and Women's Development*. Cambridge, MA: Harvard University Press.

Ginn, J. and Arber, S. (1996) Patterns of employment, gender and pensions: the effect of work history on older women's non-State pensions. *Work, Employment & Society*, 10(3): 469–90.

Gipps, C. (1995) What do we mean by equity in relation to assessment? *Assessment in Education*, 3(2): 271–81.

Gipps, C. and Murphy, P. (1994) *A Fair Test? Assessment, Achievement and Equity*. Buckingham: Open University Press.

Goldthorpe, J.H. and Heath, A. (1992) Revised class schema 1992, Working Paper 13. Oxford: Nuffield College.

Gould, S.J. (1984) *The Mismeasure of Man*. Harmondsworth: Penguin.

Greer, B. (1993) The mathematical modelling perspective on wor(l)d problems. *Journal of Mathematical Behaviour*, 12: 239–50.

Halsey, A.H., Heath, A.F. and Ridge, J.M. (1980) *Origins and Destinations: Family, Class and Education in Modern Britain*. Oxford: Clarendon Press.

Hammersley, M. (1998) *Reading Ethnographic Research: a Critical Guide*. Harlow: Longman.

Harker, R. and May, S.A. (1993) Code and habitus: comparing the accounts of Bernstein and Bourdieu. *British Journal of Sociology of Education*, 14(2): 169–78.

Hart, K. (ed.) (1981) *Children's Understanding of Mathematics*. London: John Murray.

Hayman, M. (1975) To each according to his needs. *Mathematical Gazette*, 59: 137–53.

Henderson, P. (1976) Class structure and the concept of intelligence, in R. Dale, G. Esland and M. MacDonald (eds) *Schooling and Capitalism*. London: Routledge & Kegan Paul.

Her Majesty's Inspectorate (HMI) (1985) *Mathematics From 5 to 16*. London: HMSO.

Hoel, P.G. (1971) *Introduction to Mathematical Statistics*, 4th edition. New York: Wiley.

Holland, J. (1981) Social class and changes in orientation to meaning. *Sociology*, 15(1): 1–18.

Hollingdale, S.H. (1978) Methods of operational analysis, in J. Lighthill (ed.) *Newer Uses of Mathematics*. Harmondsworth: Penguin.

Hymes, D. (1971) On communicative competence. Reprinted in J.B. Pride and J. Holmes (eds) (1972) *Sociolinguistics*. Harmondsworth: Penguin.

Keddie, N. (ed.) (1973) *Tinker, Tailor – The Myth of Cultural Deprivation*. Harmondsworth, Penguin.

Kirscher, D. and Whitson, J.A. (1998) Obstacles to understanding cognition as situated. *Educational Researcher*, 27(8): 22–8.

Labov, W. (1973) *Language in the Inner City: Studies in the Black English Vernacular*. Philadelphia: University of Pennsylvania Press.

Lacey, C. (1970) *Hightown Grammar*. Manchester: Manchester University Press.

Lave, J. (1988) *Cognition in Practice: Mind, Mathematics and Culture in Everyday Life*. Cambridge: Cambridge University Press.

Lemke, J. (1997) Cognition, context and learning: a social semiotic perspective, in D. Kirshner and J.A. Whitson (eds) *Situated Cognition: Social, Semiotic and Psychological Perspectives*. London: Lawrence Erlbaum.

Lieberson, S. (1985) *Making it Count: The Improvement of Social Research and Theory*. Berkeley: University of California Press.

Lighthill, J. (ed.) (1978) *Newer Uses of Mathematics*. Harmondsworth: Penguin Books.

Luria, A.R. (1976) *Cognitive Development: Its Cultural and Social Foundations*. Cambridge, MA: Harvard University Press

Mackenzie, D. (1981) *Statistics in Britain: 1865–1930*. Edinburgh: Edinburgh University Press.

Marshall, G., Rose, D., Newby, H. and Vogler, C. (1988) *Social Class In Modern Britain*. London: Unwin Hyman.

Mehan, H. (1973) Assessing children's school performance, in H.P. Dreitzel (ed.) *Childhood and Socialisation*. London: Collier-Macmillan, pp. 240–264.

Messick, S. (1989) Validity, in R. Linn (ed.) *Educational Measurement*, 3rd edition. London: Collier Macmillan, pp. 13–103.

Messick, S. (1994) The interplay of evidence and consequences in the validation of performance assessments. *Educational Researcher*, 23(2): 13–23.

Morais, A., Fontinhas, F. and Neves, I. (1992) Recognition and realisation rules in acquiring school science: the contribution of pedagogy and social background of students. *British Journal of Sociology of Education*, 13(2): 247–70.

Mouzelis, N. (1995) *Sociological Theory: what went wrong?* London: Routledge.

Murphy, P. (1995) Sources of inequity: understanding students' responses to assessment. *Assessment in Education*, 3(2): 249–70.

Murphy, P. (1996) Assessment practices and gender in science, in L.H. Parker, L.J. Rennie and B.J. Fraser (eds) *Gender, Science and Mathematics*. Dordrecht/London: Kluwer.

National Council Of Teachers Of Mathematics (1991) *Professional Standards for Teaching Mathematics*. Reston, VA: National Council of Teachers of Mathematics.

National Curriculum Council (1991) *NCC Consultation Report: Mathematics*. York: NCC.

Neisser, U. (1976) General, academic and artificial intelligence, in L.B. Resnick (ed.) *The Nature of Intelligence*. Hillsdale, NJ: Lawrence Erlbaum.

Newman, D., Griffin, P. and Cole, M. (1989) *The Construction Zone*. Cambridge: Cambridge University Press.

Nunes, T., Schliemann, A.D. and Carraher, D.W. (1993) *Street Mathematics and School Mathematics*. Cambridge: Cambridge University Press.

Pandey, T. (1990) Power items and the alignment of curriculum and assessment, in G. Kulm (ed.) *Assessing Higher Order Thinking in Mathematics*. Washington: AAAS.

Ruthven, K. (1986) Differentiation in mathematics: a critique of mathematics counts and better schools. *Cambridge Journal of Education*, 16(1): 41–5.

Ryan, J. (1972) The illusion of objectivity, in K. Richardson, D. Spears and M. Richards (eds) *Race, Culture and Intelligence*. Harmondsworth: Penguin, pp. 36–55.

Säljö, R. (1991) Learning and mediation: fitting reality into a table. *Learning and Instruction*, 1: 261–72.

Sayer, A. (1997) Essentialism, social constructionism and beyond. *The Sociological Review*, 45(3): 453–87.

School Mathematics Project: Book 3T (1970) London: Cambridge University Press.

Schools Curriculum and Assessment Authority (SCAA) (1994) *Mathematics Test: Teacher's Pack, Key Stage 2 1994*. London: SCAA.

Schools Curriculum and Assessment Authority (SCAA) (1995a) *Mathematics Tests Key Stage 2 1995*. London: Department for Education.

Schools Curriculum and Assessment Authority (SCAA) (1995b) *Mathematics Tests Key Stage 3 1995*. London: Department for Education.

Schools Curriculum and Assessment Authority (SCAA) (1996) *Key Stage 2 Tests 1996*. London: Department for Education and Employment.

Schools Curriculum and Assessment Authority (SCAA) (no date a) *External Marking of the 1996 Key Stage 2 Tests in English, Mathematics and Science*. London: School Curriculum and Assessment Authority.

Schools Curriculum and Assessment Authority (SCAA) (no date b) *External Marking of the 1996 Key Stage 3 Tests in Mathematics*. London: School Curriculum and Assessment Authority.

Schools Examinations and Assessment Council (SEAC) (1992) *Mathematics Tests 1992, Key Stage 3*. London: SEAC/University of London.

Schools Examinations and Assessment Council (SEAC) (1993a) 1993 *Key Stage 3 Mathematics Tests*. London: DES/WO.

Schools Examinations and Assessment Council (SEAC) (1993b) *Pilot Standard Tests: Key Stage 2: Mathematics*. SEAC/University of Leeds.

Scribner, S. (1984) Studying working intelligence, in B. Rogoff and J. Lave (eds) *Everyday Cognition: its Development in Social Context*. Cambridge, MA: Harvard University Press.

Secada, W.G., Fennema, E. and Adajian, L.B. (1995) (eds) *New Directions for Equity in Mathematics Education*. Cambridge: Cambridge University Press.

Shan S.-J. and Bailey, P. (1991) *Multiple Factors: Classroom Mathematics For Equality And Justice*. Stoke-on-Trent: Trentham Books.

Shepard, L. (1995) Using assessment to improve learning. *Educational Leadership*, 54(5): 38–43.

Silver, E.A., Shapiro, L.J. and Deutsch, A. (1993) Sense making and the solution of division problems involving remainders: an examination of middle school students' solution processes and their interpretations of solutions. *Journal for Research in Mathematics Education*, 24(2): 117–35.

Smith, M.S. and Silver, E.A. (1991) Examination of middle school students' posing, solving and interpreting of a division story problem. Paper presented at the Annual Meeting of the *American Educational Research Association*, Chicago.

Spradley, J. (1972) *Culture and Cognition: Rules, Maps and Plans*. San Francisco: Chandler Publishing.

Stake, R. (1992) Pedagogic and psychometric perception of mathematics achievement, in D. Broady (ed.) *Education in the Late Twentieth Century*. Stockholm: Institute of Education Press.

Street, B. (1984) *Literacy in Theory and Practice*. Cambridge: Cambridge University Press.

Taylor, C. (1993) To follow a rule . . . , in C. Calhoun, E. Lipuma and M. Postone (eds) *Bourdieu: Critical Perspectives*. Cambridge: Polity

Thorndike, R.L. and Hagen, E. (1973) *Cognitive Abilities Test Levels A-H*. London: Nelson.

Torrance, H. (1993) Combining measurement-driven instruction with authentic assessment: some initial observations of national assessment in England and Wales. *Educational Evaluation and Policy Analysis*, 15(1): 81–90.

Verschaffel, L., De Corte, E. and Lasure, S. (1994) Realistic considerations in mathematical modelling of school arithmetic word problems. *Learning and Instruction*, 4: 273–94.

Walkerdine, V. (1988) *The Mastery of Reason*. London: Routledge.

Walkerdine, V. (1990) Difference, cognition and mathematics education. *For the Learning of Mathematics*, 10(3): 51–6.

Walkerdine, V. and The Girls and Mathematics Unit (1989) *Counting Girls Out*. London: Virago.

Wertsch, J.V. (1995) (ed.) *Sociocultural Theories of Mind*. Cambridge: Cambridge University Press.

Whitehead, A.N. (1911/1948) *An Introduction To Mathematics*. Oxford University Press: London.

Wood, R. (1991) *Assessment and Testing*. Cambridge: Cambridge University Press.

Wood, R. and Power, C. (1987) Aspects of the competence-performance distinction: educational, psychological and measurement issues. *Journal of Curriculum Studies*, 19(5): 409–24.

Young, M.F.D. (1971) Curricula as socially organised knowledge, in M.F.D. Young (ed.) *Knowledge and Control*. London: Collier-Macmillan.

Index

EXPERIENCING SCHOOL MATHEMATICS
TEACHING STYLES, SEX AND SETTING

Jo Boaler

Jo Boaler has written a stunning book: clearly written and carefully re-
searched, it is a model of technical rigour. A wide range of qualiative and
quantitative data is marshalled to produce exhaustive case studies of two
contrasting mathematics departments – one traditional and one progressive. Boaler's findings represent a major challenge to the 'back to basics'
credo. This book should be read as a matter of urgency by politicians,
mathematics teachers, and educational researchers.

Stephen Ball, Professor of Sociology of
Education, King's College, London

Anyone with an interest in making sure that every child is numerate should
read this book.

Sally Tomlinson, Professor of Educational Policy
at Goldsmiths College, University of London

Experiencing School Mathematics is the first book of its kind to provide direct
evidence for the effectiveness of 'traditional' and 'progressive' teaching methods.
It reports upon careful and extensive case studies of two schools which taught
mathematics in totally different ways. Three hundred students were followed
over three years and the interviews that are reproduced in the book give com-
pelling insights into what it meant to be a student in the classrooms of the two
schools. The different school approaches are compared and analysed using student interviews, lesson observations, questionnaires given to students and staff
and a range of different assessments, including GCSE examinations. Questions
are raised about:

- the effectiveness of different teaching methods in preparing students for the
  demands of the 'real world' and the twenty-first century;
- the impact of setted and mixed-ability teaching upon student attitude and
  achievement;
- gender and teaching styles;

and new evidence is provided for each.

The book draws some radical new conclusions about the ways that traditional
teaching methods lead to limited forms of knowledge that are ineffective in
non-school settings. The book will be essential reading for maths teachers, parents and policy makers in education.

Contents
*Mathematics in and out of school – The schools, students and research methods –
An introduction to Amber Hill and Phoenix Park schools – Amber Hill mathematics:
experiences and reflections – Phoenix Park mathematics: experiences and reflections –
Mathematical assessments – Analysing the differences – Different forms of knowledge
– Girls, boys and learning styles – Setting, social class and survival of the quickest –
Reflections and conclusions – References – Index.*

176pp   0 335 19962 3 (Paperback)   0 335 19963 1 (Hardback)

INVESTIGATING FORMATIVE ASSESSMENT
TEACHING, LEARNING AND ASSESSMENT IN THE CLASSROOM

Harry Torrance and John Pryor

- How do teachers assess the ordinary classroom work of young children?
- How do pupils understand and respond to that assessment – does it help or hinder their development?
- How can classroom assessment be developed to be more effective in assisting the learning process?

This book brings together various perspectives from the fields of assessment policy development, theories of learning and the sociology of the classroom. The book explores how the assessment of young children is carried out in classrooms and with what consequences for their understanding of schooling and the development of their learning in particular subject areas. The book is based on extensive video and audio tape recordings of classroom assessment 'incidents' along with interviews of teachers and pupils about the process of assessment.

Contents

192pp   0 335 19734 5 (Paperback)   0 335 19735 3 (Hardback)

RATIONING EDUCATION
POLICY, PRACTICE, REFORM AND EQUITY

David Gillborn and Deborah Youdell

This research should make us extremely sceptical that the constant search for 'higher standards' and for ever-increasing achievement scores can do much more than put in place seemingly neutral devices for restratification.

> Michael W. Apple, John Bascom Professor of Curriculum
> and Instruction and Educational Policy Studies,
> University of Wisconsin, Madison

Recent educational reforms have raised standards of achievement but have also resulted in growing inequalities based on 'race' and social class. School-by-school 'league tables' play a central role in the reforms. These have created an A-to-C economy where schools and teachers are judged on the proportion of students attaining five or more grades at levels A-to-C. To satisfy these demands schools are embracing new and ever more selective attempts to identify 'ability'. Their assumptions and practices embody a new IQism: a simple, narrow and regressive ideology of intelligence that labels working class and minority students as likely failures and justifies rationing provision to support those (often white, middle class boys) already marked for success.

This book reports detailed research in two secondary schools showing the real costs of reform in terms of the pressures on teachers and the rationing of educational opportunity. It will be important reading for any teacher, researcher or policymaker with an interest in equality in education.

Contents
Education and equity – Reforming education: policy and practice – Ability and economy: 'intelligence' and the A-to-C economy – Selection 11 to 14: fast groups, 'left over' mixed ability and the options – Selection 14 to 16: setting, tiering, hidden ceilings and floors – Educational triage and the D-to-C conversion: suitable cases for treatment? – Pupil perspectives – Conclusions: rationing education – Notes – References – Index.

272pp   0 335 20360 4 (Paperback)   0 335 20361 2 (Hardback)